The
League of
Gentlemen's
Book of precious things

Published by Prion
An imprint of The Carlton Publishing Group
20 Mortimer Street
London W1T 3JW

Introductions and selection copyright © 2007
Steve Pemberton, Mark Gatiss, Jeremy Dyson
and Reece Shearsmith
Design and layout © 2007 Carlton Publishing Group

ISBN 978-1-85375-621-4

Editorial Manager: Roland Hall
Project Art Direction: Luke Griffin
Research and permissions: Bronagh Woods
Production: Peter Hinton
Typesetting: E-type, Liverpool

Printed in Great Britain

THE LEAGUE OF GENTLEMEN'S
BOOK OF PRECIOUS THINGS

SELECTED AND INTRODUCED BY

Jeremy Dyson, Mark Gatiss, Steve Pemberton
and Reece Shearsmith

CONTENTS

Dyson's Choice

Gatiss' Greatest

Pemberton's Picks

Reece's Pieces

Dyson's Choice

MONTY PYTHON
AND VIZ

(See colour plate section)

There is a quote that I found on a visit to the Barbara Hepworth Museum in St Ives several years ago that I have regurgitated far too often in interviews and articles, so I apologise for doing so once more – but it states a startling truth about the creative process that I have yet to see articulated as succinctly anywhere else. Speaking of her own work the great sculptor said: 'What one wants to say is formed in childhood. The rest of one's life is spent trying to say it.' This simple statement could not be more pertinent to the forces that helped forge *The League of Gentlemen*.

The first comedy I loved with a passion was Monty Python, which I came to know not through the original TV shows but through their spin-off products – the LPs, the books and later the films. These items by their very nature were more crafted and perfect than their source and consequently they were more alluring. It's fair to say I was seduced – with the force of a thunderbolt – picking up a copy of *The Brand New Monty Python Bok* on a trip to Miles University Bookshop in Leeds with my somewhat bohemian Aunty Freda and Uncle Les. The book's dust-jacket looked scuffed and dirty. And then I realised with a jolt that the thumbprints and grime were *printed on to the paper.* What a delicious joke. And then another shock. Experimentally I took off the wrapper and rather than seeing the same thing beneath there was instead a fake porno mag cover. Another joke – something rude being concealed beneath something plain. The magazine was called *Tits and Bums – A weekly look*

8

at Church Architecture and there was a photograph of a group of writhing nudes in the middle of some kind of orgy. A joke within a joke beneath a joke – like a secret passage into another world. Something everyday and ordinary had been wrought into something magical. It was more like a toy than a book. And it was *naughty*. I was lost to it. How could there be so much delight packed into one object? This was the spirit of Python. The gags – brilliant as they are – would not be as funny if their frame was not so *right*. The medium became part of the joke – Marshall McCluhan style. Fake continuity announcements, record scratches, end credits in the middle of the show – this vigorous tearing up and mocking of the means of representation was so alive and so much fun that it was completely irresistible. I was nine when I discovered Python. By the time I was ten I was recording comedy sketches with my best friend Steve Cook, into a cassette recorder.

V*iz Comic* is an unheralded and underappreciated national institution. There was a brief time when it was rated – admired in the broadsheets and general cultural discussion – but it rarely figures on that radar now. Yet it is still there on the shelves at Smiths, more than 20 years after I first started buying it. The great secret about *Viz* was always that it was very, very smart – the smartness concealed beneath the fog of vulgarity. It passed piercing comment on an element of British life that was not satirised anywhere else. It took on tabloid culture, popular culture and celebrity culture at a time when no-one else went near the stuff. Above all it was often hysterically, tear-inducingly, funny – mostly in the material that surrounded the comic-strip characters. Like Python it was chock full of detail – little adverts for strange inventions, mock public health campaigns and the like. It had a knack for truthful observation – admittedly of unsavoury things – but that didn't lessen the acuity. (*Roger's Profanisaurus* – a continuing dictionary of rude words hosted by proto-Tourettes TV presenter Roger Mellie – contained a definition of the phrase 'Ghost Shit' that made Mark Gatiss cry with laughter. Indeed I still think of Mark's tear-streaked face whenever the phenomenon the phrase describes, occurs.) I don't think I've ever read an interview with any comedian where they cite *Viz* as an influence, but it was undoubtedly a touchstone for me. The picture of Britain it evokes resonates resoundingly in Royston Vasey.

RISING DAMP

Even though me and my school friends were comedy 'fans' our tastes were quite catholic. Pre-adolescence things tend to be sorted into two simple camps – what one likes and what one doesn't like. *Rising Damp* was always in the former. There's nothing unusual about saying this now, but actually *Rising Damp*'s veneration is still relatively new. For a long time after its original broadcast it was seen as a poor cousin to the BBC classics simply because it was on ITV. It is in fact the only truly great sitcom ITV produced and it gets better with each departing year. If *Fawlty Towers* were viewed as the Beatles of the sitcom, *Rising Damp* could be the Stones. Not as formally or mathematically perfect, funkier, grimier, a little looser (apart from Leonard Rossiter's meticulously performed Rigsby that is) it throbs with warmth and life and a dark and desperate funniness. A perfect marriage of cast and script, augmented by gloriously seedy design and a singular theme tune (composed by Denis Wilson, who also composed that of *Fawlty Towers*) it bares seemingly infinite viewing. The scripts are brilliant for sure (and some of the funk may come from the speed at which Eric Chappell wrote them, owing to absurd production deadlines) but they are brought off the page by one of the finest comic ensemble casts ever assembled. Of course Rossiter is a genius (Stanley Kubrick worked with him twice) but Richard Beckinsale, Frances De La Tour and Don Warrington are so loveable as a group that they act as a perfect foil. In truth you love them all and it's a delight just to be in their company. Television was pretty ephemeral back then, pre-video recorders, but this show I was able to pin and mount on a series of red-labelled BASF cassettes, holding the microphone of my mum's portable cassette recorder against the single speaker of the black and white telly in her bedroom over a series of Thursday nights. I caught about five or six episodes – enough to fill two tapes. For years – well into my 20s – these tapes went with me whenever I moved home. I would listen to them in bed as a source of comfort. When we came to record the audience segments for the *League* nothing made me happier than the fact we were doing so in Studio One at Yorkshire Television – where *Rising Damp* had been taped 24 years earlier.

RISING DAMP

PART ONE

SCENE 1: EXT. PORCH. NIGHT.

Alan and Brenda enter. Alan is nervous whilst Brenda looks faintly bored.

BRENDA: Aren't we going in? It's cold out here.

ALAN: We'll have to watch out for Rigsby – he doesn't like it when we're late in.

BRENDA: It's only half-past ten.

ALAN: Is that the time? My word, it's just flown by, hasn't it? What a night, hey, Brenda?

BRENDA: [without enthusiasm] Yes.

ALAN: I thought you'd like *Dr Zhivago*. I've seen it three times.
[Pause. Clears throat] I hope you didn't mind the kiss.

BRENDA: [stares] What kiss?

ALAN: [surprised] I kissed you on the cheek. You know – when the Cossacks were cutting up the peasants.

BRENDA: Oh, I'm sorry, Alan. I thought you'd caught me with your ice lolly.

ALAN: No – that was me.

BRENDA: Well, I was a little distracted at the time. Omar Sharif's eyes had just started to fill with tears. He was lovely.

ALAN: Yes but he was up there, Brenda. Celluloid. I was next to you.

BRENDA: [without enthusiasm] Yes.

ALAN: I couldn't take my eyes off you. I'll tell you this – if those streetlights hadn't been on when we came home – anything could have happened.

BRENDA: We could have cut through the churchyard.

ALAN: Ah, well, I didn't like to – not with all the deceased lying around.

BRENDA: I don't think they'd have disturbed us. Were you scared?

ALAN: No.

BRENDA: You're scared of Rigsby.

ALAN: No, I'm not.

RIGSBY: [off] Who's that out there?

ALAN: [opening door] Quick – up the stairs.

Brenda exits.

SCENE 2: INT. RIGSBY'S ROOM. RIGSBY IS PEERING OUT OF DOOR.

RIGSBY: Oh, it's you. Another five minutes and I'd have locked that door. [Returns] Mind the milk bottles. [Crash] Clumsy twit.

Alan enters indignantly with remains of empty milk bottle.

ALAN: You left them there deliberately. I'm surprised you don't have barbed wire and search-lights. It's like being in Stalag Luft 7, this is.

RIGSBY: I like to know who's prowling about.

ALAN: Well, I wish you'd stop waiting for me to come home, Rigsby. You're getting just like my mother.

RIGSBY: You should be glad I take an interest in you. [Frowns] You haven't been drinking, have you?

ALAN: No, I haven't. And if I had – it's got nothing to do with you. If you don't mind I would like to lead my own life.

RIGSBY: I just don't want you getting into bad company, that's all. I owe it to your parents. You've already knocked off Holy Communion and the Scouts. Where's it going to end?

ALAN: I just don't want you spying on me all the time – do you mind?

RIGSBY: [angrily] Who's spying? I'm not spying. If you want to be bloody secretive.

ALAN: I'm not secretive.

RIGSBY: Where have you been then?

ALAN: As a matter of fact I've been to see *Dr Zhivago*.

RIGSBY: Oh. [Pause] Well, what did he say?

ALAN: What?

RIGSBY: [shakes head] And you say you're not secretive. I didn't know there was anything wrong with you. Is it the prickly heat again?

ALAN: Rigsby – *Dr Zhivago* is a film. It's about a man's disillusionment with the Russian revolution.

RIGSBY: You didn't have to go out to see that. I've been disillusioned with it for years.

ALAN: You should have seen it, Rigsby. It was a good film. You ought to get out more.

RIGSBY: I can see all the films I want to see on the television.

ALAN: What sort of films can you see on there?

RIGSBY: Good films.

ALAN: Such as? What good films have you seen lately?

RIGSBY: Well ... recently I've seen *Dracula ... Brides of Dracula ... Frankenstein and the Monster*–

ALAN: [aghast] Is that all you've watched?

RIGSBY: No. [Pause] I've seen *The Mummy's Hand* as well.

ALAN: Good Heavens! Doesn't that tell you anything about yourself, Rigsby?

RIGSBY: What do you mean?

ALAN: They're all horror films.

RIGSBY: I like horror films.

ALAN: But what does it indicate? I mean, what's the state of your mind?

RIGSBY: There's nothing wrong with my mind.

ALAN: Well, you wouldn't catch me watching that sort of rubbish.

RIGSBY: Yes – and we all know why. You watch anything like that and we'd have to leave the lights on all night. You get frightened watching *Scooby Doo*.

ALAN: It doesn't frighten me, Rigsby. I just happen to find it all rather childish.

RIGSBY: Oh, yes. Well, look what happened when we watched *Psycho* – you went to the lavatory fourteen times. You hardly saw any of it.

ALAN: I saw most of it.

RIGSBY: You didn't see the murders though, did you?

ALAN: Yes, I did. I saw them through a crack in the door.

RIGSBY: I shall never forget you that night. You went to bed shaking like a leaf and clutching your panda. Mind you, one good thing – it's stopped you hanging about the bathroom.

ALAN: Well, that film ought to be a lesson to you – the murderer had a split mind – probably got it from watching too many horror films.

RIGSBY: What do you mean? Those films are very interesting – very educational.

ALAN: Oh, yes, if you want to know how to kill a vampire, or hold a black mass, or invoke the devil.

RIGSBY: As a matter of fact these films are a manifestation of the eternal struggle between good and evil – revealing the darker side of human nature.

ALAN: [incredulously] Where did you get that from, Rigsby?

RIGSBY: I heard it on *Film Night*.

ALAN: But, Rigsby, it's all superstition – these things just don't exist.

RIGSBY: I wouldn't be so sure.

ALAN: Have you ever met a vampire?

RIGSBY: You go down to the tax office.

ALAN: I'm being serious.

RIGSBY: Listen – anyone could be a vampire. Except for having two rather prominent choppers and sleeping in a coffin, there's nothing to distinguish him from anyone else. Of course, if you do have any suspicions, try garlic – he won't come near you.

ALAN: Neither will anyone else.

RIGSBY: And watch your jugular vein. Oh, and carry a sharp wooden stake – but not in your trouser pocket.

ALAN: All right – you can joke, but I think you half believe it, Rigsby.

RIGSBY: Why not? You take the werewolf. By day a humble bank clerk. But at night he turns rather hairy – removes his white collar and cuff-links and dashes onto the Common – you'd probably take him for an Alsatian.

ALAN: I wouldn't take him for any-thing. I'm a man of science. You can't expect me to believe in the supernatural.

RIGSBY: You won't cut through the churchyard though – not at night. Not with all those bodies about.

ALAN: They don't worry me. I'm a medical man – when they're dead they're dead.

RIGSBY: They are when you've finished with them. Oh, it's all right talking like this with the lights on. But when you're on the stairs – under the forty watts – it'll be different. This is an old house. Strange things can happen. There's been a lot of unhappiness here.

ALAN: I've got news for you Rigsby – there still is.

Alan exits.

ALAN BENNETT

A lthough it might not be obvious, it was a short hop from *Python* and *Rising Damp* to Alan Bennett. A favourite hardback from my early teenage years was Roger Wilmut's *From Fringe to Flying Circus* – an overview of Oxbridge comedy from the late 1950s onwards. Naturally it was the Python chapters I was interested in but it didn't take long for my curiosity to take in the rest of the book. My dad often spoke admiringly of *Beyond the Fringe* – and I was particularly drawn to Alan Bennett. Besides I'd already discovered him. I had a vivid memory of seeing *Afternoon Off* – one of his LWT plays on a Saturday night in 1979 and being moved to tears at the lonely plight of Lee, the Chinese waiter looking for a good time in Hartlepool. Why I should have been thus affected at such a tender age I don't know, but its bleakness spoke to my young heart in a way that touched me deeply. I also enjoyed the fact it was funny and sad at the same time. There was the double delight too that Bennett was from Leeds and as I watched more of his output – particularly the next set of TV plays he did for the BBC in 1982 – I found great pleasure in the references to Armley and Roundhay and Park Square. Leeds wasn't exactly a cultural hotspot back then and I think there was something very encouraging in the discovery that writing television plays and being born in an LS postcode were not mutually exclusive. And of course the fact that he was so good. The sheer quality of his comic dialogue – like other comic dialogue squared – the trademark economy and ring of truth that was simultaneously fresh and familiar. The genius use of vernacular terms in just the right amount to offset the heightened turn of phrase – all this was apparent to me as a teenager even if I couldn't have articulated it. Nowadays it's nothing to say 'I like Alan Bennett' – it's like saying 'I like Mozart' or 'aren't Shakespeare's sonnets good?,' but back then it felt like it put you into a more exclusive club – certainly amongst your comedy-loving peers anyway. This wasn't *The Young Ones* or *The Comic Strip* after all. It was *Talking Heads* in 1987 that began the process of cementing Alan Bennett into the national consciousness as an unofficial laureate. You were pleased but also experienced that vague crossness at a cherished and personal passion being stolen by the mainstream. A couple of years prior to this crossover myself and Gordon Anderson (producer of the very first *League* stage show and now the director of *The Catherine Tate Show*) were sharing a house together in Leeds. One lunchtime we were walking through Leeds city centre when we spotted Alan Bennett some way off. Both of us fans, we decided to accost him and say we were writing for a fanzine so we could interview him, not expecting him to say yes. In fact he proved to be absolutely charming and told us to meet him in an hour or so at the City Varieties, where he was auditioning for a new TV play (which turned out to be *The Insurance Man*). Unable to believe our luck we sat down and wrote a list of questions and then kept our appointment. Mr Bennett was kind and generous and gave us a full hour of his time. Had we been Melvyn Bragg and Alan Yentob he could not have responded more fully or articulately. I blush now at the thought of my intense and fanatical interrogation – but am still pleased at the memory of a long and involved query about *Marks* – one of his less familiar BBC2 plays – which caused Mr Bennett to turn to Gordon and say in his inimitable manner – 'He knows his stuff doesn't he?'

A Chip in the Sugar

GRAHAM IS A MILD MIDDLE-AGED MAN. THE PLAY IS SET IN HIS BEDROOM, A SMALL ROOM WITH ONE WINDOW AND ONE DOOR.

IT IS FURNISHED WITH A SINGLE BED, A WARDROBE, TWO CHAIRS AND NOTHING MUCH ELSE.

I'd just taken her tea up this morning when she said, 'Graham, I think the world of you.' I said, 'I think the world of you.' And she said. 'That's all right then.' I said, 'What's brought this on?' She said, 'Nothing. This tea looks strong, pull the curtains.' Of course I knew what had brought it on. She said, 'I wouldn't like you to think you're not Number One.' So I said, 'Well, you're Number One with me too. Give me your teeth. I'll swill them.'

What it was we'd had a spot of excitement yesterday: we ran into a bit of Mother's past. I said to her, 'I didn't know you had a past. I thought I was your past.' She said, 'You?' I said, 'Well, we go back a long way. How does he fit in vis-à-vis Dad?' She laughed. 'Oh, he was pre-Dad.' I said, 'Pre-Dad? I'm surprised you remember him, you don't remember to switch your blanket off.' She said, 'That's different. His name's Turnbull.' I said, 'I know. He said.'

I'd parked her by the war memorial on her usual seat while I went and got some reading matter. Then I waited while she went and spent a penny in the disabled toilet. She's not actually disabled, her memory's bad, but she says she prefers their toilets because you get more elbow room. She always takes for ever, diddling her hands and whatnot, and when she eventually comes back it turns out she's been chatting to the attendant. I said, 'What about?' She said, 'Hanging. She was in favour of stiffer penalties for minor offences and I thought, "Well, we know better, our Graham and me." I wish you'd been there, love; you could have given her the statistics, where are we going for our tea?'

The thing about Mam is that though she's never had a proper education, she's picked up enough from me to be able to hold her own in discussions about up-to-the-minute issues like the environment and the colour problem, and for a woman of her age and background she has a very liberal slant. She'll look at my *Guardian* and she actually thinks for herself. Doctor Chaudhury said to me, 'Full marks, Graham. The best way to avoid a broken hip is to have a flexible mind. Keep up the good work.'

They go mad round the war memorial so when we cross over I'll generally slip my arm through hers until we're safely across, only once we're on the pavement she'll postpone letting it go, because once upon a time we got stopped by one of these questionnaire women who reckons to take us for husband and wife. I mean, Mam's got white hair. She was doing this dodge and I said, 'Mam, let go of my arm.' I didn't really wrench it, only next thing I knew she's flat on the pavement. I said, 'Oh my God, Mother.'

People gather round and I pick up her bag, and she sits up and says, 'I've laddered both my stockings.' I said. 'Never mind your stockings, what about your pelvis?' She says, 'It's these bifocals. They tell you not to look down. I was avoiding some sick.' Somebody says. 'That's a familiar voice,' and there's a little fellow bending over her, green trilby hat, shorty raincoat. 'Hello,' he says, 'remember me?'

Well, she doesn't remember people, I know for a fact because she swore me down she'd never met Joy Buckle, who teaches Flowers in Felt and Fabric at my day centre. I said, 'You have met Joy, you knitted her a tea cosy.' That's all she can knit, tea cosies. And bed socks. Both outmoded articles. I said to her, 'Branch out. If you can knit tea cosies you can knit skiing hats.' She says, 'Well, I will.' Only I have to stand over her or else she'll still leave a hole for the spout. 'Anyway,' I said, 'you do remember Joy because you said she had some shocking eyebrows.' She said, 'I hope you didn't tell her that.' I said, 'Of course I didn't.' She said, 'Well, I don't remember.' And that's the way she is, she doesn't remember and here's this little fellow saying, 'Do you remember me?' So I said, 'No she won't. Come on, Mother. Let's get you up.' Only she says, 'Remember you? Of course. It's Frank Turnbull. It must be fifty years.' He said, 'Fifty-two. Filey. 1934.' She said, 'Sea-Crest.' He said, 'No sand in the bedrooms.' And they both cracked out laughing.

Meanwhile she's still stuck on the cold pavement. I said, 'Come along, Mother. We don't want piles.' Only he butts in again. He says, 'With respect, it's advisable not to move a person until it's been ascertained no bones are broken. I was in the St John's Ambulance Brigade.' 'Yes,' said Mother, 'and who did you learn your bandaging on?' And they both burst out laughing again. He had on these bright yellow gloves, could have been a bookie.

Eventually, I get my arms round her waist and hoist her up, only his lordship's no help as he claims to have a bad back. When I've finally got her restored to the perpendicular she introduces him. 'This is Frank Turnbull, a friend of mine from the old days.' What old days? First time I knew there were any old days. Turns out he's a gents' outfitter, semi-retired, shop in Bradford and some sort of outlet in Morecambe. I thought, 'Well, that accounts for the yellow gloves.'

Straight off he takes charge. He says, 'What you need now, Vera, is a cup of coffee.' I said, 'Well, we were just going for some tea, weren't we, Mother?' Vera! Her name's not Vera. She's never been called Vera. My Dad never called her Vera, except just once, when they were wheeling him into the theatre. Vera. 'Right,' he says, 'follow me.' And puts his arm through hers. 'Careful,' she says. 'You'll make my boyfriend jealous.' I didn't say anything.

Pause.

Now the café we generally patronise is just that bit different. It's plain but it's classy, no cloths on the tables, the menu comes on a little slate and the waitresses wear their own clothes and look as if they're doing it just for the fun of it. The stuff's all home-made and we're both big fans of the date and walnut bread. I said, 'This is the place.' Mr Turnbull goes straight past. 'No,' he says, 'I know somewhere, just opened. Press on.'

Now, if there's one thing Mother and me are agreed on it's that red is a common colour. And the whole place is done out in red. Lampshades red. Waitresses in red. Plates red, and on the tables those plastic sauce things got up to look like tomatoes. Also red. And when I look there's a chip in the sugar. I thought, 'Mother won't like this.' 'Oh,' she says, 'this looks cheerful, doesn't it, Graham?' I said, 'There's a chip in the sugar.' 'A detail,' he says, 'they're still having their teething troubles. Is it three coffees?' I said, 'We like tea,' only Mother says, 'No. I feel like an adventure. I'll have coffee.' He gets hold of the menu and puts his hand on hers. 'Might I suggest,' he says, 'a cheeseburger?' She said, 'Oh, what's that?' He said, 'It's fresh country beef, mingled with golden-fried onions, topped off with toasted cheese served with french fries and lemon wedge.' 'Oh, lemon wedge,' said Mother. 'That sounds nice.' I thought, 'Well, I hope you can keep it down.' Because it'll be the pizza story all over again. One mouthful and at four o'clock in the morning I was still stuck at her bedside with the bucket. She said, 'I like new experiences in eating. I had a pizza once, didn't I, Graham?' I didn't say anything.

They fetch the food and she's wiring in. He said, 'Are you enjoying your cheeseburger?' She said, 'I am. Would I be mistaken in thinking that's tomato sauce?' He said, 'It is.' She says, 'Give us a squirt.' They both burst out laughing. He said, 'Glass cups, Graham. Be careful or we'll see up your nose.' More laughter. She said, 'Graham's quite refined. He often has a dry sherry.'

'Well, he could do with smartening up a bit,' Mr Turnbull said. 'Plastic mac. He wants one of these quilted jobs, I've shifted a lot of those.' 'I don't like those quilted jobs,' I said. 'He sweats,' Mother said. 'There's no excuse for that in this day and age,' Mr Turnbull said, 'the range of preparations there are on the market. You want to invest in some roll-on deodorant.' Everybody could hear. 'And flares are anathema even in Bradford.'

'Graham doesn't care, do you, Graham?' Mother said. 'He reads a lot.' 'So what?' Mr Turnbull said. 'I know several big readers who still manage to be men about town. Lovat green's a nice shade. I tell you this, Graham,' he said, 'if I were squiring a young lady like this around town I wouldn't do it in grey socks and sandals. These shoes are Italian. Feel.' 'I always think Graham would have made a good parson,' Mother said, feeling his foot, 'only he doesn't believe in God.' 'That's no handicap these days,' Mr Turnbull said. 'What do you do?'

'He's between jobs at present,' Mother said. 'He used to do soft toys for handicapped children. Then he was making paper flowers at one stage.' I went to the toilet.

Pause.

When I came back he said, 'I don't believe in mental illness. Nine times out of ten it's a case of pulling your socks up.' I didn't say anything. Mother said, 'Yes, well, I think the pendulum's gone too far.' She didn't look at me. 'It's like these girls, not eating,' he said, 'they'd eat if they'd been brought up like us, Vera, nothing to eat.' 'That's right,' Mother said, 'they have it too easy. Did you marry?' 'Twice,' he said. 'I buried Amy last May. I was heartbroken but life has to go on. I've a son lives in Stevenage. I've got two grandsons, one at the motorbike stage. Do you drive?' 'No,' I said. 'You do,' Mother said. 'You had that scooter.' 'It was only a moped,' I said. 'Well, a moped, Graham. They're all the same. I can't get him to blow his own trumpet.'

'I've got a Rover 2000,' Mr Turnbull said, 'handles like a dream. I think the solution to mental illness is hard physical work. Making raffia mats, I'd go mad.' 'Yes,' says Mother, 'only they do pottery as well. I've seen some nice ashtrays.' 'Featherbedding,' Mr Turnbull said. 'Do you like these Pakistanis?' 'Well in moderation,' Mother said. 'We have a nice newsagent. Graham thinks we're all the same.' I said, 'I thought you did.' She said, 'Well, I do when you explain it all to me, Graham, but then I forget the explanation and I'm back to square one.' 'There is no explanation,' Mr Turnbull said.' 'They sell mangoes in our post office, what explanation is there for that?' 'I know,' Mother said, 'I smelled curry on my *Woman's Own*. You have to be educated to understand.' I didn't say anything.

He ran us home, promised to give her a tinkle next time he was in the neighbourhood. Said he was often round here tracking down two-tone cardigans. 'Your Mother's a grand woman,' he said. 'You want to cherish her.' 'He does, he does,' Mother said. 'You're my boyfriend, aren't you, Graham?' She put her arm through mine.

GO TO BLACK.
Come up on Graham standing looking out of the window. It is late afternoon. He sits on the arm of the chair.

There must be a famine on somewhere because we were just letting our midday meal go down when the vicar calls with some envelopes. Breezes in, anorak and running shoes, and he says, 'I always look forward to coming to this house, Mrs Whittaker.' (He's got the idea she's deaf, which she's not; it's one of the few things she isn't.) He says, 'Do you know why? It's because you two remind me of Jesus and his mother.' Well, I've always thought Jesus was a bit off-hand with his mother, and on one occasion I remember he was quite snotty with her, but I didn't say anything. And of course Madam is over the moon. In her book if you can't get compared with the Queen Mother, the Virgin Mary's the next best thing. She says, 'Are you married?' (She asks him every time, never remembers.) He said, 'No, Mrs Whittaker. I am married to God.' She says, 'Where does that leave you with the housework?' He said, 'Well, I don't do as well as your Graham. He's got this place like a palace.' She says, 'Well, I do my whack. I washed four pairs of stockings this morning.' She hadn't. She put them in the bowl then they slipped her mind, so the rest of the operation devolved on me.

He said, 'How are you today, Mrs Whittaker?' She says, 'Stiff down one side.' I said, 'She had a fall yesterday.' She says, 'I never did.' I said, 'You did, Mother. You had a fall, then you ran into Mr Turnbull.'

Pause.

She says, 'That's right. I did.' And she starts rooting in her bag for her lipstick. She says, 'That's one of them anoraky things, isn't it? They've gone out now, those. If you want to look like a man about town you want to get one of those continental quilts.' He said, 'Oh?' I said, 'She means those quilted jackets.' She said, 'He knows what I mean. Where did you get those shoes?' He said, 'They're training shoes.' She said, 'Training for what? Are you not fully qualified?' He said, 'If Jesus were alive today, Mrs Whittaker, I think you'd find these were the type of shoes he would be wearing.' 'Not if his mother had anything to do with it,' she said. 'She'd have him down Stead and Simpson's and get him into some good brogues. Somebody was telling me the Italians make good shoes.'

The vicar takes this as his cue to start on about people who have no shoes at all and via this to the famine in Ethiopia. I fork out 50p which he says will feed six families for a week and she says, 'Well, it would have bought me some Quality Street.' When he's at the door he says, 'I take my hat off to you, Graham, I've got a mother myself.' When I get back in she said, 'Vicar! He looked more like the paper boy. How can you look up to somebody in pumps?' Just then there's a knock at the door. 'Get down,' she says, 'he's back.' Only it isn't. It's Mr Turnbull.

Graham stands up

New outfit this time: little suede coat, corduroy collar, maroon trousers. She says, 'You're colourful.' 'We just happen to have these slacks on offer,' he says. 'I was wondering whether you fancied a run out to Bolton Abbey?' 'Bolton Abbey?' she says. 'Oh, that's right up our street, isn't it, Graham? Graham's good with buildings, aren't you, Graham? He knows all the periods of houses. There's one period that's just come in. Other people don't like it yet but we do, don't we, Graham?' 'I don't know,' I said. 'You do. What is it?' 'Victorian,' I said. 'That's it, Victorian.

Only there's a lot been pulled down.' Mr Turnbull yawns. 'I've got a little bungalow.' 'That's nice,' Mother says. 'I like a nice bungalow, don't you, Graham?' 'Yes,' I said, 'provided it's not a blot on the landscape.' 'Mine's architect designed,' says Mr Turnbull. 'It has a patio and a breakfast bar, it overlooks a beauty spot.' 'Oh,' said Mother, 'sounds tip-top. We'd better be getting our skates on, Graham.' He said, 'I've got to pick up a load of green three-quarter-length windcheaters in Ilkley; there won't really be room for a third party. Isn't there anything on at the pictures?' 'Oh he'll be happy reading,' Mother said. 'Won't you, Graham?' 'Anyway,' Mr Turnbull said, 'you don't always want to be with your Mother at your age, do you, Graham?' I didn't say anything.

He sits on the chair arm again.

I've been laid on my bed reading one of my magazines. I've a feeling that somebody's looking at the house, only I can't see anybody. Once or twice I think I've heard a knock on the door, but I haven't gone in case there's nobody there.

GO TO BLACK.
Come up on Graham sitting on his unmade bed in his pyjamas. Night.

Today they went over to York. It was after seven when he dropped her off. He generally comes in but not this time. Just gives her a little kiss. She has to bend down. I said, 'Have you had a good time?' She said, 'Yes. We had egg and chips, tea, bread and butter, we've got a lot in common and there's a grand new car park.' I said, 'Did you go in the Minster?' She said, 'No. Frank's not keen on old buildings. We need to look more to the future. He says they've built a spanking new precinct in Bradford, so that's going to be next on the agenda. You're quiet.' I said, 'Well, do you wonder? Doctor Chaudhury says I should have a stable environment. This isn't a stable environment with your fancy men popping in every five minutes.' She said, 'He isn't my fancy Man.' I said, 'Well, he's your fancy man in embryo.' She said, 'You know I don't know what that means.' I said, 'How old are you?' She said, 'I don't know.' I said, 'You do know.' She said, 'I don't. Tell me.' I said, 'You're seventy-two.' 'That's not so old. How old was Winston Churchill?' I said, 'When?' She said, 'You think you've got it over me, Graham Whittaker. Well, I'll tell you something, my memory's better with Frank. He was telling me about the economy. You've got it all wrong.' I said, 'How?' 'I can't remember but you have. Blaming it on the government. Frank says it's the blacks.' I didn't say anything, just came upstairs.

When I went down again she's still sat there with her hat and coat on. I said: 'Do you want to knit him a tea cosy?' She said, 'I don't think he's the tea-cosy type. When I first knew him he had a motorbike and sidecar. Besides, I think it's got beyond the tea-cosy stage.' I said, 'What do you mean?' She said, 'Graham. My one aim in life is for you to be happy. If I thought that by dying I would make you happy I would.' I said, 'Mother, your dying wouldn't make me happy. In fact the reverse. It would make me unhappy. Anyway, Mother, you're not going to die.' She said, 'No. I'm not going to die. I'm going to get married. And the honeymoon is in Tenerife. Have one of your tablets.'

She made a cup of tea. I said, 'How can you go to Tenerife, you're smothered at Scarborough?' She said, 'It's a four-star hotel with tip-top air-conditioning, you get your breakfast from a long table.' I said, 'What about your bowels?' She said, 'What about my bowels?' 'Well, you said they were unpredictable at Morecambe. Get them to the Canary Islands and they're going to be all over the place.' She said, 'Who's talking about the Canary Islands? I'm going to Tenerife.' 'And what about post-Tenerife? Where are you going to live?' She said, 'Here. Frank says he'll be away on and off on business but he wants to call this home.' I said, 'What about me?' She went into the kitchen. 'Well, we wondered whether you'd prefer to go back to the hostel. You were happy at the hostel. You rubbed shoulders with all sorts.' I said, 'Mam. This is my home.' She said, 'A man shouldn't be living with his mother at your age, Frank says. Did you take a tablet?'

Now it's four o'clock in the morning and I can't sleep. There's a car parked outside. I can't see but I think there's somebody in it, watching like they used to do before. I thought all that chapter was closed.

GO TO BLACK.
Come up on Graham sitting on an upright chair. Evening

This morning I went to Community Caring down at the Health Centre. It caters for all sorts. Steve, who runs it, is dead against what he calls 'the ghetto approach'. What he's after is a nice mix of personality difficulties as being the most fruitful exercise in problem-solving and a more realistic model of society generally. There's a constant flow of coffee, 'oiling the wheels' Steve calls it, and we're all encouraged to ventilate our problems and generally let our hair down. I sometimes feel a bit out of it as I've never had any particular problems, so this time when Steve says 'Now chaps and chappesses who's going to set the ball rolling?' I get in quick and tell them about Mother and Mr Turnbull. When I'd finished Steve said, 'Thank you, Graham, for sharing your problem with us. Does anybody want to kick it around?'

First off the mark is Leonard, who wonders whether Graham has sufficiently appreciated that old people can fall in love and have meaningful relationships generally, the same as young people. I suppose this is understandable coming from Leonard because he's sixty-five, only he doesn't have meaningful relationships. He's been had up for exposing himself in Sainsbury's doorway. As Mother said, 'Tesco, you could understand it.'

Then Janice chips in. 'Had they been having sexual intercourse?' I said I didn't want to think about it. Steve said, 'Why?' I said I didn't know. So he said, 'Maybe what we should be talking about is why Graham is being so defensive about sexual intercourse.' I said, 'Steve. I am not being defensive about sexual intercourse. She is my mother.' Jackie, who's nine parts Lesbian, said, 'Graham. She is also A Woman.' I couldn't believe this. I said, 'Jackie. You're an ex-battered wife. I thought you didn't approve of marriage.' She said, 'Graham. I approve of caring marriage.' I said, 'Jackie. This is not caring marriage.' She said, 'Graham, what's Tenerife? That's caring. All I got was a black eye and a day trip to Fleetwood.' Then they all have a go. Get Graham. Steve summed up. 'The general feeling of the group is that Graham could be more open.' I said, 'How can I be more open? There's somebody sat outside the house watching.' I wanted to discuss that only Leonard leaped in and said he felt the need to talk through an episode behind British Home Stores. I stuck it a bit longer and then came home.

Mother's sat there, all dolled up. Earrings on, chiffon scarf, lathered in make-up. She said, 'Oh, I thought you were Mr Turnbull.' I said, 'No.' She said, 'I'll just go to the lav.' She goes three times in the next ten minutes. I said, 'You're not getting married today, are you?' She said, 'No. There's a new Asda superstore opened at Bingley and we thought we'd give it the once over. Frank says they have a very good selection of sun tan lotions.' I said, 'Mother, there's somebody watching the house.' She said,

'I want to pick out some tissues and Frank's looking for a little chammy for his windscreen. He's promised me something called a cheeseburger, there's a café that's part of the complex.'

Just then there's a little toot on the horn and she runs to the lav again. I said, 'Don't go. Don't leave me, Mam.' She said, 'I'm not giving in to you, you're a grown man. Is my underskirt showing?' He toots again. She says, 'Look at your magazines, make yourself a poached egg.' I said, 'Mam.' She said, 'There's that bit of chicken in the fridge. You could iron those two vests. Take a tablet. Give us a kiss. Toodle pip.'

I thought I'd go sit in the back room where they couldn't see me. I pulled the curtains and I'm sitting there in the dark and I think I hear a knock at the front door. I don't move and there's another knock. Louder. I do like Doctor Chaudhury says and tell myself it's not happening, only it is. Somebody shouts through the letter-box. 'I know you're in there. Open this door.' So I do. And there is someone. It's a woman.

She said, 'Are you the son?' I said, 'What?' She said, 'Are you the son? I'm the daughter.' I said, 'Have you been watching the house?' She said, 'On and off. Why?' I said, 'Nothing.' She said, 'I don't know what there is to look so suited about.' I said, 'You'd better come in.'

GO TO BLACK.
Come up on Graham as he puts a magazine on top of the wardrobe. He sits down in the easy chair. Night.

It's nine o'clock when I hear the car outside. I'm sitting watching TV. I say, 'Oh hello. Did you have a nice time?' She said, 'Yes. Yes we did, thank you.' 'Did you get your sun tan lotion?' She said, 'What sun tan lotion?' 'You were going to get some sun tan lotion. Never mind. You've forgotten. How's Mr Turnbull?' 'Frank? He's all right.' She took her things off. 'I'm sure you could get to like him, Graham, if only you got to know him.' I said, 'Well, you should have brought him in.' 'Well, I will next time. It'd be nice if now and again we could go off as a threesome. What have you done?' 'Nothing,' I said. 'Just sat here.' 'You've been all right?' 'Mmm.'

'You see,' she said, 'there wasn't anybody outside.' 'Oh yes there was.' She said, 'Oh Graham. Have you had a tablet? Have a tablet.' 'I don't want a tablet. I'll tell you who was sat outside. Mrs Pamela Musgrave.' She said, 'Who's she?' 'Nee Turnbull. The daughter of your hubby to be.' She said, 'He hasn't got a daughter. He's got a son down south. He hasn't

27

got a daughter,' she said, 'you're making stuff up now, have a tablet.' I said, 'I'm not making it up. And there's something else I'm not making up. Mrs Turnbull.' She said, 'There isn't a Mrs Turnbull. She's dead. I'm going to the lav.' I said, 'She's not dead. She's in a wheelchair with a broken heart. He's been having you on.'

After a bit she comes out. 'You're just saying all this.' 'The number's on the pad. Ring up. She's disabled is his wife. Has been for ten years. Their daughter looks after them. You're not the first. He's always doing it. One woman, it was going to be Barbados. Somebody spotted you together at Bolton Abbey. A well-wisher. Tenerife!'

Later on I took her a cup of tea. She'd been crying. She said, 'I bought this little bedjacket.' I said, 'I'm sorry, Mam.' She said, 'He was right enough. What can you expect at my age? How old am I?' 'Seventy-two.' 'That's another thing. I remembered with him. I don't remember with you.' I said, 'I'm sorry.' She said, 'You're not sorry. How are you sorry? You didn't like him.' I said, 'He wasn't good enough for you.' She said, 'I'm the best judge of that. He was natty, more than can be said for you.' And starts crying again. I said, 'I understand, Mam.' She said, 'You don't understand. How can you understand, you, you're not normal?' I said, 'I'm going to bed.'

In a bit she comes shouting outside the door. 'You think you've got it over me, Graham Whittaker. Well, you haven't. I've got it over you.' I said, 'Go back to bed.' She said, 'I know the kind of magazines you read.' I said, 'Chess. You'll catch cold.' She said, 'They never are chess. Chess with no clothes on. Chess in their birthday suits. That kind of chess. Chess men.' I said, 'Go to bed. And turn your blanket off.'

Pause.

Next day she's right as rain. Forgotten it. Never mentions it anyway, except just as we're coming out of the house she said, 'I do love you, Graham.' I said, 'I love you too.' She said, 'Anyway he had a hearing aid.' She said, 'What's on the agenda for today, then?' I said, 'I thought we might have a little ride to Ripon.' She said, 'Oh yes, Ripon. That's nice. We could go to the cathedral. We like old buildings, don't we, you and me?'

She put her arm through mine.

FADE OUT.

WOOD

Of course not all the subsidiary influences that fed into the fast-flowing river of *The League of Gentlemen* were comic. There was a shared enthusiasm for various dramas and documentaries, in addition to the well-documented love of all things ghoulish and macabre. Many of these tastes were esoteric and it was a surprise – and one of the things that drew us all together – to discover that various passions we had considered private were actually shared. One of these was for the great twentieth century writer of supernatural fiction, Robert Aickman – a figure me and Mark were familiar with through the anthologies of *Great Ghost Stories* he edited for Fontana throughout our childhoods. Aickman often included one of his own stories in these books, but it wasn't until his own collections began to be republished in the late 1980s that we realised quite how brilliant he was. A writer with a voice and a sensibility unlike anybody else – his ghost stories rarely featured actual ghosts. Rather there would be inexplicable occurrences, a creeping sense of dread and climaxes of such daring strangeness that one would be disturbed by them for days after reading them. He never wrote anything that one could describe as comedy – he was too dour and intense for that – but some of the episodes he described were genuinely surreal. There were many things in the *League* that would seem to me to be touched by Aickman. A running gag we had called Pram People, which is in episode 5 of the first series, had a young mother asking a middle-aged man to help her with her pram over a step and he ends up having to carry it all around the town. The climax revealed her alone again pushing the pram across a desolate moor. And then we see the hapless man is now *inside* her pram, complete with a bonnet and with a dummy in his mouth. Take away the bonnet and the dummy and I could imagine this as an Aickman story, her pushing the man off to some unspecified and lonely end.

'WOOD' BY ROBERT AICKMAN

So my niece, Elinor, has given me one of those weather houses, where the woman comes out when it is likely to be fine, and the man when it is going to rain! I did not think they were made any more. There is something about them that not many people know; at least nowadays. It is this: that just as dowsing can be used to trace many things other than water (which of course makes "water divining" quite the wrong name for it), so these little weather houses, or some of them, can be attuned to foretell more things than the merely literal state of the heavens.

It is an odd story of which I am reminded by this, and until now I have not cared to make a note of it. There is always a risk of a written record coming into the wrong hands; and so perhaps reaching the eyes or ears of the people described. Moreover, I was always very uncertain how far I could depend upon my own impressions of what happened; and naturally I am even less confident now, nearly twenty years later. Also, one is superstitious about seeming to give a new life, by writing about it, to something which has frightened one. The curious business about Munn and his wife, whatever I thought about the reality of it, even at the time, certainly frightened me – so much that I was the last person to be surprised by what happened to them in the end. But old Pell and his wife are dead now too. So here goes.

I suppose that if anyone at all reads what I am writing, it is more likely than not to be a stranger. A few sentences about myself had, therefore, better come first.

I served my articles as an architect, in the days when that was how one learned a profession, by working at practical and immediate problems from the first, instead of merely listening to lectures and doing exercises; and for several years I worked as an architect's assistant in a good office, doing well and having every prospect of starting in practice on my own. The tone was set in those days by architects such as Ernest George, and there seemed an unlimited number of costly country houses being built, pleasant work for all who had the social knack of getting it – which did not seem very difficult, as I look back on it. But then came the War, the first one, and the real one: the greatest mistake mankind ever made, in my opinion, but, curiously enough, one out of which I myself did quite well, at least in a sense. Before it was over, and to my considerable surprise, I found myself a lieutenant-colonel, though very much of the wartime kind, not the real thing, as I knew perfectly well; but then in the very last month, more or less when Wilfred Owen was killed, if I have it right, I was, not killed, but badly knocked out, since when I have never been quite right in any way, even though I made a good recovery, and a remarkably swift one.

Of course I had always intended to go back into architecture, but I never quite did. There were several factors. One was that I began to receive a pension, which at first seemed fairly good: enough, anyway, to save one from having to rush at things, and to give one time to think. Another, and much more important, was that the profession had completely changed. We were fast on the way to the state of affairs when the word "art" was seldom mentioned, still less the word "beauty". It is odd that the busy, slave-driving old offices, always with several pupils, had much to say about art and beauty – too much, many of the pupils thought; while these new Schools of Architecture lead to nothing but, for example, the buildings you can see beside and around the Festival Hall in London. A third thing was that I never succeeded in marrying and thus taking on a new incentive. The war seemed to do something to me there; or perhaps it was mainly my experiences at the end of the war. But what settled things at first was that I was offered the job of editing a series of architectural lives.

I had always been interested in the actual lives and careers of the architects of history, and the work carried me away completely for a longish time. I was enabled to travel in a modest way (though, there again, I could not have paid for a wife to travel with me), and I was in a position to appoint myself as the author of two or three of the books. I did so, and these books proved to be among the most successful of the series, for what that meant. When I was in my mid-forties, I bought an old cottage outside this Suffolk village; without clearly realizing that East Anglia is pre-eminently the part of England to which unattached and unattachable males with tiny but comparatively secure incomes tend to drift. They settle there on the outskirts of villages, and, I must admit, seem often to live on for ever, though no one quite knows what they do all day. Edward FitzGerald is the archetype and patron of us all; though, speaking for myself, I have so far managed to keep my hands off the local fishing lads. But then FitzGerald was a genius, even though an under-productive one. I, no genius, have managed to have many affairs of the more ordinary kind; mainly, indeed, with married women. It does not seem a thing one should proclaim: but it is no joke being a married woman in East Anglia, if the woman has the smallest imagination. I am, therefore, unabashed.

That odd man, Munn, on the other hand, seemed, during the first years I knew him, to be genuinely uninterested in women. Of course I did not know him really well, then or ever; and one can be utterly mistaken in such assessments. Still, many English males *are* genuinely unconcerned about women; are without the need for them, especially after the age of thirty or so.

Munn struck me in those days as one who instead of embracing a woman, embraced a grievance. Unlike most people with entrenched grievances, he was as reticent about the details as one normally is, or as one should be, about the details of a love relationship. He had been employed in the Inland Revenue, and there had been trouble of some kind, though it was hard to guess what, because he had emerged with a small allowance, upon which, like me, he lived; in his case, in rooms above the village post office. Possibly he unearthed some corruption or other, and had to be sacked, and silenced. If Munn had been still in the employ of the tax people, instead of on bad terms with them, I could never have known him even as an acquaintance; because, say what they will, I cannot accept that any kind of gentleman will, under any circumstances, make a career of prying into the private affairs of others and then mulcting them, commonly to the point of spoiling and destroying their entire lives and those of their families. Munn supplemented his allowance (which, comically enough, was "tax-free") by making funny little figures out of straw and brass wire, which were offered for sale in the post office below under the name of "daffies". It was an unusual occupation for a middle-aged man, but I mention it because it had a faint and obscure bearing upon what happened in the future. Meanwhile, the figures, though often quite clumsy, seemed to sell remarkably well; not only to passing motorists, of whom, from other points of view, there were soon far too many, needless to say, but even to the villagers and to rustics apparently from other villages. Sometimes one of our locals, having bought one of Munn's straw figures, would later buy another. Perhaps the first figure had by then worn out, but at least it proved that Munn was meeting a demand, always the great thing in the world, we are told. I have described the figures as "little" and so most of them were; but always on view were a few larger ones, some, two or three feet high. Naturally, these cost more, and it was the smaller, cheaper figures that most of the motorists went for, and that must have provided most of the turnover – again, as is usual in commerce.

Munn had taken up residence in the village before I arrived, and at first all I knew of him was his tweedy figure toddling about and sometimes bidding me Good-day. His tweeds were very hairy indeed, and more than usually shapeless. One almost felt that he made his suits himself, as well as the straw figures; and perhaps wove the hirsute fabric also. He had profuse white hair under a scarecrow hat; a nose like a reversed peg for that same hat; and a darkly red face, which made one think neither of drink nor of exposure to the elements, neither of sickness nor of shyness. It struck one simply as how he was made, how he was coloured: several shades too red, as some are made too tall, and others too dwarfish.

It was at one of the village inns (I refuse to employ the word "pub") that I first exchanged more words with Munn than the time of day. I remember the occasion very well, but I have little recollection of what we said, then or, indeed, at most of our subsequent encounters. Of course he hinted at his troubles, and I at mine. But we were neither of us, perhaps to a fault, involved or much interested in what is called "the life of the village", so that we undoubtedly ranged over wider fields: the newspapers, the world, and man's future (though, as I have said, seldom woman's). Munn seemed another who did not quite know what next to do in life, or even to aim at doing. He too was, more than anything else, marking time. The main thing we had in common was exile. All the remaining days of our lives seemed to drop upon us like dried-out snowflakes or like daily leaves from the dead calendar of a past and forgotten year. It was as well that the Marxists did not catch and roast us. Life has become more rigorous than it was then; though it is likely to become more rigorous still.

And yet—

I think I had been talking in a sketchy way to Munn, on and off, and every now and then, for as long as three or four years, when one morning, as I was on my way to something rather private, and was less than usually open to distraction, he hailed me from across the street and asked if I would look in at his place for a drink that same evening. I can see him as he did it, in my mind's eye, quite clearly: the white shutters across Gabb the butcher's window were behind him in the late autumn sunshine (so that it must presumably have been early closing day or the Sabbath). After all, it was a rather historic moment: I had never before been invited to enter the rooms above the post office. That which at the time I was about to undertake would be completed long before evening, so I accepted for half-past six.

Munn proved to have several rooms, quite a suite, reached by his own stair from the street; and, in general, seemed to be better accommodated than I had supposed, even though the trappings plainly appertained to a "furnished apartment". All that looked personal was a mill for making the straw figures. As usual with Munn, the device looked as if he had made it himself; out of rough old planks, long thick nails, and bright steel edges – very sharp, by the look of them. The contraption stood in a corner of the living room, with a bale of straw stuck away behind it, and straw ends all over the carpet beneath and around it. Of course, all was dry, or no doubt there would have been complaints from the sub-postmistress, Mrs Hextable, below. There were also two or three of the figures lying about in various stages of completion.

"My eker-out of income," said Munn, entering the room behind me and watching my gaze. He crossed to the machine and gave it a hard kick in the midriff, so that the bright cutting wheel spun round like a flying saucer. "And I wish His Majesty's bloody Commissioners were beneath it," added Munn.

"But sit yourself down," he went on, and, without consulting me, mixed a whisky that was far stronger than I normally liked or like, or than he had observed me drink at the inn, supposing that he ever took in such things. "I propose to ask you a favour."

He had provided himself with an even stronger whisky than mine. He gave me the impression of a man who so feared to find himself weak that he had both hands on the bull's horns almost before the animal had entered the field, so to speak.

"I'm getting married and I want you to be my best man."

I must admit I had feared that it was going to be something to do with money.

"I expect I can manage that," I replied, "though it's something I've never done."

"At our age, one feels such a fool at having to ask," said Munn. I saw that his hands were shaking.

I have always felt that the plural possessive is a case that should be used with caution, but all I said was "Where will it be? And who is she? And congratulations too, of course."

"It's only in the next county. In fact, just over the border." Munn expressed it a trifle histrionically, but of course there is an enormous difference between Suffolk and Norfolk, and between both and North Essex.

"I shall be hiring a motor," Munn continued, staring at me, as if the availability of private transport might make all the difference.

"I shall be delighted to do everything I can," I said, taking a goodish pull on Munn's whisky. "In fact, I shall be honoured."

Munn looked a shade doubtful about that, as well he might; but he was wonderfully relieved, and almost gulped as he said, "Thank you very much. I shall never forget it. I may be able to do the same for you one day."

"Who knows?" I responded, as the whisky began to rise within me.

"Would Saturday of the week after next suit you?" Munn really seemed to imply that if it would not, the day could be changed.

"Perfectly," I replied; though almost completely at random.

"I was afraid it might not. Unfortunately it has to be on a Saturday or a Sunday, or my future wife's people couldn't get to it."

"I quite understand."

"He's a very busy man, and his wife is closely involved in what they do."

It seemed that I was meant to take that up, even though, as will be noticed, I had not yet even learned the bride's name. "And what is that?" I enquired politely.

"It's something I think you ought to know. That's why I raised the matter," said Munn.

I nodded.

"It's a little hard to talk about," said Munn, looking at the floor.

"It's the kind of thing that makes people giggle a bit." Munn drew on himself again and gazed at me. "I don't really mind if you do giggle. I couldn't possibly blame you."

"I shall do nothing of the kind," I rejoined.

But Munn still beat about the bush. "You know that story of Maurice Baring's? Or is it a play?"

"I am not sure that I do." Maurice Baring had, after all, written an enormous amount even by the date we had then reached.

"A young man tells a girl he has a secret that he simply must confide in her before she marries him. She swears black and blue that no matter what it may be, she will love him as much as ever. In the end, he discloses that he's the hangman, and she sheers off."

"No," I said. "I can't recall having come upon that."

"My future father-in-law is an undertaker," said Munn. "Not the hangman. Just the undertaker."

"I shouldn't let that worry you. Indeed, I've always understood it's a most lucrative trade. Whatever happens in the world, the demand's still there. Indeed, as things get worse, it often increases."

"What a good chap you are!" exclaimed Munn, refilling my glass. "When I told my brother, he laughed at first, and then began to be very wary. Of course he's been a married man for more than twenty years. Really settled, is Rodney. But it was just the same with three other men I spoke to about it."

"It doesn't worry me," I asserted. It was hardly possible to say anything else, though what I had said was not the exact truth.

"It's just the two of them do the whole thing," Munn continued. "He was a merchant navy carpenter or something like that to begin with, and then began to specialize. She does the laying-out, as I believe it's still called. I'm told she can do the other things too; as well as any professional. Embalming, for example; though of course there's no great demand for that in rural England. All the same, she has an embalmer's full certificate. It's rather comic really. It hangs on their wall. It's one of the first things you see."

"Someone has to do these things," I said.

"Yes," said Munn. "And it's quite surprising how clean and calm it all is when you get close to it. 'Clean' and 'calm' are the words that have stayed in my mind all the way through."

I enquired no further, though I daresay it was obvious enough that Munn wanted to go on talking around the discouraging topic. For my part, I have always been a conventional enough person, and, drink or no drink, I was beginning very clearly to understand why the topic is half tabu.

I said I was sorry but that it was time I went, and Munn said he would call for me in the hired motor at 8 a.m. on the following Saturday week. Did I mind it being so early? Munn was once more drawing himself together. But I was past minding almost anything, as long as this absurd ceremony could be decently put into the past, and, as far as I was concerned, buried there. I said I would look for a booklet upon the duties of a best man, but Munn said quite earnestly that it wouldn't be necessary.

In all the circumstances, I never expected to receive one of those smooth cards that announce future weddings; and this was as well, because none came. Before the day dawned, I saw Munn, two or three times, stumbling about the village. After all it was not a large village, and an imminent bridegroom could hardly live as a recluse. I thought it best to make no approach, and this was clearly right, because Munn made no approach to me, except that once when we were far enough apart and unmistakably going in different directions, he winked at me. It seemed plain that Munn did not want his future plans to be generally discussed, so I said nothing about the matter to anyone. After a day or two, however, I recollected that a best man is expected to make a presentation of some kind to the bride. The answer to that was simpler than might be expected: I have a rule that when a gift is required, I give a year's membership (or, occasionally, longer) of a society which admits one free of charge to a number of buildings of diverse architectural interest. The general public has to pay for admission in every case; and the list of structures includes several important ones to which the general public is not admitted at all. I did reflect that it might not be an absolutely ideal gift for a young girl, but there was no evidence that Munn's intended *was* a young girl. I knew nothing about her. I had not enquired, because I had little doubt that if Munn had wanted me to know at that stage, he would have told me. There was also the question of gifts to the bridesmaids. I dealt with it by assuming that there would be no bridesmaids.

I was right about that, but, for some reason (no doubt, the infrequency of weddings in my life), it had never occurred to me that there might not even be a church.

"I simply couldn't face all that white stuff and slobbering about," said Munn to me in the car. "I'm sure you'll agree it's not the thing for chaps of our age."

So we were making towards a small country town with a convenient registry office. I shall not give a name to the town, because marriage is an institution so delicate that all in any way concerned are very touchy on the subject, and prone to seek legal redress for any possible dubiety or even comment. At the time, I wondered whether Munn was not perhaps a divorced man; or even a potential bigamist. It was the kind of thing that the course of events tended to bring to one's mind; but I have absolutely no reason to think there was any truth in either hypothesis.

In the car, however, Munn did let fall his bride's family name. It was Pell: in East Anglia, a gypsy name, though less eminent in that way than Mace. I did not remark upon these facts to Munn. He was now referring to the bride herself as "Vi". Munn struck me as being less uneasy than I had expected. I observed that he had not bought new clothes for the occasion, but was in his usual shapeless tweeds. I myself was at least wearing a "dark suit". I touched my pocket containing the membership card of the society I have mentioned, which I had sealed in an envelope: sealed, I mean, with scarlet sealing wax. I was far from sure what would be the best moment to hand it over. I should have to wait upon events.

The distance was not all that great and we managed to arrive before the registry office was even open. There were, in fact, six or seven minutes to go. I felt that this was the sort of thing that could be counted upon, and concentrated upon the idea that my duties must soon be all over. At least we had the car to wait in; which was fortunate, as it had begun to rain. The car was of moderate size only, and I wondered how many there would be for the return trip. The young driver began to nod to passers-by he knew. Munn had fallen silent. By way of conversation, I enquired how he and his bride had met.

"She came into the post office and liked my straw daffies. She told Mrs Hextable that she would like to meet me. She thought we had interests in common. Mrs Hextable came up and brought me down. And so it proved to be."

"You mean that you *did* find you had a lot in common?"

"So it seemed. I must admit that I'd been keeping half an eye open for a wife for some time. You may not believe that. I was feeling more and more that I couldn't let my whole life be ruined by the swinish way I was treated."

"Of course I believe you, and I'm quite sure you're right," I said firmly; "and I very sincerely hope you'll be very happy." I felt quite warm about it.

"Old Pell says he's going to build us a house," remarked Munn.

I managed to avoid any facetious reference to an abode which would last till Doomsday. Even so, Munn was blushing slightly.

"My God!" I cried. "What about the ring?" It was the first I had thought of it. I was behaving like the best man in a pantomime, but then, of course, one so often does behave like a character in a pantomime.

"It's all right," said Munn. "Here it is." He handed over a tiny grey box from his jacket pocket.

"Isn't it rather small?"

"She's a small girl."

At that point, one of the big office doors opened and a clerk emerged.

"Is either of you Mr Munn?"

"I am," said Munn.

"The Registrar's waiting for you. The bride is inside already with her family." I cannot recall that I ever learned how they had managed to achieve this: professional influence, no doubt.

We followed the clerk indoors, and, slightly to my surprise, the young driver of the car came after us. As Munn made no objection, it was not for me to speak.

The windows of the room in which the ceremony was to take place were in need of cleaning. Perhaps they were unusually difficult to reach, as they were very high in the walls. The grime on the panes and the increasing rainfall made things very dim, and somewhat obscured my first view of the Pell family.

My main feeling was that they were indeed small: small, smooth, and round was the impression they all left with me. Miss Pell, a little taller than her gnome-like parents, though only a trifle, was a pretty, round-faced, round-eyed girl, arrayed in bright colours, a selection of them. She had very blue eyes and very pink cheeks and very yellow hair, which stuck up sturdily all over her head, rather in the manner of Munn's own white tangle. She was talking as we entered the room, in a noticeably sharp, even metallic voice; there was something stocky and assured in her whole demeanour, which, I must admit, did not attract me; and from pretty well the first instant I was in no doubt at all that it was she who had carried off Munn rather than he who had captured her. Why she should wish to do that was another matter; but no affair of mine, and rather glad I was to be unimplicated. Munn's marriage, hitherto partly comic, partly pathetic, became for me, as I entered that registry office, partly disagreeable as well.... I should add that Mr Pell was dressed in a well-fitted black suit, and little Mrs Pell in a tight dress of deepest purple.

"Happy to meet you," said Mr Pell. One simply could not exclude the sinister overtones of such a greeting from one's mind, absurd though it is to say so.

I simpered.

"I often think the best man is the key to the whole wedding," continued Mr Pell. Even that implausible compliment added to my uneasiness, lacking as I was in all experience of the tasks required. Moreover, Mr Pell had a grating voice; compulsive antecedent of his daughter's.

"How do you like the bride's clothes?" enquired Mrs Pell. "Doesn't she look gay? Don't you think Leonard's lucky to get her?" I had forgotten that Munn's name was Leonard (Christian names were not used among men in the present casual way), and had to grope in my mind for what she meant.

"She looks lovely," I said.

"You'll be able to kiss her in a few minutes, you know. It's the best man's privilege."

"I shan't forget."

But the Registrar was awaiting us with some impatience, especially as he had a bad cold. The rubric was minimal, so that only a few minutes had seemingly passed before he was saying "And I hope you'll be very happy," and moving back to the fire that was smoking away in his private room. I had passed across the ring at the right moment and, at so spare a solemnization, had little other commitment. We all signed the register, including the driver of the car. There had been no one else present, except the registrar's clerk, who served unobtrusively.

The Pells were cackling away (the verb is unavoidable: though of course voices do run in families, as do handwriting and faiths), and now had come the time for me to kiss Vi. Her cheek (to which I confined myself) struck me as hard and chilly, but the bride is in a palpably false position at such moments. All the same, I remembered by contrast other kisses that were coming my way just then. I also noticed that Munn had not kissed Vi at all. He had not touched her in any way except to put the small ring on her stick-like finger. The rain had eased off when we emerged, so I suppose it may all have taken rather longer than I supposed.

To my relief, there was no further celebration. Even drinks all round at the hotel opposite were precluded by the licensing hours, as we all had to agree. Munn, the new Mrs Munn, and I re-entered the car and the Pells waved us away. I saw their squat shapes shoulder to shoulder on the pavement: Mr Pell with his right arm raised, Mrs Pell with her left. The rain was now only a light drizzle, to which the Pells seemed impervious. After all, most funerals take place in the wet, I reflected. Could it have been really so difficult for Pell to get away thus briefly and thus early on another day than Saturday? Not that it mattered. I remembered that the Pells had had to travel from somewhere or other. I do not think I then knew where Pell plied his profession: visibly, and, as I had seen for myself, happier than any lark, as are all these men of timber and satin.

Munn was taking his bride back to the rooms over the post office. I had found them, of course, to be more spacious than I had thought before I entered them. I noticed that the word "honeymoon" was never, in my hearing, mentioned. In the car, however, Vi, from the back seat, did assure me anxiously that, as Munn had said her father was going to build them a house.

"The first thing we'll do," she grated on, "is start looking for a plot. It'll have to be the cheapest we can find, as Daddy doesn't believe in buying things when he can make so much with his own hands."

There was no reference to Munn making any contribution, nor did he, installed in the back seat beside her, say a word.

"It will only be a teeny house," Vi explained in her rasping voice, "but Mummy says you're often best off when you're living small."

It was necessary to enter into it. "Have you a builder in mind?" I enquired.

"Of course not, silly. Daddy's going to build it for us."

I had sensed that this was in the background. "The whole thing?" I asked. "The plumbing included? And the electricity?" The latter had just entered our area, but was not yet truthfully in our immediate range.

"We shan't be having silly things like that. Only wood."

I was constrained to turn in my seat, difficult though it was to do, and look back at her.

"Daddy can make everything needed in this world out of wood."

There was something almost evangelical in her tone and choice of words. There was also something wild and fantastical: which seemed infectious.

"Even people?" I asked, smiling no doubt, but really asking under some compulsion that remained elusive.

"You're making game of me," she replied on the instant. Her pink cheeks had darkened, and I noticed that she, for her part, was not smiling at all.

"Lay off, you fool," said Munn, really quite sharply, and speaking almost for the first time since entering the car. "Let's change the subject. We haven't even started looking for the land as yet."

"That's right," said Vi. "Though we're going to, aren't we, Leonard?" She left little doubt that they were.

And we did manage to talk of something else. As a matter of fact, we talked of how beautiful the wedding had been: a compulsory theme, needless to say, for all such moments of time, regardless of objectivity.

Munn had been preposterously rude; but I had observed such quick gripings of rage in him before, notably when he thought about the Inland Revenue and how they had treated him.

A few weeks later, the Munns did invite me round one evening, "after supper". It was a remarkably formal visit: I must acknowledge that I found it difficult to keep the word "wooden" out of my mind. Munn's capacity to talk at large about this and that seemed entirely to have shrivelled, as happens so often to a man after marriage, sometimes immediately after; and Vi's sole interest appeared to be her own family and their conversationally equivocal trade.

Inevitably, no doubt, she took the line that there was nothing whatever to be frightened about, and that the details were most interesting when encountered from the inside. The expression "from the inside" did not appeal to me. And, with Vi, it was difficult even to make a feeble joke about it; or, I thought, about anything.

I learned that the constructions in which her father took so much pride, and she on his behalf, were passed off, at least within the family firm, as "boxes". It was not that this usage was specially defined to me. It was simply that the words "box" and "boxes", with various other special expressions, were lightly thrown about by Vi, and sometimes by Munn too; so that I quickly realized what was meant, as when one grasps a foreign idiom through contact with those to whom it is habitual.

Thus Vi remarked: "Daddy's already made our boxes"; as one might lightly describe the planting of two saplings by way of commemoration.

It was impossible not to perceive that Munn seemed already to be completely involved; to be seriously and sincerely interested in the gruesome business. Again it is something one commonly notes: that very speedily the husband is all but totally englutinated into the wife's life-pattern.

Perhaps in the present case, a kind of clue was offered – or re-offered.

"As soon as I set eyes on those daffies Leonard made," observed Vi, her round blue eyes almost alive, "I *knew*."

And, this time, suddenly, I knew too. Munn's reference to something of the same kind, when he was asking me to be his best man, had left me groping after some mere folksiness, some rural witchery and magic, which one could only hope was white. Now I realized that, at least for Vi, Munn's journeyman imitations of men (if I may cite Hamlet) were surrogates for those other imitations of men that were put into her father's boxes. (For what, at the end, is man but ravelled straw?)

Munn's cups and plates, or Mrs Hextable's, had all disappeared, and we ate little square sandwiches, with pink stuff inside, off smooth wooden platters, and drank tea out of mugs that had been not thrown but hollowed out. In the end, when Vi was out of the room, Munn offered me a whisky, and whipped out a single glass tumbler from the back of the cupboard.

He drank nothing himself, though before he had customarily exceeded me.

"I've been looking around," he said, in a confidential voice. "The daffies won't keep two of us, nor will my measly blood money." It struck me that it was the first time that evening he had referred, even indirectly, to the King Charles's head which previously had floated at almost all time, before his angry gaze.

"And soon there'll be three of us."

"Indeed?" I replied. I reflected, in a vulgar way, that it seemed quick work. "I congratulate you both."

"Vi sets great store by our having a child immediately. And so do her people."

"I see what you mean," I said. "And have you found anything?"

"No, damn it, I haven't. It's not easy at our age. But I have something in the back of my mind."

"And what is that? If you wish to tell me, of course."

"Not just yet, old man." I could hear Vi approaching from the next room. "Only if it materializes."

The door opened. "If what materializes, Leonard?" enquired Vi, in her unpleasant voice, her head on one side, like the head of a toy bird.

"If Marley's ghost materializes," said Munn; with more authority than I had observed in him during the whole of the earlier evening.

Vi projected her straight red tongue at him from her round red mouth.

"All things come to him who waits," said Munn with apparent vagueness. Married couples quickly learn to fill in with such utterances.

But I never really like drinking alone, so I soon made my excuses, and walked home to my cottage on the outskirts of the community.

I had a strong suspicion of what the something was at the back of Munn's mind.

And soon we walked into one another outside one of the branch banks. Not that either of us ran an account there: if one knows one's onions, one does not bank in one's own gossipy village.

"We're off," Munn said, "Vi and I. Next week, in fact: Wednesday, I'm told. The old man's sending one of his wagons. It's the only day he can spare one."

"Wagons" in the patois of the Pell family had an implication similar to that of "boxes"; so that the symbolism behind Munn's remarks seemed greatly too oppressive.

But Munn continued the theme. "I doubt whether we shall meet again, you and I."

For a moment I could find nothing at all to say, even though words were my trade.

Munn eased matters. "Not that I shan't send you a change of address," he said. "Of course, I shall."

"In that case," I observed, smiling, "I am sure we shall meet. I shall make a point of looking you up."

"Don't speak too soon. You don't know what I shall be doing."

"I think I do know."

"I'm going into the old man's trade."

"Yes?"

"I'm to serve a quick apprenticeship, to learn from the bottom up, so to speak. And, after that, there's a partnership offered.... So you'll hardly want to know me any more."

"Nonsense," I responded, as brightly as I could manage. "Not see that charming girl you've discovered for yourself! Miss seeing your child! Not likely." To so many married men, one has to say such things. One feels it is the least one can do; and that it is expected.

"You're a good chap," said Munn, "but, for God's sake, don't feel in the least obliged. I know what I'm doing and what the consequences are."

"All bosh," I rejoined, in the same spirit as before. "You're taking up one of the safest money-spinners there is, and I look to enjoy some pickings from the rich man's table."

I received a card bearing Munn's new address (it also bore a faint fringe of acorns), from which for the first time I learned the name of the settlement where the Pells did their work; and, as it happened, I also saw Pell's "wagon", an outsize model, looking all the blacker for its bulk, as it bore away such of the trappings as were Munn's, and Munn himself on the seat in front, with the sably accoutred driver at the other end, and little Vi wedged between them. It was evening at the time, and rapidly sinking into dusk. I reflected that public use of a "wagon" for such an uncanonical purpose as this might attract adverse comment if done during the hours of full daylight. As for me, at that moment, I too had a particular reason for sliding about inconspicuously. Indeed, I drew far back into a convenient hedge as the huge "wagon" sped smoothly by.

I did not go after the "wagon" that week, or the following week; that month, or the following month; that year, or the following year. The place where the Pells had proved to live was a small industrial town, built, in remote East Anglia, as a single entity during the nineteenth century. Though high ideals lay behind its founding, it had little current reputation for beauty of architecture. Of course, standards change remarkably in such contexts, but, at the time I am talking about, the town was represented as a place more to avoid than to visit. Nor did I receive a specific invitation from the Munns. I had not expected one. Indeed, I received no further communication at all from them; not even an undertaker's Christmas card.

Some years later, none the less, I drifted over, and so acquired some idea of what ultimately became of Munn.

By then I had acquired a small, second-hand motor; a two-seater so-called roadster. For some time, I had had a commission to catalogue all the churches in Suffolk. It was no light or brief task, as Suffolk has many churches. Moreover, the prospect of a similar assignment relating to Norfolk was held before me. As far as pleasure went, I should greatly have preferred to travel by train and on foot, which was then perfectly possible; but my employers pressed. I am not sure that by the end, time had been saved; because my second-hand roadster was always breaking down and leaving me helpless, as I have no gift with machines and no love for them.

I acknowledge that for some time I omitted consideration of the town which housed the Pells (and which I had taken to thinking of always in that way). After all, it was agreed that the place had little to offer the connoisseur of *beaux arts*; such as was expected to study my careful lists. I was even ignoring the district around it; which, indeed, was still, in the main, open heath, with few churches, and hardly more houses. (Now it has been utilized in familiar ways: varying from an "open prison" to a large mineral development.) But, in the end, necessity called, and, picking a rainy day, I set out. I should have preferred to disguise myself.

In the town itself, all went perfectly well, even though the rain inconveniently ceased to fall while I was doing my duty in the church. I recalled that the same had happened during Munn's inauspicious nuptials. The church, paid for entirely from the pocket of the founding industrialist, was splendidly ornate; after the fashion then in the 1920s, deprecated, but now once more respected. The town, as a whole, duly seemed more of sociological than aesthetic interest. But my obligation was exclusively ecclesiastical; and though, as I edged along the streets, I kept half an eye open for the name PELL surmounted by plumes or the staring eyes of black horses, I saw nothing of the kind, and in the end even plucked up courage for a coffee and cake in an anomalous tea-shop, half gentlewoman's chintz and half charge-hand's lincrusta. In those days, it was easier to "park" one's car; though, on the other hand, one's car could therefore stand out more conspicuously.

It was on a low ridge to the south of the town, as I drove homewards, that I came upon Munn's new abode. Curiously enough, I was deliberately avoiding any kind of main route, and weaving my way through lanes by the use of the map. This was not easy to combine with driving the roadster, but fortunately the lanes carried very little traffic in those days.

Possibly there was some finger of fate which pointed my way to the house. I seemed conscious all along of such an element in my relationship with Munn; and what happened next perhaps confirms it.

It was hard to believe that it had been necessary to pay money for the "plot" on which the house stood. The tiny black structure recalled what one had heard of "squatters" and their "rights". It stood on a sandy, scrubby, nondescript waste, like a thrown-away cabin trunk; or perhaps like a house built by the little people, there one day, gone the next. I am sure I should have known at once that it was the house built by Munn's father-in-law for his chicks with his own hands; but, as it happened, Vi, in her bright colours, was at work in the front garden as my open roadster snorted laboriously up the ridge. At the same time, rain began to fall once more, this time heavily. I saw Vi go back into the little house; from the other side of which Munn emerged, already clad in heavy oilskins. I suppose it was natural enough for the frail female to withdraw from the inclement weather and for the stouter male to take her place; but there seemed to be something odd and automatic about it, all the same. Moreover, on the instant two flaps opened in the house's single black gable, and a quite life-size wooden cuckoo jumped out, shouting its head off four times. I looked at my watch: it was indeed four o'clock. It seemed odd to have a clock outside a tiny private house, as if it were a town hall; but there could be no doubt about the hour of day being audible over a wide area.

By this time, Munn had looked up and seen me seated there, grinding slowly uphill. To speak plainly, I doubt whether, if I had been travelling faster, I should have stopped; though this may make me sound a cad. With Munn's gaze upon me, I had no alternative. Also, I should have to raise the hood; always a lengthy and injurious undertaking.

I brought the motor to a standstill. Munn just stood there staring at me, silent and motionless. His clothes had never appeared particularly to fit, as I believe I have indicated; but the oilskins seemed to belong to another and much larger man altogether. Munn held a hoe with a very long handle; but it was hard to see what he was doing with it, or what Vi had been doing before him. I have spoken of "a front garden", but when I stopped the car, I realized that there was nothing: no cultivation of any kind, but only the sparse and stony heath, no different in front of the house from elsewhere.

"Excuse me," I shouted, "I must put up my hood." By now the rain was bucketing down; what people call a "cloudburst", though no one knows exactly what that is. Raising the hood was always a fearful ploy, but I dashed at it and did better than usual under the continued pressures of the situation. All the same, the job took a minute or two, so that it became rather noticeable that Munn was not offering to help.

When I had adjusted the last screw (car hoods were more elaborately devised in early days), I realized that Munn was no longer there at all. Obviously, instead of coming to my aid, he had returned to the house for shelter.

I think I should almost certainly have proceeded therewith upon my way, though no doubt with qualms. But what happened was that the car refused to start; which was all too customary.

I sat there for some time with the downpour beating on the hood. I daresay I fiddled around a bit with the levers and buttons and so forth, but I had little hope in that direction.

Then I noticed that the glass in the front window of Munn's house was broken. They were narrow French windows; narrow, but a pair of them. And it was not just a matter of the glass being cracked, but of actual black holes. From the whole look of the place, it dawned on me that no one could seriously live there. And yet, without doubt, I had seen both Munn and Mrs Munn. The former had stared, quite unmistakably, at me, for an appreciable period of time.

Hitherto I had spent the day (and long before that) beating around the bush in one way and another precisely in order not to re-encounter these Munns and Pells. It now occurred to me that the tribe of them had perhaps so weighed upon my mind that I was seeing members of it where they were not. The little black house was so exactly what I was both looking for and avoiding, that the notion of an hallucination seemed slightly more plausible than it commonly does. I had even heard or read that hallucinations are most likely at just such moments between dark and light as, with the heavily gathering clouds, I had lately passed through.

Perhaps for reasons such as these, perhaps for obscurer, and less resistible reasons, at which I have hinted, I resolved to have a closer look round. I was wearing a motorist's overcoat, substantial even against such weather as this. I climbed down from the car and walked over to the broken windows. There was no hedge, gate, or boundary of any kind.

I looked in, with some caution, through one of the holes in the glass; while the rain from the wide gable above dripped down my neck. Despite the two French doors, there appeared to be only a single room within, stretching from side to side of the house; and with the inside walls painted in the same black as the outside. There were some vague items of litter lying about the floor, but no real furniture that I could see. All the same, I could hear the huge cuckoo clock ticking above my head; and some one, I reflected, had to wind it.… Or perhaps not. Perhaps Mr Pell could make entirely wooden clocks that required no winding.

I was not yet exactly frightened, but, rather, puzzled. I pushed away at both the French windows, but succeeded only in dislodging further portions of glass, which fell to the black floor inside with astonishingly much noise. I half expected the life-size cuckoo upstairs to croak in protest.

I imagined that there might be a door at the back of the structure; through which, as I could not help thinking, one "got at the works", in little houses and little artefacts made of wood. I walked round in the rain, and such a door there was. This time, I dragged it open. It stuck and shrieked, but by now I meant business and I pulled hard.

The first thing I saw inside was a child seated on a shelf with both arms extended. It was presumably clutching something out of sight at each side; as its whole posture suggested strain and effort; but I realized that it was a figure in wood of remarkable liveliness. I even managed to extend my hand and touch it. It felt like wood too.

The little house was divided into two chambers by a wooden partition which, painted in the usual black, now confronted me, and against which the child's shelf was set on wooden brackets. This rear chamber was six or eight feet deep. The door I had opened, was a large one and admitted a considerable amount of light, except into the further corners; but there was no window, and the carefully painted, elaborately lifelike figure of the child had been sitting there, it was impossible to guess for how long, in complete darkness. All things considered, it was surprisingly well preserved and spruce.

I now saw that its two hands were involved with a system of wires and pulleys which went upwards into the dimness, but was rusty, broken and drooping. Here were indeed the customary "works". I thought it might be an unusually complex scheme for manipulating the marionette that squatted before me; but it then seemed to me more as though it were the child, with its effortful posture, that was designed to do the manipulation. And the child was so shiny and glossy, where all else was so rotten. *Quis custodiet custodem?* I could not help asking myself.

Beneath the shelf was a low door into the main room of the house, this time ajar. I kicked it open, bent myself double (which was not easy in my very heavy coat), and went through.

The litter on the floor, not merely dusty and dirty, but damp and fungoid, proved to be mainly pages from a book or booklet on the collection of taxes. Against the back partition wall, to the right of the door as I looked back at it, was what appeared, after all, to be the ruin of a large, low piece of furniture. It was as dark, as black, as everything else, and I had not made it out when I peered in through the French windows at the front.

I saw that to the inside of the dwarf-sized door a piece of paper had been pasted: the instructions, one could not help thinking, on how to get the best out of the device. I went back and peered.

Instructions, after a kind, indeed they were; written out in ink and with no punctuation by a hand to me unknown. I read them; and after a considerable pause brought out my churches notebook from my jacket pocket, and copied them down. Here is what I wrote:

> When the man is sawing wood
> Wait and watch for falling blood
> Blood and sawdust are the same
> In Dame Nature's little game
>
> When the woman's blindly scraping
> Then's the hour for blows and raping
> Within the earth without a sound
> That's what makes the world go round
>
> Whatever else you need to know
> Set the man and woman so
> Let them prophesy for ever
> Curse them once and come back never

Obediently, I gazed around me. I thought that, before departing, I might as well look more closely at the low piece of crumbling furniture set against the partition wall.

There could be no doubt as to what was really there. The "piece of crumbling furniture" was a pair of old Mr Pell's "boxes"; set side by side and crumbling indeed. They had no lids – perhaps the lids had crumbled quite away; and inside were the remains, respectively, of the late Mr and Mrs Munn, in no ordinary state of decomposition, but half-merged, in fact much more than half, into the wood from which and to which I was beginning to think we all spring and return. Like a pair of Daphnes, the two of them, I thought; Daphne who was changed by Apollo into a tree. Not that the hideous amalgam in those boxes was imperishable. Far from that: it was already turning into a woody, crawling, wretchedness, damp and primeval-looking, flesh and pulp as one.... Daphne? Of what, in that wooden house, did the name remind me? Then of course I remembered. Old Munn's "daffies" ... I could only wonder.

I made a bolt for it, not looking back, least of all at the little fellow on the shelf, but slamming the door as I ran, so that it jammed fast.

Believe it or not, I had quite forgotten that my car was broken down. I gave one twirl on the starter, leapt in, and had roared on for at least a mile and a half before I recollected that by rights I should not be moving – or escaping – at all. The finger of fate once more I could not but feel.

And perhaps the spell was, in fact, now broken; because, only a few weeks later, I read in the local weekly that there had been a bad fire one night on the heath, with many sheds and shanties burnt out, and several lives lost. In the way of local weeklies, the report concluded by saying that the funerals of the victims would be conducted by Mr Pell.

RIPPING YARNS

In a far off time, still several years from viable domestic videotape, television was as ephemeral as the newspapers – barring occasional repeats. Books and records were the only way of re-experiencing such comedy 'on demand'. The Pythons' love of the book as artefact/objet d'art extended into their solo projects – Eric Idle's *Rutland (Dirty) Weekend* book was an even more Byzantine piece of design than its group antecedents and the script book that accompanied Palin and Jones' *Ripping Yarns* was a delightful evocation of a boy's adventure annual from half a century before. (The series had its genesis in Jones being given such a book by his brother for Christmas). *Ripping Yarns* was the first comedy I can remember anticipating and watching as a 'fan' – as opposed to a more innocent experiencer. By now there were a small group of us – me, Steve Cook, Simon Nicholson – confirmed and knowledgeable aficionados, all of 13 – who gathered at lunch-hours and exchanged favourite moments, sketches and scenes. Looked back on it's hard not to see this as a rehearsal for the professional conversations to come. Though to use the word 'rehearsal' maybe gets it the wrong way round – because these were the real thing that the later activities were a Hepworthian groping back to.

'The Curse of the Claw' from Ripping Yarns

I was lucky. I got a job as Captain upon the *Greasy Bastard*, a tramp steamer which carried rubber goods and things for the weekend between London and Rangoon.

Kevin, in Captain's uniform is standing on the bridge of the Greasy Bastard, *a low, chunky vessel, not much larger than an ocean-going tug.*

It seemed an unbelievable stroke of luck, but I knew that some time … somewhere – the Claw would start to work its evil influence …

Kevin walks across to the door of the wheelhouse and enters. Inside is a Helmsman and next to him a Chief Petty Officer, who is giving orders into the speaking tube to the engine room. This is Chief Petty Officer Russel.

RUSSEL: Fourteen starboard … Mr Jenkins … Three degrees sou' sou' east …

Russel starts checking and cross checking the course and being generally efficient. Kevin's eyes seem drawn to the Chief Petty Officer, but he looks away quickly and shyly as the glance is returned.

But even I was totally unprepared for the way in which the Curse was to manifest itself … We were four days out of London, when I began – to my horror – to notice what an extraordinarily beautiful Chief Petty Officer Mr Russel was.

Mr Russel turns and looks inquiringly at Kevin, having caught his eye. Mr Russel is, indeed, extremely attractive. His fine features, almost delicately beautiful: soft-skinned and un-lined … his body too, hints at a slender femininity … beneath his officer's tunic a moderately well-endowed chest is betrayed by a slight-straining of the buttons. Kevin blushes and looks away, bemused and troubled.

A few hours later, in the evening, as the Greasy Bastard *heaves its way through a heavy swell off the Portuguese coast, Kevin is lying on his bunk in his cabin. He looks troubled and is staring at the Claw in its box on a shelf beside him. He shakes his head and tries unsuccessfully to concentrate on a nautical book.*

Could the Claw be taking its revenge in this cruel way…? My shameful passion for the Chief Petty Officer grew and grew, and I was helpless in its grip …

Kevin flings the book down and buries his face in his pillow. Suddenly there is a knock at the door. Kevin jerks up, eyes wide. He tries to pull himself together.

KEVIN: Come.

The door opens and in comes Mr Russel himself.

KEVIN: Ah … Mr Russel … [He swallows.]

They both swallow.

RUSSEL: Permission to speak with you, Captain?
KEVIN: [slightly breathless]: Yes?
RUSSEL: Well it's just that I … I've noticed you *looking* at me, Captain.
KEVIN: [quickly, highly embarrassed]: Well I look at all the men, Mr Russel … [Attempts a laugh.] I'm just a born starer, I suppose …
RUSSEL: Not the way you've been looking at me, Captain.
KEVIN: Please don't be offended, Mr Russel …
RUSSEL: I'm not offended, Captain … [Meaningfully.] That's what's worrying me …

Kevin is speechless. He tries to reply, but cannot. He swallows dryly.

KEVIN: "Worrying" you?
RUSSEL: I don't know how to say this … Captain …

KEVIN: [breathlessly]: What?

RUSSEL: [dropping his eyes for a moment]: Ever since you first took over the ship, Captain ... I've ... I've felt attracted to you.

KEVIN: Oh God!

Kevin turns away, fists clenched and stares blindly out of his porthole into the night.

RUSSEL: Does that repel you?

KEVIN: [dragging it out of himself]: I wish it did, Mr Russel ... I only wish it did.

Russel comes up behind Kevin.

RUSSEL: May I touch you, Captain?

Kevin freezes and shrinks away.

KEVIN: No! No! It's bad enough with a girl ... but you're ... you're a *man*!

Russel leans his fists against the wall and closes his eyes. His breast heaves.

RUSSEL: I know! I know!

KEVIN: [focussing on Russel's chesty region]: You are a man, aren't you?

RUSSEL: Of course I'm a man.

KEVIN: I'm sorry, Mr Russel, I didn't mean ...

RUSSEL: Don't be sorry. It's me that's sorry. You don't know what it's like ... trapped in this man's body ...

KEVIN: But what about ... [Kevin nods at Russel's heaving bosom.] ... those.

RUSSEL: These. [He looks down at them.] Oh ... I've been putting on weight there ever since I was sixteen ... it's a recognised medical condition.

KEVIN: Have you seen a doctor?

RUSSEL: Doctors ... surgeons ... there's nothing they can do, they just say I'll grow out of it ...

KEVIN: [swallows tentatively, and approaches Russel]: Well ... Mr Russel

... since you are a man ... maybe it would be ... all right ... for me to ... rub something on them ... for a bit ...

It seemed as if the evil influence of the Claw was tearing away the last shreds of my manhood and dignity ...

RUSSEL: Would you ... Captain?
KEVIN: Oh yes ... Chief Petty Officer.

They fall, locked in an illicit embrace, onto Kevin's bunk, in the very shadow of the Claw itself. The scene discreetly changes and we see the small boat from a distance, tossing in the waves ... one porthole is lighted ...

And yet, at that moment, something changed. As if the power of the Claw seemed to be suddenly weakening.

Back in Kevin's cabin. He and Chief Petty Officer Russel are sitting up naked in Kevin's bunk. Russel's long dark hair spilling across the pillow ...

That night, we discovered that Russel had been wrong – he was a woman after all ... it was a mistake anyone could have made, in the sort of society in which we had been brought up.

Some time later in the voyage, Kevin is sitting on the stern of the Greasy Bastard *surrounded by his pretty crew. Their jackets hang loosely open in the sunshine. They laugh gaily and happily.*

We discovered that most of the rest of the crew were women as well ... The voyage became suddenly idyllic ... Free from the repressive society we'd left behind us, we began to talk frankly about ourselves and our bodies and our needs ... I was happy for the first time in my life until one day, with the coast of Burma almost in sight ... I realised I had once again underestimated the power of the Claw.

Kevin is in his cabin. He looks tanned and fit. He's humming happily away to himself as he does his packing. The Claw is in its box beside his bed. There is a knock at the door.

KEVIN: Come!

The door opens and a deputation from the crew enters, headed by Chief Petty Officer Russel, looking quite ravishing. All the rest are women, apart from a bearded Stoker, who is quite definitely a man. There is a slight pause. They look a little uncomfortable.

KEVIN: Ah! We'll be in Burma by tomorrow, eh men? All packed?

They look at each other.

RUSSEL: We're not going to Burma, Captain.
KEVIN: I beg your pardon?
RUSSEL: We're not going to Burma, Captain.
KEVIN: What do you mean? We're practically there.
RUSSEL: It's too good here, Captain. On board the *Greasy Bastard* we've all found a freedom and happiness we can never find anywhere else. Let's not just throw it all away ...
CHIEF ENGINEER [a flaxen-haired beauty]: Why can't we sail on like this forever?
KEVIN: Because I have to get to Burma.

The crew stand their ground, looking defiant.

KEVIN: Look ... I know we've been happy together ... I've learnt a lot about ... well ... all sorts of things I didn't know before ...
STOKER: Like stoking the boiler, sir?
KEVIN: Well that ... and ... er ... other things ... [He eyes Russel knowingly.]
STOKER: I *meant* it metaphorically, sir.
KEVIN: [highly embarrassed]: Ah ... yes ...

Kevin decides it's time he came clean, he picks up the box containing the Claw and shows it to them.

KEVIN: Look! I have a trust to return this to its rightful owners ... I cannot betray that trust.
RUSSEL: You wouldn't let that come between us and our happiness!

KEVIN: A man's life depends on it.
RUSSEL: Our happiness depends on it too, Captain!

Russel makes a sudden grab for the box, snatches it out of Kevin's hands and races out of the cabin.

KEVIN: Mr Russel!

He gives chase, elbowing his way through the other men. Russel, pursued by an increasingly frantic Kevin, who is pursued in turn by the rest of the crew, races down the steps from the bridge, and runs the length of the Greasy Bastard *until she reaches the stern, there she stops, and begins to open the box.*

KEVIN: No! You don't know what you're doing, Russel!
RUSSEL: I do, Captain … I'm saving you … I'm saving all of us!
KEVIN: Russel! No!

Russel clasps the Claw, holds it aloft, but before she can hurl it over the side, there is a tremendous explosion and a sheet of flame and debris fly hundreds of feet into the sky.
As the noise of the explosion dies down we move on in the story, and find young Kevin, many weeks later, torn, battered, and slightly charred, walking forlornly up the driveway of Uncle Jack's crumbling house.

I was the only survivor … A dreadful sense of foreboding gripped me as I returned to the house I had loved so much …

The chimney of Uncle Jack's house collapses, quite slowly, in a shower of brick dust. Kevin walks slowly up the drive. He goes in the front door, the porch collapses as usual, only more so.

… During my absence Uncle Jack had grown weaker and weaker. He had caught a rare Spanish skin disease, which cheered him up momentarily, and a bout of myxomatosis, but apart from that it had all been downhill:

Kevin walks through the house and up the stairs and into Uncle Jack's room. Uncle Jack is lying in bed at his last gasp. Flies buzz around him.

KEVIN: Uncle Jack ...

UNCLE JACK: [wearily]: Kevin ... did you return the Claw?

KEVIN: [lowering his eyes]: No ... Uncle Jack ... I'm sorry ...

UNCLE JACK: Where is it boy?

KEVIN: It's in the Indian Ocean ...

UNCLE JACK: [as if caught by some sudden, unbearable pain]: Agh! ... Oh ... no ... no

KEVIN: I couldn't help it. I was nearly there, but ...

UNCLE JACK: Of course you couldn't ... I told you boy, the Claw's too strong ... too cunning.

KEVIN: I'm sorry Uncle Jack ...

UNCLE JACK: Listen, boy ... I'm done for now, but I want you to promise me something.

KEVIN: Yes?

UNCLE JACK: That Claw must be stopped ... if it's allowed to go loose in the world for too long it'll do untold damage.

KEVIN: Yes Uncle Jack.

UNCLE JACK: One day ... it will return to this house ... you must be here, always, ready for it, when it comes.

KEVIN: How can it Uncle Jack?

UNCLE JACK: It will ... it will ... [In considerable pain.] Now boy, come here and have a look at my ... Aargh ... Aargh ... Aaaaarggghhh!

Uncle Jack dies spectacularly with prolonged gurgling, and rattling. Kevin looks on with deep sadness and utter helplessness.

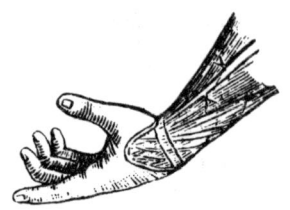

PORTNOY'S COMPLAINT

One of Gordon Anderson's questions to Alan Bennett (*see* pages 16–17) was about who he enjoyed reading. He said that he was very fond of Phillip Roth. I leapt in in my show-offy way and said that I enjoyed him too. It's fair to say however that my knowledge of Roth extended to one book only – *Portnoy's Complaint* – which had been passed to me, along with a pile of rag mags, when I was 15 by my good friend Andy Nyman (now an actor and magician of some renown). His interest in the book – and mine too – was not really literary. It was mainly for chapter 2 – descriptively titled "Whacking Off" – paragraphs which echoed our own experience to an uncanny degree in their combination of frenzied self-abuse, Jewish mothers and the guilt that attended both. The book demonstrated to me at an early age that the highbrow and the lowbrow could meet to hilarious effect – and that masturbation is a comic vein with rich potential. The trick is to stop doing it long enough to be able to write about. (A BBC comedy executive recently complained to me that he had noticed a considerable drop in the volume of unsolicited scripts submitted in the past five years or so – he had no doubt that the prevalence of internet pornography was to blame.)

WHACKING OFF

Then came adolescence – half my waking life spent locked behind the bathroom door, firing my wad down the toilet bowl, or into the soiled clothes in the laundry hamper, or *splat*, up against the medicine-chest mirror, before which I stood in my dropped drawers so I could see how it looked coming out. Or else I was doubled over my flying fist, eyes pressed closed but mouth wide open, to take that sticky sauce of buttermilk and Clorox on my own tongue and teeth – though not infrequently, in my blindness and ecstasy, I got it all in the pompadour, like a blast of Wildroot Cream Oil. Through a world of matted handkerchiefs and crumpled Kleenex and stained pyjamas, I moved my raw and swollen penis, perpetually in dread that my loathsomeness would be discovered by someone stealing upon me just as I was in the frenzy of dropping my load. Nevertheless, I was wholly incapable of keeping my paws from my dong once it started the climb up my belly. In the middle of a class I would raise a hand to be excused, rush down the corridor to the lavatory, and with ten or fifteen savage strokes, beat off standing up into a urinal. At the Saturday afternoon movie I would leave my friends to go off to the candy machine – and wind up in a distant balcony seat, squirting my seed into the empty wrapper from a Mounds bar. On an outing of our family association, I once cored an apple, saw to my astonishment (and with the aid of my obsession) what it looked like, and ran off into the woods to fall upon the orifice of the fruit, pretending that the cool and mealy hole was actually between the legs of that mythical being who always called me 'Big Boy' when she pleaded for what no girl in recorded history had ever had. "Oh shove it in me, Big Boy," cried the cored apple that I banged silly on that picnic. "Big Boy, Big Boy, oh give me all you've got," begged the empty milk bottle that I kept hidden in our storage bin in the basement, to drive wild after school with my vaselined upright. "Come, Big Boy, come," screamed the maddened piece of liver that, in my own insanity, I bought one afternoon at a butcher shop and, believe it or not, violated behind a billboard on the way to a bar mitzvah lesson.

It was at the end of my freshman year of high school – and my freshman year of masturbating – that I discovered on the underside of my penis, just where the shaft meets the head, a little discoloured dot that has since been diagnosed as a freckle. Cancer. I had given myself *cancer*. All that pulling and tugging at my own flesh, all that friction, had given me an incurable disease. And not yet fourteen! In bed at night the tears rolled from my eyes "No!" I sobbed. "I don't want to die! Please – No!" But then, because I would very shortly be a corpse anyway, I went ahead as usual and jerked off into my sock. I had taken to carrying the dirty socks into bed with me at night so as to be able to use one as a receptacle upon retiring, and the other upon awakening.

If only I could cut down to one hand-job a day, or hold the line at two, or even three! But with the prospect of oblivion before me, I actually began to set new records for myself. Before meals. After meals. *During* meals. Jumping up from the dinner table, I tragically clutch at my belly – diarrhoea! I cry, I have been stricken with diarrhoea! – And once behind the locked bathroom door, slip over my head a pair of underpants that I have stolen from my sister's dresser and carry rolled in a handkerchief in my pocket. So galvanic is the effect of cotton panties against my mouth – so galvanic is the *word* "panties" – that the trajectory of my ejaculation reaches startling new heights, leaving my joint like a rocket it makes right for the light bulb overhead, where to my wonderment and horror it hits and it hangs. Wildly in the first moment I cover my head, expecting an explosion of glass, a burst of flames – disaster, you see, is never far from my mind. Then quietly as I can, I climb the radiator and remove the sizzling gob with a wad of toilet paper. I begin a scrupulous search of the shower curtain, the tub, the tile floor, the four toothbrushes – God Forbid! – and just as I am about to unlock the door, imagining I have covered my tracks, my heart lurches at the sight of what is hanging like snot to the toe of my shoe. I am the Raskolnikov of jerking off – the sticky evidence is everywhere! Is it on my cuffs too? In my *hair*? My *ear*? All this I wonder even as I come back to the kitchen table, scowling and cranky, to grumble self-righteously at my father when he opens his mouth full of red-jello and says, "I don't know what you have to lock the door about. That to me is beyond comprehension. What is this, a home or a Grand Central Station?" "…privacy …a human being… around here *never*," I reply, then push aside my dessert to scream "I don't feel well – *will everybody leave me alone?*"

After dessert, which I finish, because I happen to like jello, even if I detest them – after dessert I am back in the bathroom again. I burrow through the week's laundry until I uncover one of my sister's soiled brassieres. I string one shoulder strap over the knob of the bathroom door and the other on the knob of the linen closet: a scarecrow to bring on more dreams. "Oh, beat it Big Boy, beat it to a red hot pulp – " So I am being urged by the little cups of Hannah's brassiere, when a rolled up newspaper smacks at the door. And send me and my handful an inch off the toilet seat "Come on, give somebody else a crack at that bowl, will you?" my father says. "I haven't moved my bowels in a week."

I recover my equilibrium, as is my talent, with a burst of hurt feelings. "I have a terrible case of diarrhoea! Doesn't that mean anything to anyone in this house?" – in the meantime resuming the stroke, indeed quickening the tempo as my cancerous organ miraculously begins to quiver again from the inside out.

Then Hannah's brassiere *begins to move*. To swing to and fro! I veil my eyes, and behold! – Lenore Lapidus! Who has the biggest pair in my class, running for the bus after school, her great untouchable load shifting weightily inside her blouse, oh I urge them up from their cups, and over, LENORE LAPIDUS' ACTUAL TITS, and realize in the same split second that my mother is vigorously shaking the doorknob of the door I have finally forgotten to lock! I knew it would happen one day! *Caught!* As good as *dead!*

"Open up Alex. I want you to open up this instant."

It's locked, I'm *not* caught! And I see from what's alive in hand that I'm not quite dead yet either. Beat on then! Beat on! "Lick me, Big Boy- Lick me a good hot lick! I'm Lenore Lapidus' big fat red-hot brassiere!

"Alex, I want an answer from you. Did you eat French fries after school? Is that why you're sick like this?"

"Nuhhh, nuhh."

"Alex, are you in pain? Do you want me to call the doctor? Are you in pain, or aren't you? I want to know exactly where it hurts. *Answer me.*"

"Yuhh, yuhh…"

"Alex, I don't want you to flush the toilet," says my mother sternly. "I want to see what you've done in there. I don't like the sound of this at all."

"And me," says my father, touched as he always was by my accomplishments, – as much in awe as envy – "I haven't moved my bowels for a week," just as I lurch from my perch on the toilet seat, and with the whimper of a whipped animal, deliver three drops of something barely viscous in the tiny piece of cloth where my flat-chested eighteen-year-old sister has laid her nipples, such as they are. It is my fourth orgasm of the day. When will I begin to come blood?"

"Get in here, please, please, you," says my mother. "Why did you flush the toilet when I told you not to?"

"I forgot."

"What was in there that you were so fast to flush it?"

"Diarrhoea."

"Was it mostly liquid or was it mostly poopie?"

"I don't look! I didn't look! Stop saying poopie to me – I'm in high school!"

"Oh, don't you shout at *me*, Alex. I'm not the one who gave you diarrhoea, I assure you. If all you ate was what you were fed at home, you wouldn't be running to the bathroom fifty times a day. Hannah tells me what you're doing, so don't think I don't know."

She's missed the underpants! *I've been caught!* Oh, *let* me be dead! I'd just as soon!

"Yeah, what do I do…?"

"You go to Harold's Hot Dog and *Chazerai* Palace after school and you eat French fries with Melvin Weiner. Don't you? Don't lie to me either. Do you or do you not stuff yourself with French fries and ketchup on Hawthorne avenue after school? Jack, come in here, I want you to hear this," she calls to my father, now occupying the bathroom.

"Look, I'm trying to move my bowels," he replies, "Don't I have enough trouble as it is without people screaming at me when I'm trying to move my bowels?"

"You know what your son does after school, the *A* student, who his own mother can't say poopie to anymore he's such a *grown-up?* What do you think your grown-up son does when nobody is watching him?"

"Can I be left alone, please?" cries my father. "Can I have a little peace, please, so I can get something accomplished in here?"

"Just wait till your father hears what you do, in defiance of every health habit there could possibly be. Alex, answer me something. You're so smart, how come you know all the answers now, answer me this: how do you think Melvin Wiener gave himself colitis? Why has that child spent half his life in hospitals?

"Because he eats *Chazerai*."

"Don't you dare make fun of me!"

"All right," I scream, "how *did* he get colitis?"

"Because he eats *Chazerai*! But it's not a joke! Because to him a meal is an O Henry bar washed down by a bottle of Pepsi. Because his breakfast consists of, do you know what? The most important meal of the day – not according to your mother Alex, but according to the highest nutritionists – and do you know what that child eats?"

"A doughnut."

"A doughnut is right, Mr. Smart Guy. Mr. Adult. And *coffee*. Coffee and a doughnut, and on this a thirteen-year old *pisher* with half a stomach is supposed to start a day. But you, thank god, have been brought up differently. You don't have a mother who gallivants all over town like some name I could name, from Bam's to Hahne's to Kresge's all day long. Alex, tell me, so its not a mystery, or maybe I'm just stupid, – Only tell me, what are you trying to do, what are you trying to prove, that you should stuff yourself with such junk when you could come home to a poppyseed cookie and a nice glass of milk? I want the truth from you, I wouldn't tell your father," she says, her voice dropping significantly, "but I *must* have the truth from you." Pause. Also significant. "Is it just French fries darling, or is it more?... Tell me, please, what other kind of garbage you're putting into you're mouth so we can get to the bottom of this diarrhea! I want a straight answer from you, Alex. Are you eating hamburgers out? Answer me, please, is that why you flushed the toilet – was there hamburger in it?"

"I told you – I don't look in the bowl when I flush it! I'm not interested like you are in other people's poopie!"

"Oh, oh, oh – thirteen years old and the mouth on him! To someone who is asking a question about *his* health, *his* welfare!" The utter incomprehensibility of the situation causes her eyes to become heavy with tears. "Alex, why are you getting like this, give me some clue? Tell me please what horrible things we have done to you all our lives that this should be our reward?" I believe the question strikes her as original. I believe she considers the question unanswerable. And worst of all, so do I. What *have* they done for me all their lives, but sacrifice? Yet that this is precisely the horrible thing is beyond my understanding – and still, Doctor! To this day!

I brace myself now for the whispering. I can spot the whispering coming a mile away. We are about to discuss my father's headaches.

"Alex, he didn't have a headache on him today that he could hardly see straight from it?" She checks, is he out of earshot? God forbid he should hear how critical his condition is, he might claim exaggeration. "He's not going next week for a test for a tumor?"

"He is?"

"Bring him in," the doctor said, "I'm going to give him a test for a tumor."

Success. I am crying. There is no good reason for me to be crying but in this household everybody tries to get in a good cry at least once a day. My father, you must understand – as doubtless you do: blackmailers account for a substantial part of the human community, and, I would imagine, of your clientele – my father has been "going" for this tumor test for nearly as long as I can remember. Why his head aches him all the time is, of course, because he is constipated all the time – why he is constipated is because ownership of his intestinal tract is in the hands of the firm of Worry, Fear and Frustration. It is true that a doctor once said to my mother that he would give her husband a test for a tumor – if that would make her happy, is I believe the way he worded it; he suggested that it would be cheaper, however, and probably more effective for the man to invest in an enema bag. Yet, that I know all this to be so does not make it any less heartbreaking to imagine my father's skull splitting open from a malignancy.

Yes, she has me where she wants me, and she knows it. I clean forget my own cancer in the grief that comes – comes now as it came then – when I think of how much of life has always been (as he himself very accurately puts it) beyond his comprehension. And his grasp. No money, no schooling, no language, no learning, curiosity without culture, drive without opportunity, experience without wisdom... How easily his inadequacies can move me to tears. As easily as they move me to anger!

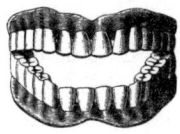

LES DAWSON

O nce I saw Les Dawson filming a sketch, dressed in cricket whites on Woodhouse Moor – the park which adjoined our school. My first instinct was to run up and say hello, as I would have done to a favourite uncle. Fortunately I remembered in time that I didn't actually know him. There was a particular family tie to Les in the Dyson household in that when he dragged-up to perform Cissie and Ada with Roy Barraclough, Les was an almost exact double for Grandma Dyson – right down to the absent false teeth (Grandma Dyson was always happiest with her teeth in a glass, rather than in her mouth. She had a ladies' fashion shop called Lafayettes in Leeds city centre and she would take her dentures out while she dressed the window. Often they would remain there all afternoon, glistening pinkly beneath the couture, until one of the shop-girls – or a passing customer – drew attention to them.) I was enchanted by Cissie and Ada, not realising that the routine itself was inspired by Norman Evans' 'over the garden wall'. I just recognised the absolute truth of the portrayal of those women – who could still be seen everywhere in Leeds, even in the 1970s. The lowering of the voice in order to talk about taboo subjects was another Grandma Dyson trait, although she adopted the double precaution of saying the unsayable in Yiddish. Not really a natural performer – at least not in the sense of adopting funny voices and personas – I did find it easy to do Ada myself, right down to the slapping of the back of the wrist and the heaving of the imaginary bosom. When me and Mark wrote the Iris and Judee scenes for the *League* we quite consciously tapped into the rhythms of these exchanges – the posh woman with airs and her earthier foil. We definitely enjoyed the fact that some of our gags were as shameless as Terry Ravenscroft's, (Mark's and my favourite – 'Do you have Retsina Iris?', 'No, I'm just tired.')

CISSIE AND ADA

1. ART GALLERY

An art gallery. Cissie and Ada are looking at a large painting, a landscape by Pissarro. Cissie is obviously very taken by the painting.

CISSIE: Oh yes. Very artistic, isn't it Ada.

ADA: Well if you like trees, yes.

CISSIE: French, if I'm not mistaken. [She refers to her brochure] Yes, I was right. It's a Pissarro.

ADA: They'll do it anywhere, these foreigners, won't they.

CISSIE: Camille Pissarro was a famous impressionist, Ada.

ADA: What, you mean sort of an French Rory Bremner?

CISSIE: Honestly Ada, I can't take you anywhere. You're pig ignorant, you really are. For your information impressionists were painters who paint without elaborate finish or detail.

ADA: Well the Co-op decorators do that, have you seen the state they left my front room skirting boards in, I've seen less streaks on two pound of belly of pork.

CISSIE: If, as I suspect, you are totally uncomprehending in matters of good taste and breeding Ada, kindly keep your gob shut!

ADA: Well there's no need for that, I'm sure.

CISSIE: Well you'd test the patience of a Saint, you really would. I mean you were just the same when I took you to that exhibition of 'Clothing Through The Ages' when we went to Rhyl. Showing me up like that!

ADA: What do you mean?

CISSIE: You know very well what I mean. When the Guide pointed out those corsets and said they were from William and Mary. And you said 'Are they as good as Marks and Spencers?'

ADA: Well I'm very sorry I'm sure, but some of us haven't had the benefit of your education, have we. I mean I could only go to school every other day, what with being a twin and only one pair of knickers between us.

CISSIE: But you were in the school hockey team, weren't you, what did you do then?

ADA: If it wasn't my day for the knickers I prayed it wasn't going to be windy.

CISSIE: Yes well accompanying me round this art gallery will give you the chance to catch up on your education, won't it. It can do you nothing but good.

ADA: It's not doing my feet much good, they feel like a couple of globe artichokes.

CISSIE: Oh stop complaining will you, we have a lot to get through yet.

They walk on. Suddenly Ada sees a statue of a naked Greek god. It stops her in her tracks.

ADA: Ooooooh! [She quickly covers Cissie's eyes and tries to walk her past the statue]

CISSIE: What the…. what do you think you're playing at, Ada!

ADA: Just keep walking.

Cissie pushes Ada's hands away.

CISSIE: Get your hands off me, you daft…. [she sees the statue]…oooh! Oh I say.

ADA: Well I did try to save you from it.

CISSIE: Yes. Thank you Ada, love.

ADA: Disgusting, isn't it.

CISSIE: Positively scandalous.

They both carry on looking at the statue.

CISSIE: I wonder who sculpted it?

ADA: I don't know, but he wasn't short of clay.

CISSIE: It could be Moore, I suppose.

ADA: Oh not much more, surely.

CISSIE: I meant *Henry* Moore, the sculptor! Or on second thoughts it could be Rodin. He did 'The Thinker' you know.

ADA: Well that would give you something to think about, that's for sure.

CISSIE: Honestly Ada, your mind! You've got a point though, because he's certainly a big lad isn't he, and no mistake.

ADA: I thought he had three legs at first.

CISSIE: I wonder what it's called? [She notices a plaque and leans forward to read it]

ADA: Be careful Cissie, it could poke your eye out.

CISSIE: [Reads off the plaque] It's called 'Waiting'.

ADA: Yes and he'd be waiting a hell of a long time if he was mine. Hey, can you keep a secret, Cissie?

CISSIE: Well of course I can.

ADA: That's the first grown-up one I've ever seen.

CISSIE: Oh come on Ada, you don't expect me to believe that, surely. What about your Bert, you must have seen him undressed?

ADA: Not once, Cissie. the whole time we've been married. No he's always got undressed in the dark. He says it's because when his mother was carrying him it was during the war and she was frightened by a searchlight operator.

CISSIE: Well now that you've seen one, what do you think?

ADA: I think I'm going to go back to the vicar who married us and ask for a rebate on my marriage licence.

They walk on.

2. HOLIDAYS

A travel agency. Cissie and Ada walk in. Cissie notices that there is nobody at the counter so they sit down to wait.

CISSIE: There doesn't appear to be anyone here, Ada love.

ADA: Perhaps they've gone on their holidays.

CISSIE: Well while we're waiting it will give us the chance to decide where we want to go this year.

ADA: Well anywhere as long as it isn't Greece, I didn't like that Rhodes place last year.

CISSIE: I told you, you should have gone to Athens, you'd have liked it there, it's lovely, they have an acropolis there.

ADA: They had one in Rhodes, I was never off it.

CISSIE: Oh you're pig ignorant Ada, you really are, it's an old ruin!

ADA: Well this one had a crack in it and a loose board.

CISSIE: I quite fancy Italy, myself.

ADA: Me too, a coach tour would be nice.

CISSIE: How about the Dolomites?

ADA: Well if they start to play me up I can always sit on a rubber ring. I quite fancy Blackpool too, to tell you the truth.

CISSIE: Oh I find it so uncouth, Blackpool.

ADA: Yes, nice isn't it. Me and Bert had our honeymoon there, you know. It's the place where I finally became a woman – that first night at the Seaview guest house.

CISSIE: And when you went there, were you virgo intacta?

ADA: No, just bed and breakfast.

CISSIE: I mean that prior to your honeymoon you and Bert hadn't done it?

ADA: Oh no. Can you keep a secret, Cissie? Bert didn't know how to do it.

CISSIE: I must say I find that very hard to believe, knowing your Bert.

ADA: May God strike me dead, Cissie. He hadn't got a clue. My mother told me to lie back and think of England. I'd time to think of England, Scotland, Ireland, Algeria.....

CISSIE: Oh you poor dear.

ADA: And I did everything in my power to tempt him, everything in my power Cissie.

CISSIE: Did you wear a sexy night-gown?

ADA: Yes, one I got it from Silky Billy's on the market, off the bargain rail.

CISSIE: Was it see-through?

ADA: Oh yes, you could see my vest and liberty bodice through it as plain as day. Anyway I went to the doctor to see if he could suggest anything and he told me to try taking Bert past the Tower a few times.

CISSIE: Auto suggestion.

ADA: No we drove past in a landau. And I walked him past it several times.

CISSIE: And did he rise to the occasion, as it were?

ADA: Well I'll put it this way, I think he must have been looking at the Central Pier instead.

CISSIE: Well I don't know about us going to Blackpool for your holiday I would have thought you would want to steer well clear the place after an experience like that.

ADA: That's why I want to go, I'm hoping he'll leave me alone again.

CISSIE: And where does Bert want to go?

ADA: Well he did once mention that he'd always wanted to return to the place where he spent the war.

CISSIE: What, the glasshouse at Colchester?

ADA: No, I mean before he stole that tank. Normandy.

CISSIE: Now that's not such a bad idea, because my Leonard would like that. He saw action at Normandy, you know. That was where he almost got the V.C.

ADA: Well that's the chance you take when you go with foreign women. The hussies!

CISSIE: I think we'll settle for Normandy then. Now how shall we travel there, on the cross-channel ferry or shall we fly?

ADA: Oh the ferry, because it cost us an extra thirty quid the only time me and Bert ever flew.

CISSIE: Thirty pounds? Whyever was that?

ADA: Well you know that little paper bag they give you?

CISSIE: Yes.

ADA: Well Bert asked the stewardess what it was for. And she told him it was to be sick in.

CISSIE: So why did that cost you another thirty pounds?

ADA: Well he had to drink three bottles of whisky before he felt sick.

THE SHUTTLEWORTHS

'PILLOCK OF THE COMMUNITY'

Gratifyingly John Shuttleworth has become a national institution – singular, without precedent, enduring, often unexpectedly beautiful. He began life on the radio – or rather he flowered into life on the radio. The first time I actually remember seeing him was on the short-lived *Saturday Zoo* series doing a spoof masterclass on drunk acting. But his first late-night Radio 4 series a year or so later was a whole other deal. This was the best use of radio as a comic medium since *The Hitchhiker's Guide to the Galaxy*. It had taken what some might see as limitations and turned them into glorious strengths. Using one man's voice, a multi-track recorder, a pitch-shifter and a few sound effects Graham Fellows created a complete world that bloomed in your head as you listened. He performed all the characters – but they interacted so fully and spontaneously that it was hard to believe they weren't all in a room with one another. The observation of life's minutiae and the richness of the personalities made it a delight to listen to again and again. John's wife Mary, a crotchety dinner-lady, is evoked with a scant few words – but her permanent state of irritation is so *real* that she brings you out in a cold sweat – a chilling reminder of the constant fear felt as a child in the presence of a shouty mum. And this was just the start of John Shuttleworth's treasures. The comic songs are some of the most warming ever written – 'Karen's Tangerine', 'Alone With The Day,' 'Modern Man' to name but three. Ken Worthington – John's neighbour and agent (John is an unlikely aspiring singer/songwriter) – rivals the main character in his richness and lovability – a preening fool and would be Don Juan, who is in fact a lonely and desperate bachelor. And John himself – a complex figure – sensitive, loving, stern, tough, gloriously innocent – absurd but true. It's the combination of silliness, truth and warmth that makes John Shuttleworth such a delight. And the excellence of the comic dialogue. Many of John's, Ken's and Mary's turn-of-phrases are lodged deep in my consciousness and I find I have been trotting them out on a regular basis for over a decade. From John's simple 'Ooph' to Mary's rebuking 'No love', to Ken's 'You'd better believe it John, it is happening' – these little soundbites get adopted in all kinds of situations. To me this is a mark of absolute quality – when somebody's work becomes so ingrained that quite spontaneously you find it coming out of your mouth. Ultimately the thing I admire most about John Shuttleworth is the humanity that lies at its heart – never sentimental, always true – the older I get the more I think that this is the real gold of comedy. It might not shout the loudest but it will endure beyond anything else.

PILLOCK OF THE COMMUNITY

JOHN: Ooh! Some banging next door. Hello! Er, I'm afraid I'm in a bit of a rush today because I've got to go and mow the lawn. Of a halfway house that, er, opened near us recently. It's run by Lesley, a lovely lady, from Louth, Lincolnshire. And in return for mowing the lawn I get to use her typewriter you see, for me letters. To record companies. But, er, I'd better get a move on because there's some clouds forming, er, over Gleedless, I'd say, you know. They look pretty ominous and they're heading this way. So, um, ohhh! Excuse me! I've just witnessed a crime being committed. Stay there please, I'll be back in a minute.

[Intro music]

[Radio 4 voice:] We present, *The Shuttleworths*. Episode 4, 'Pillock of the Community'.

JOHN: Ken, what d'you think you're doing?
KEN: Pardon? Hello! Whooo!
JOHN: What're you doing with that hosepipe?
KEN: I'm watering the garden. What's it look like?
JOHN: But why Ken?
KEN: What d'you mean? Cos needs watering, that's why.
JOHN: Yes but you're contravening the hosepipe ban. Are you not aware of that fact?
KEN: No. No I'm not. I thought that was last year.
JOHN: No, no, the restriction's not been lifted. It still applies Ken.
KEN: [interrupting] Oh!
JOHN: So I'll ask you please, to, er, turn off your tap and, er, roll up your may-
KEN: Hosepipe?
JOHN: Hosepipe.
KEN: No, no I won't John.

JOHN: Kenneth, come on. Look, hey, it's going to rain in a couple of hours anyway.

KEN: It isn't.

JOHN: Look-

KEN: Keep away! Don't come any closer.

JOHN: Ken! Stop that.

KEN: Well I warned ya.

JOHN: You can't see ladies and gentlemen, but Ken's just splashed me. Er, bit of water. Just caught me trousers.

KEN: Yes. And I'll do it again if you don't get off my land.

JOHN: Look-

KEN: Go on clear off. You're trespassing.

JOHN: Ken. Co-operate. Offff.

KEN: [giggles]

JOHN: See, Ken's laughing.

KEN: I am, yes.

JOHN: And that's because I've become, er, ensnared in his rose bush.

KEN: [grunts]

JOHN: There's a thorn gone right through me sweater.

KEN: That's right.

JOHN: Mary'll be furious.

KEN: She will.

JOHN: In fact, can you come and disentangle me please Ken?

KEN: No. No. You can stay there till the police arrive.

JOHN: Look, I'm getting angry now.

KEN: Oh? Well maybe you need cooling off then.

JOHN: Ken! No! Please! No! Ken! Stop it.

[Music starts, then singing]

I'm a modern man
I'm a modern man
I do the household chores
Whenever I can

I'm a modern man
I'm a modern man
I get the hoover out
And I put it away again

[Spoken] When me wife's finished with it, you know.

On Saturday morning I take an hour or two out of my life
To go shopping with Mary, my wife

[Spoken] Yeah, that's right. Nice country ditty this one, in't it? Yeah, on a Saturday morning I accompany Mary to Morrison's or Asda and we do the weekly shopping. I carry the heavier articles such as breakfast cereal, big box powders... It's teamwork, you know. Holding the bags open for each other. I enjoy it. We both do.

[Singing] Then we may go for a cappuccino in the new arcade
It's more pricy than the ordinary but it's... freshly made

[Spoken] It is, lovely and frothy in't it? They put a bit of chocolate on top. Yeah, fantastic. Had some tarama salata as well the other day.

[Singing]
I'm a modern man oh ho oh
I'm a modern man oh ho
I'm a modern man oh ho oh

[Spoken] Well I think I am. You may disagree. That's your privilege. Ah, ooh...

KEN: Hello! No. There doesn't seem to be anybody here. [tuts] Lesley's jeep isn't in the drive. She's got a Suzuki. You know, a purple one with a big bumper. S'got a funny name. Aw, this is frustrating. Because, here am I, you know, with me Concord in the boot. I'm all raring to go. Got me extension lead but unless I have a power source, I can't do a damn thing. Sorry to swear but, what do they suggest I do? Break in? Oh! There is somebody. Ah no, that's Roger. Sitting in the window, looking at me. Now he's, erm, wheelchair bound. He's an ex-solicitor. Er, very sad case, er, at one time anyway he was very successful. He had an E-type Jag. A succession of dollybirds. He married his secretary I believe. But, um, he suffered a collapsed spine in the early eighties and this turned him to drink and, er, it affected his brain. He started doing strange things you know, ah, and in the end he was struck off. Then rejected by his family.

And now he's just er, well, um, his hair sticks up, like Ken Dodd. You know. But whereas I suspect Ken does that, er, purely for comic effect, in Roger's case it's, um, just gone like that, you know, naturally. I mean, there are moments of mental clarity, when Roger will give out bits of useful legal advice, and you know I've been there wishing I had a pen and paper, because he's said things like, er, the husband has the right to do this, and the wife can do this if she- you know, it's very interesting but, er, sometimes he turns the air blue, you know, he starts swearing. At meal times he has to be wheeled out. Ooh, now, look at that! Oh you can't obviously, but there's a little bird in a bush, just sitting there blinking away at me. Don't think he's injured. Hello. You alright? What's he sitting on? Looks like a Curlywurly wrapper. Ha, it is. Mm, probably discarded by one of the local schoolchildren. Cos, um, they do walk past this road, with their sweets you know. Mind you, it looks like the older style. Remember the big size wrapper they don't do any more? So it must be a few years old. It's preserved quite well. It's probably cos, plastic coated in't it? [bird tweets] Oh, he's off, disappearing into the foliage. Me trousers are dry now. What was he playing at? Why did he do that? It's a good job I wasn't dressed as Alderman Fitzwarren in't it? With me silk britches, me velvet cap. He'd have had a hefty cleaning bill plonked on his desk. [car passes] Talk of the devil. You know who's just driven past? Ken Worthington. [shouts] KEN! Oh, no, he's going too fast to hear me. Which reminds me, he's still got my copy of Miss Saigon. Now, ooh, he's just turned left, which suggests he's going into town. Now, he could also be heading for the M1, junction 33. Going South that would take you to Chesterfield, er down through Woodhouse way. Or if he goes North – that's, of course, yes. He'll be going to Leeds, to see his new signing. Julie Satan. Cos she's Leeds-based. She's a personality vocalist, um, she works for Barclay's Bank in the daytime, but she mimes to tapes you know, she has a broadsword and a leather gauntlet and a basque. I don't think she's very good myself. But Ken seems to rate her. Hey – she nearly killed him the other night apparently. Er, this was in a pub, after she'd done a show and Ken had told a joke and she, er, sort of punched him, playful, on the chest. You know, as if to say like, er, ooh duckie, you know, get you, that sort of thing. But she caught him on the windpipe and he started to choke. And she thought he was laughing at his own joke, you know. She said, hey, you shouldn't be laughing at your own joke. But he wasn't, he was fighting for his life.

Where is this Lesley? This is getting ridiculous. You see, this is an impossible situation, because if I go, she's almost certain to come, erm, but it, um, those cl-, those clouds are not advancing, I would definitely say that. They're going towards Glossop. And yet, there's going to be a problem with dew, in't there? In a couple of hours' time. The dew's settling. And it's a big lawn, it's going to take a while to do it. Ooh. She's just gone – what you doing? She's just gone past, Lesley, in her jeep. She didn't look at all, just went straight past. I don't know what's happening here. Hang on, hang on, was, oh, Mary's just gone past as well, my wife. Now this is funny, because she's not with Patricia MacMahon. She's supposed to be, because Patricia has just quit the prison service after 18 years. Mary's going to spend some time with her. She's with Joan Chitter, in Joan's Mini Metro. The two of them smiling at something, don't know what. This is very odd. It's a funny day, in't it? That bird's come back as well. P'raps because she wasn't in. Look at him, don't know what to do with himself [tweeting] Do ya? [tweeting] Eh? What are you making such a noise at? Oh, it's Roger, ah, see, Roger's started talking. But is he swearing or is he, er, giving out legal advice. S'hard to tell, ah, no, no, I was just going to go and put me ear against the window but I've just remembered they've got double glazing so I probably wouldn't hear anything. Tis a nice house, they've done it up very nicely. Right, I'm going for a drive, myself, because I'm wasting my time here. Erm, we could go up to Ladybower Reservoir, near Bamford, but the level probably hasn't changed much since yesterday. I know, let's go to, er, Peniston, because there's a nice little electrical shop up there and I need a new 5-din to phono, lead. Also, there's a cheap petrol station on the way, so I'll kill two birds with one stone. Yeah, that's what I'll do. See you later Roger. Ooh, he's gone all silent again. His eyes are boring right into me. It's a bit disquieting really if you don't understand. That bird's got something in its beak. Oh, that's a Jameson's Ruffle Bar wrapper, in't it. Do you remember those? Purple. Could open a sweetshop at this rate.

[Car starts and drives away, incidental music plays]

Follow that stream
See that chimney lean
Eat your ice cream
Where have those sandals been?
I'll go for the green
Are you watching closely our Dean?

Catch that train
Meet a soldier called Shane
Get off that train
Get back on it again
Avoid that rain
Buy some flowers for Elaine

And pubs and clubs
The bus to Crooks
And scouts and cubs
And Doberman pups

And woodland paths
And parks and calves
A shandy Bass
In a lady's glass

Did you hear about Lorna?
She's opening a sauna
Did you hear about Brian?
He's bought an Orion
Did you hear about Dale?
His computer's for sale

And pubs and clubs
The bus to Crooks
And scouts and cubs
And Doberman pups

And woodland paths
And parks and calves
A shandy Bass
In a lady's glass

[music fades]

BARTON FINK

I wonder if the Coen Brothers have ever read Robert Aickman.
The Hotel Earl in *Barton Fink* is not a million miles from the
titular institution in Aickman's 'The Hostel'. I suspect the literary
antecedent they both have in common is Kafka – a writer who is much
funnier than he is given credit for. Another example of how the most
singular and distinct voices, given free reign can be the most engaging
and memorable, *Barton Fink* is among the Coen's finest. It's hard to
describe the Coen's universe in cold prose. It's something people seem to
either get or not get – a description that can be applied to all the comedy
that we feel most passionate about. In the Coens' case it's a world-view,
a particular taste made manifest – a chimerical creature that wears its
manifold influences brazenly on its sleeve yet often succeeds in being
greater than the sum of its disparate parts. I've never forgotten a BBC2
debate I saw about the nature of comedy back in the early 1980s. The
panel consisted of Jonathan Miller, the critic Waldemar Januszczak and
Ben Elton (in his edgier, counter-cultural incarnation). Jonathan Miller
observed – as succinctly and acutely as you might expect – that nothing
made you laugh as hard as a private joke and that therefore the funniest
comedy – the stuff that lodges under people's skins and that they take
to their heart – always has the quality of a private joke made public. It
is singular, distinct and particular, and once clasped to your bosom the
world becomes divided into those who get it and those who don't. And it
always feels that to be in the former group is to be in a superior position
to those in the latter. This is a brilliant definition of the funniest comedy
that we've seen played out again and again over the years. You can discern

it going back to the Goons and Python right up to the present day. I have a vivid recollection of watching Reece performing Papa Lazarou for the first time in his and Steve's shared front room and I thought to myself (though didn't say) that it was just too private and personal a thing – something Reece had designed to make Steve laugh – a joke about their landlord – and that it would prove impenetrable to any audience. How telling that Papa Lazarou went on to become one of our most popular characters.

BARTON FINK

Late afternoon sun slants in from one side. The lobby has the same golden
*   ambience as when first we saw it.*
Barton is walking toward two wing chairs in the shadows, from which two
*   men in suits are rising. One is tall, the other short.*

POLICEMAN: Fink?
BARTON: Yeah.
POLICEMAN 2: Detective Mastrionotti.
POLICEMAN 1: Detective Deutsch.
MASTRIONOTTI: LAPD.
BARTON: Uh-huh.

All three sit in ancient maroon wing chairs. Mastrionotti perches on the edge of
*   his chair; Deutsch slumps back in the shadows, studying Barton.*

DEUTSCH: Got a couple questions to ask ya.
MASTRIONOTTI: What do you do, Fink?
BARTON: [still hoarse] I write.
DEUTSCH: Oh yeah? What kind of write?
BARTON: Well, as a matter of fact, I write for the pictures.
MASTRIONOTTI: Big fuckin' deal.
DEUTSCH: You want my partner to kiss your ass?
MASTRIONOTTI: Would that be good enough for ya?
BARTON: No, I – I didn't mean to sound –
DEUTSCH: What *did* you mean?
BARTON: I – I've got respect for – for working guys, like you –
MASTRIONOTTI: Jesus! Ain't *that* a load off? You live in 605?
BARTON: Yeah.
DEUTSCH: How long you been up there, Fink?
BARTON: A week, eight, nine days –

MASTRIONOTTI: Is this multiple choice?
BARTON: Nine days – Tuesday –
DEUTSCH: You know this slob?

He is holding a small black-and-white photograph out toward Barton. There is a long beat as Barton studies the picture.

BARTON: …Yeah, he… he lives next door to me.
MASTRIONOTTI: That's right, Fink, he lives next door to you.
DEUTSCH: Ever talk to him?
BARTON: …Once or twice. His name is Charlie Meadows.
MASTRIONOTTI: Yeah, and I'm Buck Rogers.
DEUTSCH: His name is Mundt. Karl Mundt.
MASTRIONOTTI: He's also known as Madman Mundt.
DEUTSCH: He's a little funny in the head.
BARTON: What did… What did he –
MASTRIONOTTI: Funny. As in, he likes to ventilate people with a shotgun and then cut their heads off.
DEUTSCH: Yeah, he's funny that way.
BARTON: I…
MASTRIONOTTI: Started in Kansas City. Couple of housewives.
DEUTSCH: Couple of days ago we see the same MO out in Los Feliz.
MASTRIONOTTI: Doctor. Ear, nose, and throat man.
DEUTSCH: All of which he's now missin'.
MASTRIONOTTI: Well, some of his throat was there.
DEUTSCH: Physician, heal thyself.
MASTRIONOTTI: Good luck with no fuckin' head
DEUTSCH: Anyway.
MASTRIONOTTI: Hollywood precinct finds another stiff yesterday. Not too far from here. This one's better looking than the doc.
DEUTSCH: Female caucasian, thirty years old. Nice tits. No head. You ever see Mundt with anyone meets that description?
MASTRIONOTTI: But, you know, with the head still on.
BARTON: …No. I never saw him with anyone else.
DEUTSCH: So, you talked to Mundt, what about?
BARTON: Nothing, really. Said he was in the insurance business.

Deutsche indicates Mastrionotti.

DEUTSCH: Yeah, and he's Buck Rogers.

MASTRIONOTTI: No reputable company would hire a man like that.

BARTON: Well, that's what he said.

DEUTSCH: What else?

BARTON: He... I'm trying to think... Nothing really... He... He said he liked Jack Oakie pictures.

Mastrionotti looks at Deutsch. Deutsch looks at Mastrionotti. After a beat, Deutsch looks back at Barton.

MASTRIONOTTI: Ya know, Fink, ordinarily we say anything you might remember could be helpful. But I'll be frank with you: That is not helpful.

DEUTSCH: Ya see how he's not writing it down?

MASTRIONOTTI: Fink? That's a Jewish name, isn't it?

BARTON: Yeah.

Mastrionotti gets to his feet, looking around the lobby.

MASTRIONOTTI: Yeah, I didn't think this dump was restricted.

He digs in his pocket.

...Mundt has disappeared. I don't think he'll be back. But...

He hands Barton a card.

...give me a call if you see him. Or if you remember something that isn't totally idiotic.

Gatiss' Greatest

THE TWO RONNIES

Saturday night was always the best night for telly and, in our house as in most others, a fantastic ritual was observed that took you from Final Score on *Grandstand* through *Basil Brush* to *Doctor Who*, *The Generation Game* and *The Two Ronnies*. There was a tremendous sense of security watching the Ronnies. It had a sort of scale to it that meant you could put on your slippers, have your tea and relax into Ronnie B's hysterical ministerial broadcasts, Ronnie C's straight-to-camera pieces in that funny beige chair (which introduced me to a strange grown-up world of fey BBC producers with handbags) and a seemingly endless supply of sketches set at cocktail parties. Then there were the serials: Piggy Malone and Charlie Farley, The Worm That Turned (in which women took over the world and Diana Dors dressed as a sort of Nazi dominatrix) and best of all, the Phantom Raspberry Blower of Old London Town – "written by Spike Milligan and a gentleman" – a joke that used to make me cry with laughter. The one thing I never got on with, Ronnies-wise, were the comedy songs, which I used to find vaguely depressing for reasons I can't quite fathom. Years later, *Not The Nine O'Clock News* mercilessly parodied the Ronnies' innuendo-laden songs and I felt a shadow enter my soul; I was a grown-up. The parody was cruel but spot-on and Saturday night would never feel quite the same again. Better then to remember The Two Ronnies at their absolute peak, and there can be no better example than David Renwick's 'Mastermind' sketch: a simple, brilliant idea perfectly executed that remains completely gettable to this day.

"Mastermind"

Q: "And so to our first contender. Good evening, can I have your name, please?"

A: "Ah… good evening."

Q: "In your heat your chosen subject was answering questions before they were asked. This time you have chosen to answer the question before last, correct?"

A: "Charlie Smithers."

Q: "And your time starts now. What is paleontology?"

A: "Yes, absolutely correct."

Q: "What is the name of the directory that lists members of the peerage?"

A: "A study of old fossils."

Q: "Correct. Who are Len Murray and Sir Geoffrey Howe?"

A: "Burke's."

Q: "What is the difference between a donkey and an ass?"

A: "One's a trade union leader, the other's a member of the Cabinet."

Q: "Correct. Complete the quotation … "To be or not to be…" ""

A: "They're both the same."

Q: "Correct. What is Bernard Manning famous for?"

A: "That is the question."

Q: "Correct. Who is the present Archbishop of Canterbury?"

A: "He's a fat man who tells blue jokes."

Q: "Correct. What do people lean on in church?"

A: "The Right Reverend Robert Runcie."

Q: "Correct. What do tarantulas prey on?"

A: "Hassocks."

Q: "Correct. What would you use a ripcord to pull open?"

A: "Large flies."

Q: "Correct. What sort of person lived in Bedlam?"

A: "A parachute."

Q: "Correct. What is a jockstrap?"

A: "A nutcase."

Q: "For what purpose would a decorator use methylene chlorides?"

A: "A form of athletic support."

Q: "Correct. What did Henri Toulouse-Lautrec do?"

A: "Paint strippers."

Q: "Correct. Who is Dean Martin?"

A: "Erm..he's a kind of artist."

Q: "Yes...what kind of artist?"

A: "Erm...pass."

Q: "That's near enough. What make of vehicle is the standard London bus?"

A: "A Singer."

Q: "Correct. In 1892, Brandon Thomas wrote what famous long-running English farce?"

A: "British Leyland."

Q: "Correct. Complete the following quotation... [hooter sounds to signal that time has run out] I've started so I'll finish. Complete the following quotation about Mrs Thatcher... "her heart may be in the right place but her..."

A: "Charlie's Aunt."

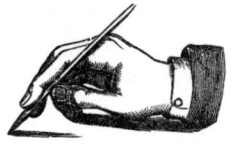

PRICK UP YOUR EARS

I t seems incredible now that Alan Bennett and Stephen Frears' *Prick up your Ears* had a theatrical release. These days the life of a dead gay playwright would more likely find a home on BBC4. In some ways, then, this fantastic and under-rated film is as much a last hurrah for the British film industry as a perfect example of screenplay writing. Apparently Bennett struggled for a while with finding the right vehicle for the bitter-sweet story of Orton and his tortured companion Kenneth Halliwell, but eventually hit upon the very clever notion of writing the story as a marriage and paralleling it with biographer John Lahr's relationship with his own wife. The film reeks of the 1960s, it seems to me, without having to over-egg the pudding, and I love its slightly damp English atmosphere, suddenly leavened by the Morocco scenes or the headiness of a casual pick-up in the park ("Oooh nice bum!" A line that Reece and I used to quote endlessly for our amusement.) It's one of Gary Oldman's best performances and Orton's casual cruelty is mesmerizing. But it's Alfred Molina's Halliwell to which I've always been drawn, not least because I'm convinced that he based the whole character on Tony Hancock, someone he played only a few years later on TV. ("Have a wank? Have a wank? That's very nearly an armful!") The screenplay is an absolute gem and remains for me – like so much of Alan Bennett's work – *"how to do it"*.

PRICK UP YOUR EARS

EXT. STREET. NIGHT. 1964

Cut to Orton and Halliwell running. Halliwell takes off his wig to run more easily. They eventually slow down. Halliwell puts on his wig again. They have come back to the Arts Theatre. They look up at the neon sign 'Entertaining Mr Sloane' (Written by, Joe Orton.]

HALLIWELL: Thank you.
ORTON: Thank *you*.

He checks no one is looking then kisses him.

INT. ORTON AND HALLIWELL'S FLAT. DAY. 1967

Orton is sitting at his desk, above which is a collage made by Halliwell of the notices and comments on Loot.

ORTON: My second play *Loot* is a bigger hit than my first. It's also a better play. And it is the critics' choice: Best play of the year. The film rights have been sold for a record figure. Currently I am working on a screenplay for four boys who are nudging Jesus Christ for position of Number One Most Famous Person Ever. But have I met these fabled creatures? Have I met their manager, Miss Brian Epstein? Have I been paid? No. Then why am I doing it?
HALLIWELL: Vanity.
ORTON: Answer supplied by the envious queen with whom I share what is laughably called my life. Well, I'm going to jack it in, Beatles or no Beatles. What I would like to do at this moment would be to ease down their Liverpudlian underpants and ram my Remington up their arses. The lovable mopheads.

HALLIWELL: What about me?

ORTON: What about you?

HALLIWELL: I can't remember when you last touched my cock. Well, I can actually, it was about two years ago, only I don't know the actual date. Pity. If you'd said, 'Ken, this is the last time I'm going to touch your cock', I could've done something to mark the occasion. Cracked a bottle of champagne, maybe, or put in my diary 'The last time Joe touched my cock. Grouse shooting begins'.

ORTON: Maybe we should go away. Somewhere there's plenty of sex. And I don't mean Southport. Somewhere even you might be happy. Morocco maybe. What do you think?

HALLIWELL: I don't want to go away. I just want to go to the awards. I could. Look. [Shows him the invitation] 'Joe Orton and Guest'. I'd behave. I wouldn't say a word. Promise.

ORTON: No.

HALLIWELL: Why?

ORTON: Because it's for me. I wrote it.

HALLIWELL: I gave you the title.

ORTON: OK. So when they have awards for titles you can go to that. [Halliwell launches himself at Orton with a carving knife.] Jesus!

They wrestle. The telephone rings.

HALLIWELL: Yes? No. This is Mr Orton's personal assistant. No. He's tied up at this moment. [His tone changes.] Oh, I see. Yes. Yes. Thank you. [To Orton] Paul McCartney is calling to see you. He's on his way now.

ORTON: Here? [Halliwell nods.] Shit!
[He immediately starts taking off his clothes. Halliwell immediately starts tidying the flat. Both rushing around, Orton changing, Halliwell tidying, and having this conversation.]
Was that him?

HALLIWELL: No. Someone more cultured. The chauffeur I think.

ORTON: Did you tell him the address?

HALLIWELL: He knew the address. I wish I'd known. The place is a pigsty.

ORTON: He won't mind. He's used to it. He's an ordinary working-class boy. They all are.

HALLIWELL: [Putting on some make-up] He's the nicest though. I've always liked him. The others are more ... instinctive. I won't stop. Just introduce me and say whom I am then I'll make myself scarce. [They are now sitting side by side on one of the beds, waiting. There is the sound of a car door slamming.] This is what it must feel like when one's about to meet the Queen.

ORTON: Except when one meets the Queen one normally hasn't just threatened to ram a typewriter up her arse.

The bell rings downstairs. Orton jerks his head for Halliwell to answer. Halliwell goes out, leaving Orton sitting on the bed.

INT. ORTON AND HALLIWELL'S FLAT: DOWNSTAIRS. DAY. 1967

Halliwell opens the door.

CHAUFFEUR: Mr Orton?
HALLIWELL: I'm his personal assistant.

He glances over the Chauffeur's shoulder at the waiting Rolls.

INT. ORTON AND HALLIWELL'S ROOM. DAY. 1967

Orton sitting on the bed. Sound of Halliwell running up the stairs.

HALLIWELL: He's waiting for you in the car.

Orton goes out leaving Halliwell.

EXT. NOEL ROAD. DAY. 1967

The Chauffeur opens the door. Orton gets in and closes the door. The Chauffeur goes round and is about to start when Halliwell runs out of the house with the script. He bangs on the window.

HALLIWELL: Joe.

[The window slides down and Orton takes it, maybe with a wink. Halliwell gazes after the car as it drives off.]

That was Paul McCartney.

MRS SUGDEN: Was it? Oh Kenneth, you are going to have some memories.

MAD ABOUT THE BOY

I visited Noel Coward's house in Jamaica a couple of years ago and it turned out to be a curious afternoon. My partner and I had been lured to the island by its Ian Fleming associations, but had found it disappointing. Indolence hangs over the island like a cloud of tobacco smoke. Never-to-be-completed buildings litter the countryside, the funds to finish them long since embezzled, but way back it seems to have been a kinder, less homophobic place. Coward's holiday home, Firefly – just up the road from Fleming's Goldeneye – seemed in need of more than a little TLC. We were shown round by a confused Jamaican lady, rattling off Sir Noel's biography in the usual tour guide monotone and only really flashing into a semblance of life when she became embarrassed about the great man's rather rotten paintings of naked youths. Ludicrously there was a set of tea things preserved just as they were the day the Queen Mum came to tea. The staff seem to regard this visit with almost religious awe, not shared by those of us who regarded her as a quasi-Fascist brown-toothed old sow. Reece always makes me laugh when he reminds me that, as a child, he thought the Queen Mum pooed out of her mouth – hence the brown teeth. BUT wonderfully here in the house was the Master's piano, cluttered with pictures of his glamorous friends and lovers – and here was the desk at which some of the later plays and songs had been written. I'm not sure where 'Mad about the Boy' was composed but it's a song I have always admired. It tells a story, but most importantly I think it speaks with poetic and heart-rending directness of the pain of falling in love. ("I've been and spent my last half-crown/To weep about a painted clown") Although my partner Ian cherishes a memory of a curious

Japanese girl who stalked him at drama school massacring the number, of all the versions, it's the one Marianne Faithfull recorded for Neil Tennant's *Twentieth Century Blues* Coward tribute album which remains my favourite. Perhaps because – in the old dame's cracked, ruined fag-ash delivery – there is a very real feeling that her love has sent her over the edge. She is *mad about the boy*.

MAD ABOUT THE BOY

I'm...
Mad about the boy
I know it's stupid to be mad about the boy
I'm so ashamed of it but must admit the sleepless nights I've had
About the boy

On the silverscreen
He melts my foolish heart in every single scene
Although I'm quite aware that here and there are traces of the cad
About the boy

Lord knows I'm not a fool girl
I really shouldn't care
Lord knows I'm not a school girl
In the fury of her first affair

Will it ever cloy
This odd diversity of misery and joy
I'm feeling quite insane and young again
And all because I'm mad about the boy

So if I could employ
A little magic that will finally destroy
This dream that pains me and enchains me
But I can't because I'm mad...

I'm mad about the boy

HUMAN REMAINS

I think I first met Julia Davis on the corner of a street. Neither of us were working as prostitutes, and yet that is what we have become to each other. The otherwise ill-fated *Sex Lives of the Potato Men* will always be special to me because it was the means by which Julia and I first started working together. By working, I mean being unable to stop laughing whilst the camera is rolling. I'd always loved her work and the sensational 'All Over My Glasses' episode of *Human Remains*, which she wrote with Rob Brydon is a favourite. Harking back to the foundations of great sitcom, here are two people – Steven and Michelle (Spindalero!) trapped in a miserable, bullying relationship. Michelle's only escape being her sympathetic relationship with the late "Lady Diane". There's too much wonderful stuff to list but favourites include: Julia moving her face next to the Lady Diane plate, the description of Steven's gay brother (the fact that Julia is clearly laughing whilst Rob speaks lifts it even higher) and the ABC of bands scene – included here.

'All Over My Glasses'

(Episode 3)

Michelle and Stephen play a 'simple game'.

MICHELLE: You start then.
STEPHEN: Abba.
MICHELLE: Abba... [long pause]
STEPHEN: Abba... Abba, Beatles.
MICHELLE: Abba... Beatles... [long pause]
STEPHEN: Abba, Beatles, Christians.
MICHELLE: Abba... Beatles... Christians... [long pause]
STEPHEN: Abba, Beatles, Christians... Doors.
MICHELLE: Abba... Beatles... Christians... Doors... [long pause]
STEPHEN: Abba, Beatles, Christians, Doors, Eagles.
MICHELLE: Abba... Beatles... Christians... Doors... Eagles...
STEPHEN: F. F.
MICHELLE: F... F...
STEPHEN: [With more emphasis] *F. F.*
MICHELLE: Abba... Beatles... Christians... Doors... Eagles... F.
STEPHEN: No! F. A band beginning with F – Fleetwood Mac.
MICHELLE: Abba, Beatles... Fleetwood Mac.
STEPHEN: No! You stupid–
   He throws a handful of pilau rice at Michelle. It sticks to her hair and glasses.
   It's a game! It's a simple game! God 'Chelle, you ruin everything...
   Simple bloody game.

DOCTOR WHO

My affection for *Doctor Who* is so well documented it is in danger of becoming a bore. Suffice to say, it was my inspiration, my first telly love affair and has formed the spine of my career in many ways. Now I'm actually part of the real programme, I'm happy as a Dalek in a Spiradonian icecano. Of all the writers who have contributed to the programme over 40-odd years, the shining genius was a gangly ex-policeman called Robert Holmes. You can see his name on many of the fantasy shows of the 1960s and 1970s. Yet it is with *Doctor Who* that he seems to have found his perfect niche. His impeccable comic timing and love of gothic horror found their acme in the 1977 story 'The Talons of Weng-Chiang' – a giddy compote of Sherlock Holmes, Jack the Ripper, Fu Manchu and the Phantom of the Opera. What elevates it above simple pastiche is the unique *Doctor Who* element – the fact that what appears to be a lurid nineteenth century masked villain is in fact a war criminal from the fifty-first century, whose deluded time travel experiments have pitched him up in Limehouse. Holmes had a genius for opening a little window onto tantalizing possibilities, and in this scene the Doctor off-handedly mentions that he was with the Phillippino army during the last advance on Reykjavik. Imagine that strange future world! How spooky, how exhilarating and what a lesson for the George Lucases of this world to keep your back-story an alluring shadow rather than punching people on the nose with it.

THE TALONS OF WENG-CHIANG

A carriage drives off into the night, we hear laughing and a howl. The Doctor and Leela kneel before a dead body.

LEELA: Doctor!
DOCTOR: [Removing an axe from the body] Litefoot's got visitors.

They enter the house. The Doctor leaves his cane in a wicker basket by the door. They burst into the next room, where Litefoot is slowly getting to his feet.

DOCTOR: [Exclaiming] Neehhaama! [Upon seeing Litefoot] What happened?
LITEFOOT: Chinese... dozens of them. Oh, the devils. [He sits down]
DOCTOR: Well, they got what they came for.
LEELA: What?
DOCTOR: The time cabinet.
LITEFOOT: Damn scoundrels.
DOCTOR: [to Leela] Get him a drink.

She picks up a decanter and takes the top off, sniffs it and turns towards Litefoot.

DOCTOR: In a glass, in a glass. [To Litefoot] Professor, how did they get in?
LITEFOOT: I- I've no idea. I locked and bolted all the doors as soon as you left. [accepts drink from Leela] Thank you my dear.

The Doctor looks outside in the corridor. He tears the label off the wicker basket by the front door and returns.

DOCTOR: Were they all Chinese?

LITEFOOT: Tod-wallers. Criminals. Gutter-scrapings of Shanghai.

DOCTOR: And one midget.

LITEFOOT: Yes, but Doctor, how on earth did you deduce that one of my attackers was a midget?

DOCTOR: Elementary my dear Litefoot, he came in the laundry basket and let the others in.

LEELA: The same creature that attacked me!

DOCTOR: The Peking Homunculus.

LITEFOOT: Who?

DOCTOR: Yes, the time of manufacture, its disappearance, it all fits.

LEELA: Doctor what is the Peking Hum-un-

DOCTOR: [Interrupting] Homunculus.

LEELA: Homunculus.

DOCTOR: It was made in Peking for the commissioner of the Icelandic Alliance. It was in the Ice Age, about the year 5000.

LITEFOOT: Preposterous!

LEELA: Shh. Go on Doctor.

DOCTOR: The Peking Homunculus was a toy. A plaything for the Commissioner's children. It contains a series of magnetic fields operating on a printed circuit and a small computer. It had one organic component. The cerebral cortex of a pig. Anyway, something went wrong. It almost caused World War Six.

LITEFOOT: What!

DOCTOR: Yes, somehow the pig part took over... So Weng-Chiang has bought the Peking Homunculus back through time. He could have done. It disappeared completely. It was never found.

LITEFOOT: [pouring himself another drink] I say, I may have had a bang on the head but this is a dashed queer story... time travel?

DOCTOR: Unsuccesful time travel, professor. Findicus' discovery of the double nexus particle sent human science up a technological cul-de-sac.

LITEFOOT: [to Leela] Are you following this?

LEELA: Not a word.

DOCTOR: This pig thing is still alive. Needs an operator of course. But the mental feedback is so intense that somehow the swinish instinct has become dominant. It hates humanity and it revels in carnage.

NUTS IN MAY

I first saw Mike Leigh's *Nuts in May* at Bretton Hall College. Steve and I had embarked on, I think, the second term at our so-called drama school and were meant to be discovering naturalism. What this was supposed to mean was improvising whole afternoons around existing plays. What it actually meant was pissing around trying to make each other laugh. My mental patient in the Marat-Sade improv as I recall would say nothing but "Is Alan coming?" (not 'Is Alan Cumming") whilst another student had made the bold decision to be unable to use his arms and legs, something he must have regretted after rolling around on the dusty floor for most of the day. Another afternoon was spent watching the telly, but this time watching *Nuts in May* proved a valuable and lasting influence. For a long time I used to think of this play as a kind of horror film, dealing as it does with embarrassment and pain. It's a domestic tragedy. Keith has always been master of his own little world, patronising and controlling his wet wife Candice-Marie until he meets an unexpected challenge to his authority. The film is replete with memorable moments – Keith telling Candice-Marie how much to chew her food, 'Froggy Went A-courting', the moment when Keith cracks, screaming "I'll knock your head off" at Finger the biker, whose carefree attitude threatens to destroy all of Keith's certainties. But I think I like the beach scene best of all. I remember sitting in that stuffy room at Bretton Hall 20 years ago, thinking I could watch *Nuts in May* till the cows came home, and also thinking *this is what I'd like to do.*

Nuts in May

CANDICE-MARIE: [from cliff-top – shouting] Keiiiiiith! Keiiiiith!

KEITH: [on the beach – shouting] Hello! It's marvellous down here. The sea has worn through the limestone and formed an arch. And it's pushed back the weald clay and it's a little cove, it's lovely. Don't come too near the edge. Candice-Marie, you're standing on sedimentary limestone. It's been folded and it's in the shape of a stair. That's why it's called stair hole; there's a stair there and a hole down here.

CANDICE-MARIE: [from cliff-top, faintly] I can't hear you!

KEITH: What?

CANDICE-MARIE: Can't hear you!

Cut to view of Ray. He looks up a hill to see Keith and Candice-Marie walking down.

Cut to Keith and Candice-Marie walking along a shingle beach.

KEITH: Come on!

CANDICE-MARIE: It's pouring with rain. I can hardly see, my glasses are all steamed up.

KEITH: Aw, it's all right. It's only a shower from low strata, it'll pass over soon. Come on, there's a jump here.

CANDICE-MARIE: I'm not crossing over there Keith, I'm going up here.

KEITH: What? Come on? Aw come on, it's only a little jump.

CANDICE-MARIE: It's all right for you Keith, always rushing ahead. Why don't you wait for me sometimes?

Cut to walking along shingle beach.

CANDICE-MARIE: Isn't it lovely Keith?

KEITH: Yes, splendid, it's choppy out to sea and calm inside the cove here. What are you doing?

CANDICE-MARIE: I'm collecting some pebbles to take back.

KEITH: Well you shouldn't do that you know.

CANDICE-MARIE: Why not?

KEITH: Well if everybody did that there wouldn't be any pebbles left.

CANDICE-MARIE: Don't be ridiculous Keith.

KEITH: Well there wouldn't.

CANDICE-MARIE: There's thousands of pebbles on this beach.

KEITH: I told you what happened in Brighton in Victorian times. [spotting some rubbish] Look at that. People leaving their litter all over the place…

DINNER AT EIGHT

I first met Rufus Wainwright about six years ago when I interviewed him for a magazine. I'd been a fan since I took his first album with me on a solo holiday I took just after finishing filming on the first series of *The League*. I intended to read and swim and paint and little else but found myself going a bit mad being on my own. Rufus' fantastically florid, achingly touching music got me through the chilly Andalucian nights and so I was delighted when asked to interview him. We got on at once, became friends and I have thrilled at his rise to global acclaim in the intervening years. We've been collaborating on a project on and off for some time now. A couple of years ago, holed up in a snowy Montreal cabin, we'd go off and scribble away at our various ideas, returning to eat and discuss stuff. I'll never forget the feeling of offering up my poor scribblings only to have Rufus say "I've just written this little thing" and belt out the most glorious, shattering piece of genius!

I could have picked so many of his songs that I love but I think it has to be 'Dinner at Eight' from *Want One* which continues to inspire and move me. It documents, unflinchingly, Rufus' troubled relationship with the father who abandoned him ("Put up your fists and I'll put up mine/ No running away from the scene of the crime") yet, despite its specificity, I think of it as an eloquent hymn to the oddness of all families and relations. And in its heart-breaking, harp-string-soaring arrangement, it's one of the most beautiful and moving things I've ever heard.

Dinner at Eight

No matter how strong
I'm going to take you down with one little stone
I'm going to break you down and see what you're worth
What you're really worth to me

Dinner at eight was o.k. before the toasts full of gleams
It was great until those old magazines
Got us started up again
Actually it was probably me again
But why is it so
That I've always been the one who must go
That I've always been the one told to flee
When in fact you were the one
Long ago, actually, in the drifting white snow
Who left me?

So put up your fists and I'll put up mine
No running away from the scene of the crime
God's chosen a place
Somewhere near the end of the world
Somewhere near the end of our lives
But till then no daddy don't be surprised
If I want to see the tears in your eyes
Then I know it had to be
Long ago, actually in the drifting white snow
You loved me.

Rufus Wainwright

PORRIDGE

As a kid I could never get over the fact that the big man in canary-yellow jacket and specs from *The Two Ronnies* was also Norman Stanley Fletcher in *Porridge*. I still can't. *The League* are always asked about our inspirations and always cite Leonard Rossiter, Alistair Sim and Ronnie Barker amongst others. But who else but Barker could so completely inhabit the brilliant everyman character of Norman Stanley Fletcher? I've spoken of feeling secure watching television in those days, and there was a similar feeling that you were in the hands of master craftsmen with Dick Clement and Ian La Frenais' *Porridge*. As with their *Whatever Happened to the Likely Lads?*, the show is about real people whom we all recognise: the wishy-washy liberal governor, the morally crucified Mr Barraclough, the anal martinet Mr Mackay and the vulnerable, loveable Godber: all perfectly cast. What could have been an impossibly grim scenario is constantly undercut by the sheer warmth and humour of the characters. Towering above it all is Ronnie Barker's performance as Fletch; a deeply corrupt man who is nevertheless one of us; the sort of bloke you'd love to have on your side. It's testament to the brilliant writing in that trying to select a piece from the *Porridge* script book, I simply sat down and read one after another without stopping. The best sitcoms are about slightly desperate people trapped and 'A Night In' takes this to its logical conclusion. It's tender, sad and yet incredibly funny.

PORRIDGE

Episode Three: A Night In

1. PRISON

It is association hour. Lennie goes down stairs.
He walks past other prisoners on his way to Fletcher's cell.

2. FLETCHER'S CELL

Lennie walks in. Fletcher is sitting on the lower bunk writing a letter. Lennie is a bit diffident.

LENNIE: Oh er ... hello, Fletch.

He is met with silence.

LENNIE: You er ... you was expecting me? I mean they informed you?
FLETCHER: They informed me, yes.
LENNIE: Only temporary they said.
FLETCHER: You bet your life it's only temporary. Single cell this is, by rights.
LENNIE: Not my fault.
FLETCHER: I'm just saying.
LENNIE: Only temporary.
FLETCHER: Look, park your stuff, get out the light.

Lennie pauses awkwardly, indicating the lower bunk.

LENNIE: Er ... is this where you want me to sleep?

FLETCHER: What?

LENNIE: Well, I presume I'm in the bottom bunk. I mean, top bunk's status in the nick.

FLETCHER: 'Course it is. You're in the bottom bunk, yes.

LENNIE: Well, if you wouldn't mind shifting your stuff, I could—

FLETCHER: What? Oh, all right. God Almighty.

He moves his stuff to the top bunk.
Lennie begins to unpack his stuff and make up his bunk.

LENNIE: Not my fault.

FLETCHER: No no, so you keep telling me.

LENNIE: Not my fault if they have a riot on my landing. My cell mate, Banksy, he was one of the ringleaders, like. He set fire to his mattress. And mine.

FLETCHER: Head case, that Banks.

LENNIE: He's being transferred.

FLETCHER: Head case.

LENNIE: He wasn't a bad bloke to share a cell with. He was always very nice to me. He showed me the ropes and taught me cribbage. And he never displayed no violence. He was the gentlest of men.

FLETCHER: Oih ...

He nods to Lennie indicating that he should go to the other washstand.

LENNIE: [Crossing over] Oh ... He found this kitten and smuggled it into the cell and from the way he handled it you could see the gentle side of his nature.

FLETCHER: You what? Before he lit his mattress I heard he threw a screw off the top landing.

LENNIE: Well, he weren't hurt. He hit the safety net.

FLETCHER: That, Godber, is somewhat academic. The point is that a fifteen-stone prison officer was hurled from a top landing by your cell mate, mighty Joe Banks.

LENNIE: Only because he said he couldn't keep the kitten.

FLETCHER: Hardly an excuse, sonny Jim. Hardly an excuse. Can't see that cutting much ice with his parole board.

LENNIE: Where's the harm in keeping a kitten?

FLETCHER: It's not allowed, that's the point. It's against prison procedure. Caged birds, well yes, sometimes they'll let you keep caged birds. Insects in a matchbox. But you can't keep cats. And Banks knows that, the porridge he's done.

LENNIE: It was only a little kitten.

FLETCHER: A kitten differs from a cat only in scale. They share the same lavatorial tendencies, they pee on your blankets.

LENNIE: Just don't see the harm.

FLETCHER: There are rules. For example, I have certain rules in this cell here. Well, not so much rules as standards. This is my cell, in which you're a temporary resident, and as such you will honour those standards.

LENNIE: Which are?

FLETCHER: You don't rabbit, you don't snore, and you don't pick your nose.

LENNIE: I don't think I do any of them.

FLETCHER: Good, good. Then we should get on passably well.

LENNIE: Banksy never complained anyhow.

FLETCHER: Well, he wouldn't, not an animal like Banksy.

LENNIE: But I don't.

He sits down.

FLETCHER: Good good, fine fine – you're sitting on my paper.

LENNIE: Oh, sorry.

He gets up off a crumpled copy of the Sun and passes it over.

FLETCHER: Oh another thing. Newspapers. You can read the paper, but when, and only when I've finished with it.

LENNIE: All right.

FLETCHER: Right — get out of the way.

There is a pause while Fletcher climbs up into the top bunk and settles down with his paper. His shoes are off, and there is a big hole in one of his socks.
Lennie starts to set out a few personal possessions, including a photograph of his fiancee, only inscribed "Lennie — for always, Denise". He has also got some needle and thread, a tin of shag tobacco and some papers, a tin of throat lozenges, a box of liquorice all-sorts and shaving kit.

LENNIE: I've got some grey darning thread.

FLETCHER: [Irritably] What?

LENNIE: I've got some grey darning thread if you want that hole darned up.

FLETCHER: [Politer] What? Oh yes, thanks — yes.

He takes off his sock and hands it down to Lennie, who by his reaction registers that he had not expected to do the darning himself. He decides not to make a stand.

LENNIE: Your standards don't include sweaty feet, I notice.

FLETCHER: Man who don't sweat ain't healthy. Like a dog with a dry nose.

LENNIE: [Getting the darning kit] Settling in OK, are you?

FLETCHER: I'm all right, keep me pecker up. Can't grind me down. Bide your time, that's what it's all down to, bide your time.

Bells start to ring and doors start to slam, signalling lockup time. Voices are heard in the distance.

LENNIE: Unnatural in't it, men in cages.

FLETCHER: Bide your time.

LENNIE: I don't mind work. And as I'm in the kitchens I always get plenty of grub. And the screws ain't too bad, by and large …

A prison officer appears, gives a cursory check, then slams the door and locks it.

FLETCHER: Goodnight, sunshine … Charmless nurk. Oh dear, I forgot to put me shoes out to be cleaned.

Lennie walks across to the window.

LENNIE: This is the bit I can't stand though.

FLETCHER: What?

LENNIE: Lockup. It's only quarter-to-eight. Barely dark. If I was at home now I'd just be going out for the evening.

FLETCHER: That's the point you see, son. We're here to be punished, ain't we? Deprived of all our creature comforts. And the little things you've been taking for granted all these years. Like a comfy shirt, decent smoke, a night out.

LENNIE: A night out ...

There is a pause.

FLETCHER: Look, if you're so keen we'll go out. We could find a couple of girls – two of them darlings what dance on *Top of the Pops*. Yes, Pan's People. Beautiful Babs – don't know what her name is. Arrange to meet them in some dimly lit Italiano restaurant. Then we could go on somewhere if you like. Some night club ... dance till dawn. Then back to their luxury penthouse, and wallop. But you see I done all that last night so I'm a bit knackered. Also we'd have to get all ponced up and you'd have to darn me socks. So why don't we just have a quiet night in? All right?

LENNIE: If you say so, Fletch.

FLETCHER: That's what you've got to tell yourself. You're just having a quiet night in.

He goes back to the Sun. There is a pause.

LENNIE: [Gloomily] Trouble is I've got six hundred and ninety-eight quiet nights in to go.

FLETCHER: Less than some.

Lennie looks at the picture of Denise.

LENNIE: D'you think she'll wait?

FLETCHER: [Abstractedly] What?

LENNIE: D'you think she'll wait?

FLETCHER: Who?

LENNIE: Denise. My fiancée.

FLETCHER: Oh yes, Denise, fiancée.

LENNIE: Well, do you?

FLETCHER: I dunno. I shouldn't think she'll wait *in* for six hundred and ninety-eight nights.

LENNIE: She is my fiancée.

FLETCHER: Yes, I know, but when she said she'd love you for ever she didn't know you were going to get put away for two years, did she?

LENNIE: I miss her so much. I can't sleep for thinking about her.

FLETCHER: Doesn't do no good that. Don't do no good lying awake at night brooding and twitching about what you ain't going to get no more. Carnal thoughts – well, best to give them the Big E, the elbow. Less you think about women the better – cor, look at that. 'Beauty Queen shocks Council. Lovely Sharon Spenser, twenty-two, shocked members of her town Council when they learned that she played the title role in the new sex-sational film *The Virgin and the Vicar.'*

LENNIE: I wonder which she played?

FLETCHER: '"Had we known," said a Council spokesman, "We would never have crowned her floral Queen." "I don't know what all the fuss is about," said Sharon, a former convent girl, whose hobbies include water ski-ing and carpentry. "I am proud of my body and what I do with it in my spare time is none of the Council's business".' She'd never get planning permission for that.

Both stare at the photograph for several seconds, their eyes glazing with obvious relish.

FLETCHER: Yes … yes … got every right to be proud of a body like that. Oh yes. Ravishing little thing, isn't she? Mischievous little mouth. Look at that mouth. Full of mischief. I bet that's been up to some mischief. Yes … what was I saying?

LENNIE: You were saying the less you think about women the better.

FLETCHER: Oh yes, yes, carnal thoughts, yes, fatal.

LENNIE: She reminds me of Denise a bit.

FLETCHER: Which bit?

LENNIE: No – Denise. My fiancée.

FLETCHER: Oh yes, the lovely Denise, yes right.

LENNIE: Not that they're similar in appearance, but they're both … physical. Know what I mean?

FLETCHER: You're not telling me your Denise is a star of the silver screen, are you? Albeit a grubby one in a backroom.

LENNIE: Oh no, nothing like that.

FLETCHER: Not a model, then?

LENNIE: Oh no, though I once took some provocative Polaroids of her when we were caravanning in the Gower Peninsula. I don't mean mucky, like. But she was sort of expressing herself ... Posing, like.

He gives his impression of Denise posing provocatively on the Gower Peninsula. Fletcher looks disapproving.

FLETCHER: Come on, son! Leave it off! What will the neighbours think?

He is aware of the spyhole in the cell door.

LENNIE: Oh sorry, Fletch.

FLETCHER: Ain't thinking of me, son. They know which side my bread's buttered ... It's you. Harm can come to a growing lad. You're the one could drive the fairies round here into a frenzy.

LENNIE: But I'm engaged to Denise.

FLETCHER: Means naff all to them, my son. They're all engaged to each other. Denise is a thing of your past. A letter in your top pocket. A photograph under your pillow. A warm tingle in your loins.

LENNIE: In me what?

FLETCHER: Your loins.

LENNIE: What are loins?

FLETCHER: [Exasperatedly] Loins is ... look, when you think of her, when you thinks of Denise in the still of the night, think of the times you once had, don't you ever get a warm tingle?

LENNIE: Oh – yes.

FLETCHER: Well, where you gets it, that's your loins.

There is a pause.

LENNIE: I thought they were my –

He lies down on the bottom bunk.

FLETCHER: Well there's lots of words for them.

LENNIE: She is a very physical girl, Denise. She was a Beauty Queen. Finalist at the Office Machinery Exhibition. Miss Duplicating, she was. And her picture was in the paper and she became a pin-up of two thousand sailors in an aircraft carrier in Gibraltar. They wrote to her and said she was the girl they'd most like to ink their rolls.

FLETCHER: That must have made you very proud, Lennie, knowing that your fiancée was the sexual fantasy of an entire aircraft carrier.

LENNIE: Oh, I didn't know her then. That was before she moved to Smethwick, before that never-to-be-forgotten day when I met her at a supermarket in the Bull Ring – oh that's in Birmingham. She was stamping 'Special Offer' on giant-sized jars of pickled onions. I came round the corner from condiments and sauces and my wire trolley went over her foot. It was a magic moment. We both knew. I said to her straight off 'Will you meet me outside?' I said. And she said, 'All right.'

FLETCHER: God preserve us, Godber. Romance.

Pemberton's Picks

SELF-SERVICE

I first met Victoria Wood, along with the other members of TLOG, at the Montreux Festival in 2000 and my first reaction was to smile broadly and utter a very familiar "Hi, how are you?", before realising that we'd never met before. She just has one of those faces and personalities, especially if you've grown up watching her on TV as we all had. Her writing voice was spot-on Northern in a way that we all immediately connected with. Each of us had Victoria's scriptbooks *Up to You Porky* and *Barmy*, and characters such as Iris and Judee, Stella and Pauline are all directly influenced by Wood (and Walters) creations. In fact Pauline's "Hokey cokey pig in a pokey" is a direct lift from one of Victoria's characters, but then we gave her a part in our film and let her dress up as an olden-days Queen, so that just about makes up for it. I've chosen 'Self-Service' – I can never look at prawns without being reminded of it – because the use of language is inspired: "So why hence the hoohah?" Another of her great sketches, 'Giving Notes', is just one quotable line after another – indeed I spent a wonderful afternoon in Benidorm recently piecing the whole sketch together line by line with my friends Derren and Siobahn. "Any news on the skull Connie? I'm just thinking if your little dog pulls through we'll have to fall back on papier maché." If I thought that something I'd written could bring people together in such a joyous way over 20 years after I'd written it, I'd be more than happy.

SELF-SERVICE

Department store, upmarket self-service counter. Extremely long slow queue. A couple of girls serving behind. Our two nice ladies are at the end of the queue by the trays. Enid has a beret and no hair visible.

ENID: [taking a tray] Do you know, I've scoured this store from top to bottom, can I find a side-winding thermal body belt, can I buffalo?

WYN: What did you want one for?

ENID: [handing her tray over the counter] Excuse me – I think you'll find there's spam on that. [Taking another tray] That gippy kidney.

WYN: Flared up?

ENID: I'll say – it's like being continually poked – can you imagine that? [Wyn can't.] Dr Brewster says if I don't keep it lagged for the winter I could be spending a penny every twenty minutes come March.

WYN: Can't they operate?

ENID: I haven't time to go in. I'm on the phone day and night about that carpet. What's the soup, dear?

GIRL: Country vegetable.

ENID: What country – Taiwan?

WYN: Have they not sent it? Your carpet? [Rootles round the counter.] There's croutons.

ENID: With my molars? Filthy French habit. Oh they sent it – I sent it back. I said, 'Do I look like a woman who would grace her lobby with a bordered Axeminster?' I've told them time beyond number, I'm the wall-to-wall elephant.

WYN: Is that steak?

ENID: I would doubt it. Probably some poor beast that came a cropper at Beecher's Brook. Er, dear – is this fish boned?

GIRL: No.

ENID: I should check your insurance. Then I had a huge to-do and hoohah at the hairdressers.

WYN: What about these Dublin prawns?

ENID: Never touch prawns. Do you know, they hang around sewage outlet pipes treading water with their mouths open – they love it!

WYN: Still going to Maison Renée?

ENID: Chez Maurice was putting out feelers…

WYN: Oh no, he reeks of neutralizer.

ENID: And he's forever dabbing at his cold sores with *Old Spice* –

WYN: Aren't prawns an aphrodisiac?

ENID: I wouldn't put it past them. Well, I'm at Renée's – waiting to be shampooed – flicking through a Woman's Weekly – lovely piece on Alma Cogan. [They've now reached veg, and the queue's stopped.] Sorry – what's the hold-up here, dear?

GIRL: We're waiting for fresh cauli…

ENID: Fresh! You might as well wait for Maurice Chevalier. So I'm called into the cubicle – it's all separate at Renée's – not like these terrible modern places where you find yourself sharing a perm trolley with footballers [annoyed at the delay] this is ridiculous [pushing past the veg waiters]. Can I thrust by – I'm a diabetic.

They are now at the sweet section.

So in comes Renée.

WYN: She must be getting on.

ENID: Well, this is the trouble. If she leans too far forward with a sponge roller, she topples out of her walking frame – and you really have to shout up – I don't particularly want the whole world knowing I'm not a natural conker.

WYN: Is that trifle?

ENID: It may have been in a previous existence. [Elaborately casually looking away] Don't have the gateaux – I just saw her scratching her armpit with the cake slice. And Renée's very set in her ways, style-wise – I don't mind – I'm a great admirer of Phyllis Calvert.

WYN: So why hence the hoohah?

ENID: Well, I decided to go a shade mad because we've the Smoked Meat Purveyors Buffet 'n' Mingle at the weekend.

Irate voice from a woman a couple of people further down the queue.

WOMAN: Could we get by please; we're not having a sweet.

Women and friend push by our two.

ENID: Very wise, with those hips. So I said, 'Skip the conker, Renée – I'll have burnished beech-nut and to heck with it.'

WYN: So?

ENID: Well, you know she's colour blind and they've only a glass mantle round the back?

WYN: Colour blind?

ENID: Can't tell red from blue. Once tottered into a brothel thinking it was a police station.

They reach Tea, Coffee and the Till.

SECOND GIRL: Tea, Coffee?

ENID: No.

WYN: She didn't.

ENID: Oh, it was all right – one of the girl's came out and helped her pump her tyres up.

SECOND GIRL: Sorry, are you still waiting for something?

ENID: Yes, a small mineral water and an orange squash please.

SECOND GIRL: Water and squash back down the end by the trays. [To next customer] Tea, Coffee?

Enid and Wyn leave their trays behind and push past everybody to the starting point. They pick up two trays and rejoin the queue.

ENID: You've a look of Eva Braun, did you know? Well, – what Renée mixed up in the back – burnished beech-nut it was not – more like varicose violet – I could have wept.

Engrossed, they move off again – past the water and squash – people behind them as before.

WYN: Did you have to pay?

ENID: Well, she knocked off my bourbons, but – [they move along]. Then in comes Maxine, waving her whitlow…

WYN: Is she the bodybuilder?

ENID: No that's Lois [starts to fade]. No, Maxine's the one I told you about – excuse me – grey eggs – is that an Arab custom?

A CHANGE OF SEX

A Change of Sex was first broadcast on the BBC in 1979. I don't know when I first saw it (I suspect Reece had a copy on video, though he'd probably level the same accusation at me), but it became one of a select group of documentaries we'd watch over and over again to scour for comic gems. The meetings which pre-op transexual George/Julia has with the hugely unsympathetic – and unseen – psychiatrist could well have been scripted. Indeed, you will no doubt recognise chunks of this dialogue from our Dr Carlton sketches in series three. Wanting to make notes for an unsympathetic doctor character, I watched *A Change of Sex* for inspiration and just ended up copying out whole tranches of their conversation. Some of it went to Barbara – "I'll go to Casablanca and be butchered" – but most of it went to Carlton. Particular favourites are the greeting "Come in, sit down as usual", and the dismissal "Go out would you". I love the way he diagnoses her as "mildly obsessional" because of the harmless comment "I plan well", and the contemptuous, "Your need is not paramount. What matters is that it should be done properly, and medically". Comic gold. Documentaries such as this can inspire us more than a hundred Monty Python repeats.

A Change of Sex

DOCTOR: Do you have a letter from your doctor please? Thank you very much. Just one or two details. Your name is George Roberts?

JULIA: George William Roberts.

DOCTOR: And how old are you?

JULIA: Twenty-four.

DOCTOR: Right. Well, what is the problem?

JULIA: Well, I feel, erm, I've been having a fight with myself for a long time… coming to terms with the fact that I believe I'm a woman trapped within a man's body.

DOCTOR: What do you mean by being a woman?

JULIA: Well, my whole… all my thoughts and everything, are feminine. There's nothing masculine; I tend to reject my masculine body.

DOCTOR: You know it to be masculine?

JULIA: I identify it as masculine because society identifies me as masculine.

DOCTOR: It's not a matter of society, it's a matter of anatomy.

JULIA: True, but I look at myself and I hate the body I have to—

DOCTOR: Well, you see, there it is, anatomically male. Well, this has a bearing upon what we can do, and what we want to be doing for you. You say you feel like a woman?

JULIA: Yes, I believe everything I do is feminine; I believe I'm a woman inside.

DOCTOR: Oh. Michelle, how does it feel to be a woman?

MICHELLE: It just feels like being me – I can't describe it as anything else.

DOCTOR [to other woman present]: You see, she's right – nobody knows how anybody else feels inside.

JULIA: Well, I feel I don't … I believe I don't actually feel how a normal man would feel.

DOCTOR: It may be that you identify with certain stereotypes of a female gender role, that is; the traditions, the behaviour, the ideas – but that doesn't make you a woman. But I have to go into the background a bit. When did this idea first occur to you?

JULIA: It made sense to me when I was about fourteen or fifteen; there'd been occasions before, from about the age of about five—

DOCTOR: Let's go back to five – as early as possible. What then?

JULIA: When I was five I didn't like mixing with the, sort of male, with boys at school, I always mixed with girls. [fades to black before continuing] The gay scene upset me, I didn't like the gay scene at all. I couldn't identify myself with the gay scene. I met a young girl, who I eventually got pregnant, and we got married. The day after we got married we both realised we'd made a mistake. We saw the first child being born, and, er, shortly after she was pregnant again and once the second child was born we decided that we were—

DOCTOR: She was pregnant by you?

JULIA: She was pregnant by me, yes.

DOCTOR: On both occasions?

JULIA: On both occasions.

DOCTOR: Well, what's happened since the marriage was dissolved?

JULIA: I've spent – I now spend 50% of my time as a female, and I've had to approach the district authority I work for – I work within the health service – and they've agreed for me to actually go into work, which is within the psychiatric unit anyway, to work as a woman.

DOCTOR: When are you planning to be full-time as a female?

JULIA: 18th March.

DOCTOR: That's an important date as far as you're concerned.

JULIA: It is.

DOCTOR: Were you a nervous or timid child?

JULIA: Not really. Erm, I used to, sort of… when I was with the girls I could mix and—

DOCTOR: No, I meant something rather more than that; such as bedwetting?

JULIA: No.

DOCTOR: Nailbiting?

JULIA: No.

DOCTOR: Fits, convulsions?

JULIA: No.

DOCTOR: Walking in your sleep?

JULIA: No.

DOCTOR: Nightmares?

JULIA: No.

DOCTOR: Afraid of things like dogs, heights, fire, water?

JULIA: No.

DOCTOR: Would you describe yourself as a neat, tidy sort of person?

JULIA: I try to be.

DOCTOR: Everything in order? Checking—

JULIA: Yes. I plan well.

DOCTOR: Methodical?

JULIA: Yes.

DOCTOR: So you're mildly obsessional – which is a trait attributed to transvestites and transsexuals. Right. Have you any wish to be cured of this desire to live henceforth as a female?

JULIA: No.

DOCTOR: What would you really like to happen to you?

JULIA: Well, I would like to eventually be able to say that I had got the body of a woman, and to be as perfect a woman as I could see.

DOCTOR: Though you never actually can be so. Well, I want you to listen carefully, because what I'm saying now has medical and legal significance. If you can demonstrate to me, by your own decision, that you can live in society and pass as a female, be accepted as a female and support yourself, and any dependants, as a female, I may be able to refer you to a surgeon when I've known you long enough. But I want to repeat that, if you do this, you do it by your own decision, at your own risk, and on your own responsibility in relation to the civil authority – that means the police. Two further things, whatever is done to you, you won't be a woman legally, because one, you can't change your birth certificate, because that is a definition of sex attributed at birth – whatever you may think of yourself now. And, secondly, it is a criminal offence for you to attempt to marry another biological male. So, if you like, I'll take you under my care to see how I think you do, and if I think you do reasonably well, I may feel it possible to refer you to my surgeon. Who, I may say, adopts the same protocol, same criteria, as I do. So, what I would suggest you do, is that you make an appointment to see me, say in about eight weeks, and we'll have another discussion and see how far you've got. Now, one thing I would like to do, because I've seen quite a few transsexuals, is to take a photograph, and I'm going to do that now, if you don't mind. So, if you would stand over there.

Dialogue ends; Doctor narrates over footage of Julia having her photograph taken.

THE WICKER MAN

The *Wicker Man* has been much discussed and acknowledged as a major influence on our TV show, especially the 'Local Shop' characters. It wasn't so much there in the first sketch, which pays more of a homage to the tearoom scene from *Withnail and I*, but the realisation that a Scots policeman could come into the shop looking for the missing boy was what really turned Tubbs and Edward into fiercely 'local' murderers. A film like this is best viewed accidentally, tuning in after the first five minutes on a tiny black-and-white portable with no knowledge of what is about to unfold. That was how I first saw it anyway. And boy did it scare me: I just couldn't believe the ending. How did the hero die? How was he not saved by his colleagues from the mainland? We're so attuned to the catharsis of Good triumphing over Evil, that to see this reversed was truly distressing for an adolescent boy. How audiences in 1973 could sit through a double bill of *The Wicker Man* and *Don't Look Now* is beyond me (though both films do offer free busts). When Reece and I shared a flat we would watch *The Wicker Man* every May 1st, and during one mad period we watched certain scenes every day. The maypole song became a favourite, as we dissected each of the boys in the dance to see who was doing "too much" and "not enough", marvelling at the performance of the creepy teacher with his *Play Away* shirt and 'Childcatcher' movements.

After our first TV series aired, a fan sent me a copy of the original *Wicker Man* shooting script, which had been signed by Ingrid Pitt. When I was asked in 2000 to contribute to a *Wicker Man* panel discussion alongside Christopher Lee and the late Anthony Schaffer I jumped at the chance to add their signatures. Both men grudgingly obliged. I wanted to include an extract from the script in this book, but due to Schaffer's will being in dispute we were sadly unable to get the copyright. So here instead is the Local Shop scene from our first episode which pays tribute to this enduring classic – watch the film and spot the lines we borrowed!

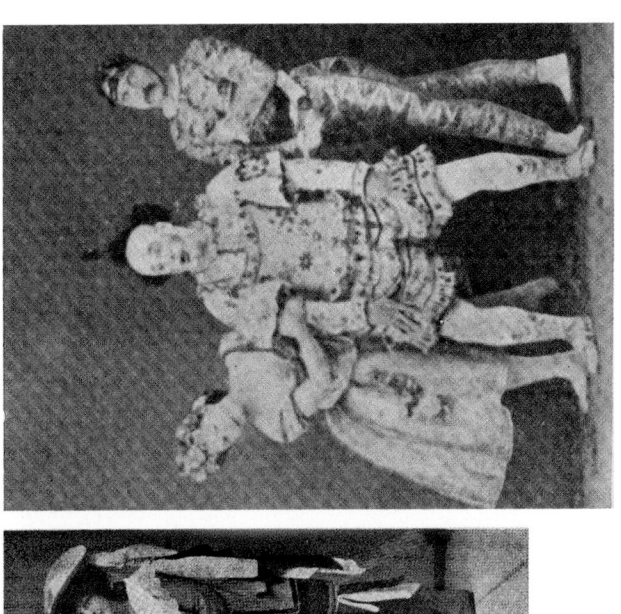

The Tiller Troupe and Master Lupino Lane in 'Jack and the Beanstalk'

Grandma, Grandad and Great Uncle

Images from Lupino Lane's *How To Become A Comedian*

**Did you know....
that El Greco's real name was E. L. Grecott?
Chuck Berry wrote many of Shakespeare's plays?
the Everly Brothers turned down a knighthood?**

The Hackenthorpe Book of Lies

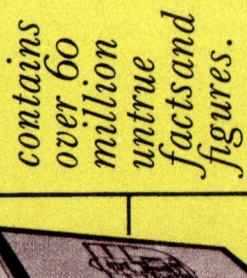

contains over 60 million untrue facts and figures.

* Did you know that the reason why windows steam up in cold weather
  is because of all the fish in the atmosphere?
* Did you know that Moslems are forbidden to eat glass?
* Did you know that the oldest rock in the world is the famous Hacken-
  thorpe Rock, in North Ealing, which is 2 trillion years old?
* Did you know that Milton was a woman?
* Did you know that from the top of the Prudential Assurance Building in
  Bromley you can see 8 continents?
* Did you know that the highest point in the world is only 8 foot?

**** These are just a few of the totally inaccurate facts
in **THE HACKENTHORPE BOOK OF LIES**

It's all in THE HACKENTHORPE BOOK OF LIES

**A thorough and exhaustive source of misleading and untruthful information, compiled and edited by
ex-Nobel Prizewinners Ron Hackenthorpe, Derek Hackenthorpe, Jeff 'The Nozz' Hackenthorpe and
the library of the Hackenthorpe in the stand volumes which can be purchased individually.**

A monthly look at the world of ~~fish~~ and books.

The latest from Slater-Methuen: a Wonderful New Coffee-Table Book:

A Complete History of World Art and Everything Else By Eydie Gormé. An ideal coffee-table book. Comes complete with 4 attractive mahogany-style legs which screw into each corner of this beautifully produced art work. The cover is an exquisite detail from Caraveggio's 'Rape of Lucrece', covered in laminated plastic to withstand the most unpleasant stains.

Other Wonderful Bargains

The Complete Works of Virginia Woolf in high-quality asbestos. Line your fireplace with **Night and Day, Jacob's Room, To the Lighthouse.** Yes! This new edition of Virginia Woolf retains the heat all through the night.

At Last! A chance to wear one of England's greatest novels. The new flimsy nylon edition of **The Mayor of Casterbridge.** This exciting exploration of love, guilt and failure in 19th-century Dorchester can be worn as a nightie or as an eye-catching adornment to any cocktail or evening dress.

You'll find all eyes on you when you wear The Mayor of Caster-bridge (£4.95).

For the commercial traveller or the busy bachelor – the **Drip-dry edition of Dead Souls by Nicolai Gogol.** This great Russian novel can be washed through in the evening, hung in the bathroom overnight, and be clean *and* fresh in the morning. **Needs no ironing.**

Kids . . . shy, embarrassed . . . ? Going through that difficult time

when you think your face will never look lovely? Well, here, for you is *the Teen-Read Edition of the Rubaiyat of Omar Khayyam* complete with retractable hinged arm for dealing with facial problems. Tears off scabs, bursts pimples and rubs on Valderma while you are immersed in the exciting, mysterious world of Omar Khayyam.

For the discerning intellectual . . . the first **All Nude Version of Pride and Prejudice.** See Jane Austen's immortal characters in a variety of interesting positions. All nude!

Other Great Beaver Classics:

War and Peace: The Battle on the Ice—see everything!
The Ascent of F6: Derek and Nigel explore the kitchen–and each other!
Hard Times: Puts the Dick back in Dickens. Foreword by Rod Laver.

In next week's *Books and Book-men* ~~and hot Fish~~:

Barry Bucknell shows you how to make a bathroom extension from the works of Zola. **The Royal Signals Reading Champion** tells how he hopes to jump the **Complete works of G. K. Chesterton**—on a motor-bike! And **'Was Milton really batty?'**— a new and controversial look at the seventeenth-century poet and writer, by one of **Jacques Cousteau's** most trusted divers.

Some highlights from
MASTURBATORS OF HISTORY

Fully illustrated, with a foreword by Alan Brien.

- '*Juste avant la grande bataille d'Austerlitz, et aussi les batailles d'Ulm et de Borodino, je m'avais preparé avec la main droite.*'
  (*Before the great battle of Austerlitz and also the battles of Ulm and Borodino, I prepared myself with a quick one.*)
  Napoleon (1813)

- **George Washington** *(from his Diary July 1776)*: '*The struggle is over, the battle is won, today the independence for which we have given so much is ours by right and deed. I could never have done this without regularly twanging the wire.*'

- **Nansen** *(Norwegian Explorer)*: '*I find I explore better after punishing Percy in the palm.*'

- **Olof Palme** *(Swedish Prime Minister)*:
  No comment.

- **Verdi**: '*Composing operas is tough work, and I find the one sure way to relax is the man's way.*'

- **Leopold I** *(1640–1705)*: '*Being Holy Roman Emperor is tough work, you have enormous territories to defend, and in*'

● **Michaelangelo:** *'E parate di pristavere e dimaggione con brio Sistine marvelloso giondore.'*
(Painting the roof of the Sistine Chapel is tough work. Self-abuse keeps me going.)

Masturbators of History **is** an entirely new way of looking at history (writes Kenneth Onan, rather shakily). For the first time we glimpse the behind-the-scenes happenings that may have influenced the course of history: the famous cross-hand during the signing of the Treaty of Utrecht, the Papal Bull making the practice compulsory during the Thirty Years War (owing to a misprint), and the reason Pilate really washed his hands. We see how it has shaped the careers of writers, musicians (especially pianists), generals and politicians. Why did Beethoven go deaf? Why was Toulouse Lautrec so small? What did Sir Walter Raleigh do in the Tower? All this and more in this fully illustrated Historical handbook. Published by Slater-Wristjob.

new and forthcoming PYTHON LECTURES

A series of lectures by people of little or no importance on very dull topics delivered somewhere near the Royal Academy in April or May 1973'ish.
We reprint here in full the text of the inaugural Python lecture given by Professor Enid Gumby of the Institute of Brick Throwing at Leicester!

Well . . . . Blimey ! . . . . Well . . . . WELL . . . .
I think giving lectures is smashing . . . I really like giving lectures . . . WELL ! ! ! . . . . I really. (HERE THE WORDS BECOME INDIS-

TINCT) . . . . Ow ! . . . . OOOOOOOHHHHHHH !
. . . Bloody hell ! . . . . My head's stuck . . . . .
OH GOD ! . . . . My head is stuck !

In the next of the four Python Lectures Aldous Huxley will talk about why he is dead.

Remember ! It's all in *The Listener* . . . out Thursdays . . . To make sure of getting your copy of *The Listener*, let your newsagent know, and we will print an extra one.

Map of 'The Shittish Isles' from *Viz*

THE LEAGUE OF GENTLEMEN

SCENE 1:1/31 INT. LOCAL SHOP. NIGHT.

Close-up of a photograph of Martin wearing his distinctive brightly coloured walking boots. We hear a policeman's voice over the photo.

POLICEMAN: (OOV) Twenty-eight years old. Fair hair. Name of Martin Lee.

Cut to Tubbs looking at the photograph closely. As the policeman continues talking the camera pans down to reveal that Tubbs is wearing the boy's distinctive walking boots.

POLICEMAN: I found his wallet outside your shop. He must have been walking in the area. Has he been in today?

TUBBS: No, I don't know anything. Now if you'll excuse me officer, the shop is local.

POLICEMAN: Perhaps your husband might have seen him. Is he on the premises?

TUBBS: He's up the stairs, cleansing the precious things of the shop. He can't walk you see, and he's blind.

Edward enters via the shop door. The bell tinkles as he comes in. He wears Martin's rucksack on his back.

EDWARD: Hello, hello, Tubbs? What's going on? What's all this shouting? We'll have no trouble here.

POLICEMAN: Are you the proprietor?

EDWARD: Yes, yes?

POLICEMAN: Your wife said you were up the stairs, sir.

Edward realises that something is wrong and tries to act casually.

EDWARD: I slipped out, Tubbs, for a walk. Didn't want to disturb you. Fine evening. The town. We're very proud.

TUBBS: He's looking for a boy.

Edward moves towards the policeman.

EDWARD: Poofter, eh? Little bummer boy. Come across your type before in the forces. You won't catch me with my trousers down.

POLICEMAN: Sir. I'm here on police business. I found this boy's wallet.

EDWARD: Local boy?

TUBBS He's not from our town.

EDWARD: Ah. Do we know his parents?

TUBBS: I said we'd never seen him before. Did Tubbs do right?

EDWARD: You did it beautifully, Tubbs. There's your answer, sir. Never seen this boy before. Now, if you'll excuse us, we've a shop to run.

POLICEMAN: Yes, of course. Thank you for your co-operation. Good day to you.

The Policeman turns to go. Tubbs stares at the picture.

TUBBS: We didn't burn him.

POLICEMAN: I beg your pardon.

The Policeman is astonished.

EDWARD: You're not from round here, are you officer? Not the local bobby we're used to. You see, Tubbs… my wife Tubbs and I, we know everyone around here. The people don't change… We don't like change.

TUBBS: We don't even give change.

EDWARD: Strangers come to the town, to the shop, young, most of them, in gangs of one or two. They leave the gates open, trample the crops.

TUBBS: Strangers make the crops fail.

POLICEMAN: And if the crops fail?

EDWARD: They must not fail. If the crops fail the town fails. If the town fails the shop fails and that must not happen. We are a community.

TUBBS: We are legion.

EDWARD: We are local.

POLICEMAN: I think we'd better continue this conversation down at the station.

TUBBS: Edward?

EDWARD: You heard the man, Tubbs. Get undressed.

Tubbs loosens her cardigan.

I, AN ACTOR

One of the chief joys of Christopher Douglas and Nigel Planer's *I, An Actor* is the (genuine) quote on the back from the *Yorkshire Post*: "He could almost be doing a send-up of a theatrical biography." As a student I'd read Antony Sher's *Year of the King* and Simon Callow's *Being an Actor* in an effort to connect with my chosen profession, but couldn't quite put my finger on why they didn't chime with me. Then somebody lent me a copy of Nicholas Craig's spoof confessional and suddenly I understood. When I was 16 I had to choose speeches to perform for my LAMDA Acting Medals. I chose characters such as Bottom in *A Midsummer Night's Dream*, The Actor in Brecht's *The Resistable Rise of Arturo Ui* and The Player in *Rosencrantz and Guildenstern Are Dead* – perhaps playing my idea of what actors were all about: theatrical, slightly camp, larger than life. But I also enjoyed the haughty affectation of these characters, and pricking that pomposity is what *I, An Actor* is all about. If you know anyone who wants to act, please don't waste your money on Stanislavsky, buy this book instead. You won't regret it.

I, An Actor

To the Young Actor

If a youngster comes to me and says, 'Mr Craig, I want to be an actor,' I tell him to go and boil his head. Only a complete and utter lunatic becomes an actor.

If the youngster insists, 'But, Mr Craig, I really do want to be an actor,' I clip him round the ear, kick him and tell him to go and do his A-levels.

If the obstinate young shaver sets his jaw, stamps his feet and shrieks, loud enough to wake the whole street up, 'Mr Craig, I mean to act!' it is at that point that I begin to take some notice of him. I turn to him, take a long cool look at him and then I ask him these eight basic questions: are you prepared to sweat and slog and suffer and slave? Are you ready to starve for very little money? Are you prepared to work so hard in your movement classes that your feet come off? Are you willing to work in the North of England? Do you have the dedication to spend your dole on silly little presents for people at the BBC who might possibly employ you? Do you have the sensitivity to sympathize with your agent's interior decor problems? Do flattery and apologizing come easily to you? And, above all, will you be able to learn the language of the profession and say things like 'Onwards and upwards', 'Oh well, we survive' and 'Never stops, love, he *never* stops'?

If he answers all these questions in the affirmative, I tell him to go away and work in an office for five years and then, *then*, if he still wants to act he should join an amateur theatre company as an assistant stage manager and there undertake the most menial and humiliating tasks he can find. If, when he has done all these things, he is still intent on making a career in the theatre then – well, I suppose he might as well go to drama school or he could try getting a job with a children's theatre company, it doesn't really make much difference, but it's no good him asking me for help because you're on your own in this business. It's tough with a capital 'T'. Look at Bette Davis, she suffered, but she survived.

So, my young friend, if you are determined to take your chance on the boards, then be assured you will know poverty, pain, despair, illness, you may even die, but you will have chosen the greatest profession in the world; a way of life that will take you to the stars and back and make you a king, an emperor, a goddess, a vicar, a pirate, a nosey neighbour, a 2nd interfering bystander – anything. Whatever glittering prize or foaming chalice of ambrosia you want is yours for the taking.

Choosing a Drama School

Drama schools go in and out of fashion very quickly; some years LAMDA is the place to show your promise, other years the agents and casting directors will be beating a path down to Webber Douglas to pick up talent. It is impossible to say which schools will be 'in' two years hence.

Do not be seduced by glossy prospectuses. You only need to know two basic facts: how many prizes and medals are handed out at the end of the final year (you will want to have some sort of award to put on your CV when you leave), and how often are the study trips to the zoo (imitating animal behaviour is of course the most important skill for a young actor to acquire).

RADA has a splendid selection of awards for the final-year students, but the Central School is within walking distance of Regent's Park. Rose Bruford and East 15 are probably too far away from any zoos to merit a place in the first division of drama schools.

While alumni of the Birmingham School of Speech Training and Dramatic Art loyally defend the virtues of the aviary in the botanical gardens at Edgbaston, a better all-round bet is the Bristol Old Vic Theatre School – a goodly clutch of awards, and practically next door to Johnny Morris's old stamping ground.

For me though, the King of Drama Schools is my old alma mater, Biddy Lanzarote's Academy of Dance and Dramatic Art. I had an absolute ball at BLADDA; not only was it handy for Whipsnade but, being the only male student, I had the pick of all the best heroic roles (I had a fair breadth of choice in matters amorous, too, but perhaps this isn't the time or place).

Choosing a Name

Remember! Once you've chosen it, you're stuck with it.

One of your first tasks on leaving drama school will be to choose a name. Possibly, you will find, as I did, that someone in the profession is already using yours. I simply dispensed with Parsons and adopted Mim's maiden name – easy. The trick is not to go too far in trying to project this image or that. It's a great mistake to put all your eggs in one basket in this way. You will look bloody silly asking for a job at the Woolwich Tramshed if you've called yourself Barrington Savoy.

Two christian names is the best combination; neutral, unintimidating and conveying to the director a reassuring sense of dependability. I wonder if we would have seen a second series of *To the Manor Born* if the leading lady's stage name had been Pip Trotsky. No, the people with the right idea are those who have opted for the two christian name format: Nigel Terry, Harriet Walter, Oliver Tobias, Anna Karen, John Neville, Suzanne Danielle, Robert Lindsay, Colin Douglas, Paul Henry, Murray Melvin, Leslie Caron, Brenda Bruce, Lance Percival, Ralph Michael, Jonathan Cecil, Robert Ralph, Raymond Francis, Robin Ray, Helen Cherry, Terence Alexander, Patrick Allen, Nigel Anthony, Emrys James, Christopher Benjamin, Alan Howard, Ann Lynn, Millicent Martin, Wendy Richard, Sylvia Kay, Christopher Douglas, Debbie Harry, Jane Seymour, Toni Arthur, June Barry, Susan George, Eleanor David, Lindsay Duncan, Peter Jeffrey, Peter Duncan and, if I may add my own name to this illustrious list, NICHOLAS CRAIG.

Of course, I would be absolutely mortified if any of these dear colleagues bought this book only because they're mentioned in it. I hope very much that they *will* buy the book, but for the right reasons.

Getting That Job

But anyway, how to get yourself started, that's the question. Well, it's tough. You needn't think that within two tenths of a second of your leaving drama school, hordes of stampeding directors are going to besiege you with offers of starring roles and bury you under a mountain of thousand-pound notes, because they won't. In fact, you might as well forget altogether about being a star, and if you have got it into your silly head that you are even remotely talented, well let me tell you, young sir or madam, that you aren't, and if you have any sense at all you will take yourself off to a remote rep and stay there for twelve years, by which time you should have learned to be a little less cocksure.

'OK,' you are probably saying, 'that's all very sound advice, but how do I, as a fledgling artist, a gosling on the duckpond of world theatre, how do I actually get a job?'

Right. As a beginner you can start by sending off a couple of dozen of these:

Dear—
I am asking to inquire whether or not it would be at all feasible for you to spare some time in your most busy schedule to glance at the enclosed photograph and CV booklet with a view to possibly granting me the opportunity to give an albeit brief audition for you at your convenience at some point in the future.

I have recently learnt to juggle / play tabor / lute / drive H.G.V. / folk dance / basic scimitar.

Sorry to trouble you but I am at home in the following accents: Northern / Dover / King's Lynn / Continental.

Not too familiar, you see, and most important, not too clever-clever. After you have been going for a year or two, your status changes subtly, and it is then that you must take full advantage of any mutual contacts you may have with a director:

Dear—
Another year has gone by and I realize that I haven't been in touch for yonks.

It's extraordinary to think that after all these years we've never actually met, but I know that, like me, you're an old mate of —'s. And as I sat me down to pen this missive I bethought me, 'I wonder how he/she is.' Any news your end?

Anyway, I don't want to bore you any longer, so I'll just say that it would be smashing to work with you at long last.

The enclosed pic shows me with/without a beard but I can easily shave it off/grow one.

You can vary this according to circumstances, but it is important to maintain the light, bouncy, obedient tone of a good company member (GCM). However, a letter like the following will immediately brand you as a BCM (bad company member):

Dear—
I would like to apply for an audition on 28th August, and would be grateful if you could let me know which plays you will be doing so that I may prepare an appropriate speech.

    Please return the enclosed photograph in the SAE provided.

Such presumptuous, self-important nonsense (this was a real letter, believe it or not, shown to me by a director pal) will place you fairly and squarely beyond the pale rep-wise. A director is not some secretary whose sole function is to carry out your every instruction. He, or she, is an extremely important person who always wears the same clothes every day.

Finally, when you've knocked around the profession for a good few years, all the little cards and notelets you send to directors can have a much chattier tone:

Dear—
How goes it with you then, you old bugger/ravishing creature? Christ, how long is it since we worked together? Yonkingtons. Any chance of a joblet?

    You owe me a drink, you rotten sod/fickle temptress. But seriously though, I'll buy you one.

    Not to nag, but if you happen to have a family solicitor or doctor or even a defending counsel sitting on your desk with a question mark by their names, you might push one of them me-wards.

    Anyway, better wend. You must come to dins one of these fine days.

But it will be a long time before you have acquired sufficient professional stature to use tricks like this.

Finding an Agent

I have never grovelled to anybody. Nevertheless there were times early in my career when it was necessary, shall we say, to 'perform' in ways not touched upon at drama school. I have no reason to be ashamed of this, nor did I at the time regard anything I did as humiliating, unhygienic or inhumane. It was simply good business.

The best time to look for an agent is, obviously, when you are in a play in London and your talents are there for all to see. Being in a play in the provinces is not so useful since agents rarely leave London for other than adulterous reasons.

I hasten to point out that I have the best agent in the world (Miriam) who is completely wonderful and a saint and to whom I am devoted. I would never dream of signing with any of the other agents who have offered to represent me and get me American TV work because I know that now she's nearly better and the office is redecorated she can hustle with the best of them, the lamb. When she puts her mind to it, she can be a *very* tough cookie indeed, which is exactly what I need because if it was up to me I'd just give in and say yes to anything. I'm hopeless.

Spotlight

The simplest way of advertising your wares (for what are we but humble hawkers in the bustling bazaar of Thespis Street?) is to advertise in the casting directory Spotlight. This will cost you about £70 and it is money well spent (though God knows, I haven't paid mine this year). It is vital to pick the right photo of yourself; remember, this is the one directors, producers and casting directors will be looking at for the next five years or so. It is very, very important that you look your best.

Equity

Equity is a trade union is a trade union is a trade union. Has to be, got to be, must be. It's unavoidable. Sorry, but there we are.

I'm pretty much of a middle-stump trade unionist, myself. Basically, I believe that anyone who has a burning desire to act (to be an actor) should be allowed, nay required, to join Equity, but not if he's just some yob who runs a string of launderettes in Leytonstone and is going to deprive 'real actors of small parts in *Minder* and *EastEnders*. If we let anybody in we might as well all go and work in a factory and have clocking-on cards because that is what it will be like.

All political parties and ideologies have some support within the membership of Equity. Once you have joined, you will have to affiliate yourself to one of the following pressure groups:

S.W.E.E.T.I.E. (Socialist Workers for Enforcing an End To Imperialist Enslavement)

L.U.V. (Lock Up Vanessa)

C.R.A.V.A.T. (Centre Right Actors Against Anarchist Trots)

S.O.P.P.I.E.S. (Silly Old Politics Prevents Important Engagements in South Africa)

K.I.S.S. (Kill Imperialists, Smash Sexists)

C.U.D.D.L.E. (Chorus Understudies and Dressers Demand Longer Engagements)

Jobfacts

A few more facts and figures which may be of interest to the young actor.

Casting Directors	Work no.	Home no.	Gift ideas
Doreen Bones	387 1359	982 8060	Dissecting equipment/ fluffy gonks
Irene Hunter	261 4345	750 6140	Snoopy ephemera/raw offal
Esther Gore	759 2388	897 9761	Live poultry/pink roses/pre-war electrodes
Maud Charnel	837 2452	402 3261	New born babies/ dentist's instruments

How To Become
a Comedian

As students at Bretton Hall in Yorkshire, Mark and I would take occasional trips to Holmfirth, which was best known as the location for *Last of the Summer Wine*. We'd take tea in Sid's Cafe and try to find Nora Batty's doorstep. People do similar things now in Hadfield, Derbyshire, which doubles as Royston Vasey, except they'd be eating Tubbs's Toasted Teacakes and Briss's Special Sausages. Anyway, on one such trip Mark bought a book from one of the many second-hand bookshops and gave it to me for my birthday. It was called *How To Become a Comedian* and it became my Bible for the next 20 years. You'll see from these extracts that I have followed the advice of Lupino Lane assiduously. Particularly useful was the list of characters to draw on for inspiration: 'The Major from Poona, The Dude, The Simpleton, Horsey Individual, Tramp or Hobo, Village Yokel, Porter, Old Man, Jew.' Incidentally, the book was inscribed 'Felicitations, and with apologies, to Cecil from Jennie – Xmas 1950.' (*See* colour plate section).

How To Become a Comedian

Chapter III

How to use an old gag

There are many ways of using an old gag. My cousin, the late Stanley Lupino, was an expert in twisting and making an old gag take on a new lease of life. His method was first to find an old one that would fit the situation, then crack it with such speed you hadn't time to recognise it. (He went further than this – most of his first plays were based on 'Turned Up', a comedy written by Mark Melford and first produced in 1886).

Again he would get someone purposely to tell an 'ancient' joke; then Stanley would solemnly lift his hat, and on being asked why he did so, he'd reply: 'I always raise my hat to an old friend', thus successfully getting a laugh by the use of an 'old 'un'. When he died at the early age of forty-eight, the comedy world and my family in particular lost a valued member.

Another good trick is to give an unexpected reply to a well-known gag. For example, in 'Radio Revue' produced by John Watt and Harry Pepper at Olympia, they suddenly found at the last minute that they wanted an act before a Front Cloth to enable them to set the scene at the back. They rushed into my dressing room and appealed to me to do something. Bobbie Comber (a very experienced comedian) and I were having a friendly argument about the use of old gags. Bobbie remarked: 'Here's your chance to prove your point – go on and crack some old stuff and we'll see whether you *can* get away with it. This put me on the spot. I agreed to have a 'pop at it', providing he would be my 'feed'. (A feed is supposed to help the comic to get his laughs.) Bobbie was willing, so, on the stage we went, and proceeded to *ad lib* on the following lines:

BOB: It's no use, I don't believe you can get a laugh with an old joke.
ME: I'll bet you five bob!
BOB: Right.

ME: Now, all I want you to do, is to suggest a couple of old ones.

BOB: Right: when I say to you, I've just been run over ...

ME: You were standing under a bridge!

BOB: Yes! Then I say I've just seen a goat with no nose ...

ME: That one's so old it smells without one!

BOB: Well, you try and get a laugh with them. Are you ready? [He goes off and comes back brightly] Good morrow! Good morrow!

ME: Good morrow! I thought it was to-day – you look upset – have an accident?

BOB: No thanks, I've just had one ... I've just been run over.

ME: You should be more careful.

BOB: That's the wrong answer.

ME: It's always the wrong answer when you get run over!

BOB: *No.* You should ask me if I was hurt.

ME: Why? You were standing under a bridge!

BOB: You're not cracking it properly.

ME: But I got a laugh out of it.

BOB: Well try the other. I've just seen a goat with no nose.

ME: Had *it* had an accident?

BOB: No!

ME: So it was standing under the bridge too?

BOB: A bridge has nothing to do with it.

ME: I know – it had no nose!

BOB: That's right, no nose.

ME: [singing] 'No nose in all the world ...'

BOB: I tell you *I've just seen a goat with no nose.*

ME: Well, you needn't shout about it; after all if you were the goat you'd be a bit sensitive, it's not quite the right thing to go about telling everybody about someone else's misfortunes. I'm surprised at you.

From now on Bobbie used all kinds of guilty expressions

ME: [continuing] *You* ought to be ashamed of yourself. After all, what has the poor goat done to you? There you stand with all the nerve in the world boasting about your knowledge of a goat that has no nose. Have you got the goat's permission to give this information? No! You don't know whether the goat arranged to have no nose, to save handkerchiefs, etc., etc.

This went on until Bobbie burst into tears and sobbed with remorse.

ME: [continuing] *You* wouldn't want everyone to know if *you* hadn't a nose. Besides, look at the things you'd miss in life, smelling is one of the senses that brings us joy and comfort – the smell of food when you're hungry, the scent of beautiful flowers – that reminds me, you remember that funny little dog you gave us sometime ago?

BOB: Yes, I remember – he used to love smelling flowers; it was most unusual!

ME: [sorrowfully] He loved them. The poor little chap died a few weeks ago.

BOB: [sympathetically] I'm sorry to hear that.

ME: Well, we buried him at the end of the rose garden and laid a lot of beautiful roses on his grave.

BOB: Why did you do that? How can a dead dog smell?

ME: Like the goat – TERRIBLY.

You will notice that the 'Feed' appears to get all the laughs, but by an exaggerated look of exasperation, and 'double takes' [explained in another chapter], most of the laughs came my way. This dialogue was, of course, much longer, but it proved that two old gags could still get laughs.

There is another method of cracking an old one, by apologising before you crack it. 'I expect you've heard this one.' 'Stop me if you've heard it', etc. But when you come to the point of the gag, it has a new twist.

Take, for instance, that old and ancient one:

Q. Why did the chicken cross the road?
A. To get to the other side.

This can be twisted, changed, and modernised in a hundred and one ways, for instance:

Q. Why did the chicken cross the road?
A. Because the road won't cross the chicken.

Another example:

Q. Why did the chicken cross the road?
A. It wanted to get there.

A. Her Rooster was waiting.
A. It was time for her daily dozen.
A. It was opening time, etc.

Look how many versions there are of the humorous announcement:

'A little song entitled "she was only a Corporal's daughter, but she
    knew what Reggie meant".'
... Put away your tweezers till your eyebrows meet again. ... An apple
    a day keeps the Doctor away, but for real peace, try an onion.
... I will now sing a song to prove the theatre can be cleared in
    three minutes.
... I will now render a song – limb from limb.

There are hundreds of mottoes that can be changed:

If at first you don't succeed, suck an orange.
You can lead a horse to water, but *I* don't like the stuff.
Thirty days have September, April, June and November, all the rest
    have thirty-one. *It's not fair!*
Never let the grass grow under your feet, you might get nettles up
    your trousers.

'That wasn't a lady, that was my wife' can be used in various ways:

FEED: I've just seen your wife sitting on the lap of your best friend and
    kissing him.
COMIC: Oh, did you? [Goes off quickly and returns, laughing] You were
    wrong, I don't even know him.

Mother-in-law stories are inexhaustible.

Many of the advertising slogans can take on a new meaning when
altered.

Again, there are many versions of the Englishman, Irish-man and
Scotchman joke.

Answers to Historical questions can be changed in numerous ways.
Here is a couple of my favourite schoolboy howlers:

Where was the Magna Charter signed? At the bottom.

Solomon had 300 wives and 700 porcupines.

Then there's the avenue of short Limericks and you can use a short Nursery Rhyme by giving it a new end:

Mary had a little lamb
With feet as black as soot
And into Mary's bread and jam
His sooty foot he put.

You can also use the *'Lunacy Gag'* [you know the type] – 'It must have been two other fellows' in many ways. Here are three examples:

Two men met the morning after the night before and were a bit regretful. 'How did you find yourself this morning?' asked one man. 'Oh, quite easily', said the other, 'I just looked under the table, and there I was.'

A Reporter was sent to interview the famous 'Tom Thumb' at his hotel. He got the number of the room, knocked at the door; it was opened by a giant of a man. 'I want to interview "Tom Thumb." said the reporter. The giant replied, 'Come in, I'm "Tom Thumb".' 'But,' the reporter said, ' "Tom Thumb" is a dwarf.' 'I know,' said the giant, 'this is my day off.'

A harassed mother dressed her little girl up in her best white dress and let her go out to play, saying, 'Now, if you come home with your dress dirty, I'll strangle you.' The little girl fell in a puddle and came home very dirty indeed, so her mother strangled her.

The *'Invisible Gag'* has many forms:

Selling an invisible dog,
"   "   "   banjo.
"   "   "   a piece of fresh air.

I am very fond of these kinds of comedy routine. They give so much scope for expressions and miming.

'Sharing of Articles, Money, etc.,' can be done in various ways. Here's the 'father' of them all: it was performed in the Harlequinade by the Clown and Pantaloon. Here's the old man himself:

[Clown steals a basket of *ten* fish]

PANTALOON: Share and share alike, Joey.

CLOWN: All right, 'Old 'Un'. Share and share alike. I'll count 'em out ... now there's one for you and one for me.'

PANTALOON: That's fair, go on!

CLOWN: There's two for you [giving him one] and one, two for me [taking two for himself].

PANTALOON: [not noticing] Ha! Ha! Ha! I love fish, go on.

CLOWN: There's three for you [again gives one], and there's one, two, three for me, [takes three] then there's four for you [gives last fish, then taking Pantaloon's four fish] and there's one, two, three, four for me. [Puts them in basket and exits].

PANTALOON: Share and share alike. [Realises he hasn't any and exits shouting.]

Sometimes a *'Pun'* can be useful. This method of comedy is now-a-days considered rather old-fashioned, but my experience is that providing the pun is bad enough it never fails if the performer puts an expression of pain on his face.

You can get a lot of routines from the following style of *'Misunderstanding Gag'*.

A. Name, please.

B. Watts' my name.

A. I'm asking *you!* What's your name?

B. That's right.

A. What is?

B. Yes.

A. Yes what?

B. You're telling me!

A. Telling you what?

B. Watt's my name.

A. How do I know?

B. How do you know what?

A. Oh dear, now let's start all over again – etc.

There's the *'Example Gag'* that can be changed:

A. Do me a favour, I want to propose to a girl. You are very successful with the ladies, give me a few hints.

B. O.K.

A. I'll make a few notes.

B. Now we'll say the girl is over there.

A. [Writes in notebook] Over there [Chalks cross on stage].

B. Then you cross over to her and look in her eyes! [He swaggers over.]

A. [Making notes] Cross-eyes.

B. Then you say: 'I'm known as a man of few words.'

A. [Making note] Few words.

B. [Goes on one knee] Before I met you my past was wrapped in a murky fog.

A. [Notes] Murky fog.

B. You are like a red, red rose.

A. [Making note] Red rose.

B. Then you give her diamonds.

A. [Still writing] Diamonds.

B. Then she's yours!
   [Girl enters and stands away from chalk mark]

A. [Whispers] There she is!

B. Well, go on, you know how to do it!

A. [Goes to girl] You're standing on the wrong place.
   [Puts her on the chalk mark, she looks bewildered. A. pulls himself together and gives an exaggerated imitation of B.'s swagger. A. looks at notebook] Cross eyes! [Girl looks indignant. A. looks at notebook] I'm a man who has known a few birds.

B. Words!

A. [Kneels] Before I met you I was fast and a dirty dog!

B. No! You fathead!

A. No, you fathead! [Girl starts to look cross] I mean you've got a red, red nose.

B. Rose!

A. Rose!

B. Go on – Diamonds.

A. [Gives her a few diamond playing cards, looks again at notebook] Now you're mine!
   [Girl slaps his face – exits leaving him sitting on floor.]

The '*Come Back Gag*' has many twists, the formula is:

> A. Here's a jug, go and get a pint of beer.
> B. Where's the money?
> A. Anybody can get beer with money, but to get beer without money, that's clever, get the beer!
> [B. goes off stage, returns with jug. A. takes jug and goes to drink, shows the jug is empty.]
> A. Where's the beer?
> B. Anybody can drink beer when there's beer to drink, but to drink beer when there's no beer to drink, that's clever; drink the beer!

The changing of the first letter of a word when properly placed will always be good for a laugh:

> 'I'm in *a bath* of *perspiration.*'
> becomes
> 'I'm in *a pirth* of *barspiration.*'

> 'Ammoniated tincture of quinine'
> becomes
> 'Animated picture of Queen Anne.'

> 'I want a pair of Sporn ring hecticles. I mean hen ring spornicles, no, spinrorn hornecles, himlock spinnicles, oh – glasses!

The source *of 'Rhyming Slang'* follows on. These you can modernise by using well-known names:

> It wants a new Ivor Novello – meaning
> "   "   "   Bellow.
> Where's my Bob?
> Bob Donat?
> My Hat.

Then there's the '*What's the difference Gag*'.

What's the difference between you and a cocoanut?

I don't know!
You can get a drink out of a cocoanut!
[There are many forms of that one.]

'Mean Gags' can be changed around:

'He's so mean he wouldn't spend Xmas.'
'He stopped his watch because he lived opposite the Town Hall.'
'He'd keep a candle alight all night to save a match in the morning.'
'He wouldn't give you the skin off a rice pudding.'
'If he was a ghost he wouldn't give you a fright.'

The *Reading of Letters* is always amusing, Here's one I used in the Musical Play 'Me and My Girl':

'Dear Bill,
Thank you for your wedding present – my wife is very proud of it and wears it on her – P.T.O. – (funny place to wear it!] Oh, yes, "please turn over" wrist! (I thought she couldn't wear it anywhere else!] We have a lovely new home but it is near the soap works and I'm sorry to say we get a most horrid smell from your old pal, Bill Barking.'

We mustn't forget our old friend the *Conundrum.* There are several ways of handling them.

There's the ridiculous answer to a ridiculous question. One of the earliest I can remember is:

Q. Why is a mouse like when it spins?
A. Because Portsmouth is a Seaport Town.

Well, that is a rough idea and short summary of 'old friends'. Of course it is only elementary. Remember, there's a new generation every seven years and this means there's a new audience waiting for the old friend to turn up. Some of the older generation may sneer, but they more often enjoy hearing the youngsters laughing at the same joke that *they* once got a kick out of. Like the old soldier, old gags never die, they fade away into a new version.

FORTUNE COOKIE,
DEAD BABIES AND
MAPP & LUCIA

I've chosen three very different fiction writers in Hubert Selby Jr., E.F. Benson and Martin Amis. I love the fact that New York lowlifes rub shoulders with Tilling high society on my bookshelves. Amis creates wonderfully vivid characters, so much so that I wouldn't even bother trying to watch a film of one his novels (I'm seemingly not alone in this) as there is nothing to beat his power of description. The prose perfectly creates the images, even if they aren't images you necessarily want in your head. The character described in the extract is Keith Whitehead, "an almost preposterously unattractive young man". Crouching in a field with his trousers round his ankles, Keith is said to expell "a pint of air" from his buttocks. His podgy nipples are said to be turned into "bloody puddings" by a rough cheesecloth shirt as he runs in it. When a film was made of *Dead Babies*, our friend Andy Nyman played the role of Keith, and I'm happy to report he's nothing like the character described in these pages.*

One of the first things I remember seeing on Channel 4 was an adaptation of E.F. Benson's Mapp and Lucia books, and once I'd seen them I devoured the novels very quickly. I don't know if seeing the faces of Geraldine McEwan, Prunella Scales and Nigel Hawthorne enlivened the books for me but I loved Benson's style, his understatement and

* He's worse.

cutting wit. I've read these books more than once – which is very rare for me – and they always make me smile.

When I was a student I went into a second-hand bookshop in Chorley, thinking that this was one of the requirements of studentdom (like buying a smelly overcoat from Affleck's Palace in Manchester). I bought, for no particular reason other than having vaguely heard of them, *Last Exit to Brooklyn*, *Titus Groan* and *The Catcher in the Rye*. Inspired choices it turns out (*Titus Groan* remains unread, but I was in the TV version so that's OK, I get the gist). What struck me most about Selby Jr.'s writing was his genuine compassion for his characters, no matter how low they'd stooped in life. *Last Exit to Brooklyn* made a huge impact on me, but I couldn't sneak an extract into a humour book, it's too violent and bleak. The short story I've chosen comes from an anthology called *Song of the Silent Snow* and is a little more light-hearted. Selby's everyman character, Harry Black, tells a story of obsession, hope and redemption which is one of the most perfect short stories I've read (after J. Dyson's).

'FORTUNE COOKIE'

Harry sat in a rear booth of the Chinese restaurant, alone and worried, toying with his chicken egg drop soup, occasionally eating a spoonful. The boss had not said anything to him directly, but he knew his time was coming ... soon. He had not given Harry an ultimatum, but the looks and remarks – more than that, the feeling Harry got when he was around him, and was starting to get when he stepped into the office, and even over the phone, forced Harry to accept the fact that his time was coming. And he did not mean a feeling of anxiety. Harry knew what that felt like. He should, he had been living with it all his life and lately it had been getting worse by the day ... day? Krist, it was getting worse by the hour and right now by the minute. It was more than anxiety, it was a realization.

A salesman sells. It is that simple. A salesman sells and when he doesn't he is not a salesman and who needs a salesman who is not selling. Firms do not carry non-selling salesmen for long. Actually he was lucky they carried him this long, even giving him his draw. But last week was his last draw and today could be his last chance. No sale today and ... he stared at the soup for a minute, then pushed it away from him, the waiter quickly picking it up and replacing it with a dish of food. Harry moved his mouth into a quick smile then took a deep breath and started mixing the soy sauce into his chow mein.

He had to make that sale today. He had no choice. It was do or die ... the knot in his stomach quickly started gnawing its way up to his throat and Harry took a deep breath and tried to relax, at least enough to eat. He ate some food and tried a little positive thinking. After all, he can do it. He can make this sale. He'll just go in there, smile and relax, and let the product, and the customer, do the selling. Right! That's all there is – but I've been doing that for months and still no order. The chow mein looked heavy and soggy. But I lit another candle this morning and prayed and made the stations of the cross and I can't fail with all – but I've been doing that for months too. He took another deep breath and tried to relax ... then took a few mouthfuls of food. Can't get all caught up in superstition – not that praying is superstition, but I mean all that business about a lucky tie or suit … have to forget all about that … Yeah, even if I had a lucky tie or suit. Pretty soon I might not have a suit or tie – this is ridiculous. This suit and tie are just as lucky as any I have. He shrugged, I've lost as many sales with them as with any other suit and tie … he chuckled inwardly and even smiled and turned his attention to the food for a while, the noodles seeming to be a little crispier. The knot of anxiety started growing and travelling again and he suddenly thought of his shoes, maybe these are my lucky shoes, and he started his silent chuckling again and kept the anxiety enough in control to finish most of his chow mein.

The waiter quickly cleared away the plates and brought a fortune cookie and the check. Harry played with the cookie for a few minutes, tapping it on the table, then eventually, almost absentmindedly, he broke it open and tugged the fortune out and glanced at it, the words not getting through his preoccupation at first, but a glimmer of something registered and he looked carefully at the fortune: Take courage, today is your day for success. He nodded his head. Yeah … sure. Then he stopped frowning and read it again and straightened, Why not? Why shouldn't it be my day? It has to be somebody's day and I've had enough losers. Yeah … that's right, I've had enough losers. This *can* be my day as well as anyone else's…. That's right … absolutely right. They need our material and they may just as well buy it from us as anyone else. We're just as good as anyone and better than most. And we can deliver on time. That's the big thing in this industry, guaranteed delivery as well as guaranteed quality. And we have it … all! He'd be doing himself and his firm a favor to place the order with us. You're damn right! Harry nodded his head emphatically and reached in his pocket for his money, then stopped and reached instead for his credit cards, the ones he had been afraid to use for many months, and dropped one on the tray with the check and sat back, relaxed, exhilarated. He smiled broadly as he added a generous tip, then signed the slip with a slight flourish. He pocketed his card and stepped briskly from the restaurant.

His appointment with Mr. Dasher went smoothly and was successful beyond all expectations. Harry seemed to speak at exactly the right time and say exactly the right thing and was quiet at exactly the right time in the right way, listening intently and exuding an aura of relaxation and confidence. His whole attitude was one of having already made the sale and he was here to simply help Mr. Dasher in whatever way he could. At the end of their meeting Mr. Dasher was as happy as Harry and their final handshake and words were extremely cordial. Harry knew he had a lifetime customer.

Harry of course was elated as he headed back to the office with the signed order, so happy over making the sale he did not stop to figure out what his commission would be. When the thought did enter his mind he quickly shrugged it off knowing he would probably still be behind on his advances anyway. And he did not want to ruin the way he felt by thinking about the state of his finances. He had made a sale, a big sale. That was the important thing. He had broken his losing streak. He was a winner and for that he was grateful.

As soon as he gave the order to the proper people in the office he called his boss and told him. At first Mr. Wells sounded surprised, but that quickly changed to a tone of delight. That's wonderful, Harry. Congratulations. I knew you could do it. Harry beamed and leaned back in his chair, nodding his head and thanking Mr. Wells for the compliments. He hung up and just sat for a few minutes allowing that good feeling to flow through him … then called his wife and told her the good news.

Harry sat quietly for a few more minutes, then looked at his watch, and started calling and making appointments, having no trouble getting appointments with the people and before he stopped his calendar was filled for the next couple of weeks.

Harry lit a candle the following morning, not wanting to break any part of the routine that led to the previous day's success, but his attitude was different. He did not kneel and beg like a condemned man going through a ritual for the sake of propriety, knowing all along that it was useless and he would be led to the gallows anyway, but rather like a friend bringing a feeling of gratitude for the gift he knew he would be receiving.

Naturally Harry had lunch in the same restaurant. He was even going to order chicken egg drop soup and chow mein, but thought it safe to deviate slightly and have won ton soup and sub gum chow mein. The big difference today was again his attitude. He sat at a small table in the middle of the restaurant, smiling, and ate the food with deep enjoyment and relish.

When the plates were cleared away and the waiter brought his fortune cookie he leaned back in the chair, one arm over the back of the chair, nonchalantly toying with the fortune cookie and feeling a warm glow inside. He picked the cookie up and smiled as he rolled it around in his hand, tapped it on the plate, spun it around playing spin the fortune cookie and eventually leaned over and snapped it in half and extricated the fortune: Today is a day to assert yourself. He pulled his shoulders back, yeah, that's right. His back was straight as he walked from the restaurant, and self-confidence exuded from him.

He had scheduled two appointments for the afternoon and both went smoothly and ended in large orders just as he knew they would. He had the right combination now and had the world by the tail. He could not lose. That he knew. He could not lose. He was a winner.

The following day he started to get a slight premonition, a tremor, when he realized he would have to change his routine, but was steadfast in his refusal to allow it to shake his confidence. He had made a lunch appointment with one of his prospective clients who was across town and so there was no way they could have lunch in the Chinese restaurant next door. So Harry checked the yellow pages for Chinese restaurants in the vicinity of the customer's office and found one listed only a block and half away. When he suggested going there for lunch the other man agreed quite readily.

Harry's relaxed attitude helped relax his customer and they had a very enjoyable lunch. Harry did not toy with his fortune cookie, but ignored it as long as possible as they continued their discussion, then casually cracked it open and smiled as he read his fortune: Success comes to the successful man. Harry nodded inwardly, that's right, success breeds success and I'm for inbreeding. The other man did not bother with his fortune cookie, so when they got up to leave Harry surreptitiously picked it up and put it in his pocket. Just might come in handy.

When Harry left the man's office 45 minutes later he had another large order. He called it in to his office then walked around for a short time until it was time to go to his next appointment. This one too went exactly as Harry knew it would – the other fortune cookie said it would – so that made two orders so far. Harry knew that sooner or later he would leave an office without a signed order, that was inevitable, but for now he was riding a hot streak and was going to give it all he had.

He also knew that the fortune cookies did not really have anything to do with the sales, but he was not going to take any chances and so he continued with the candles in the morning and the Chinese restaurant in the afternoon. And business was good. It was great! As a matter of fact his sales were mounting so rapidly that it looked like he would be a shoe in for the salesman of the year award. And as the sales mounted so did his commissions and it was obvious that he would have to start looking for some sort of tax shelter. He smiled and grinned when he thought about it, not exactly a bad position to be in.

Things continued going almost perfectly for several months. Even the people who did not give him an order were very favorably impressed, telling him they would keep him in mind if their situation ever changed. But eventually the inevitable fly came into the ointment and Harry had to find a way to get rid of the fly without throwing out the ointment. He became a victim of the Chinese restaurant syndrome.

The first time it struck he ended up being late for an appointment but fortunately no harm was done and he survived the attack and got an order. At first, as he sat on the commode doubled up with cramps and sweat pouring from his pores, he knew he would have to stop going to the Chinese restaurant every afternoon. Then, after he returned with the order and relaxed in his office, he realized that he was being hasty. It's not that he was being superstitious you understand, but it just did not make sense to change a routine that was working so well.

The following day convinced him. And though he knew that his sales did not depend upon his eating in a Chinese restaurant every day, he still tried to find some way of continuing to do so without getting sick. Or more specifically, to get the fortune cookie he needed – no, no, he didn't really need it, but ... well, what the hell, everybody has some sort of good luck charm. Certainly no different than a rabbit's foot. He shrugged inwardly, what the hell.

The next day he went to a small Chinese food take-out store and took the fortune cookie out of the bag and dropped the rest in the first litter can, then went to lunch. He glowed with pride at his ingenuity and the ease with which he had solved the problem. Each day he went to the take-out stand and ordered a few items and threw them away after taking out the fortune cookie.

One day he noticed a couple of girls from his office at the stand and continued walking, then came back ten minutes later, looking around carefully to make sure no one else from his office was there. Now when he left the office for lunch he glanced over his shoulder to be certain no one who knew him was in the vicinity, carefully looking around again before dropping the bag of food in a litter can as nonchalantly as possible, studying the sky and whistling as he hurried away.

Soon the pressure of this routine started to create anxieties so he would eat lunch in the area first, then go to a take-out stand some distance from the office to get his fortune cookie.

After much testing, and some trepidation, he found he could safely eat in a Chinese restaurant every fourth day without fear of an attack. And so he sampled the Chinese food from one end of town to the other. He was in Chinatown one day when he made a happy and astounding discovery: a store that sold fortune cookies by the bag. Now he truly had nothing to worry about.

He kept a bag of cookies in his desk drawer and rationed them out to himself, one at a time. But then it started becoming a little difficult to understand some of the fortunes. Well, it wasn't that they were hard to understand exactly, it was just that they were ambiguous or simply did not apply to the immediate situation. So Harry was forced to open another … and another, until he found one that was pertinent to the day before going out on his appointments. Soon he had to buy bags by the dozen, wanting to be certain he did not run out, and when he left the office he was covered with cookie crumbs, the old anxiety giving him a slight twinge from time to time.

One morning Harry was studying reports and getting together information to present to a prospective customer. This was an international corporation and if Harry could close this particular deal it would be the largest in his firm's history and would open undreamed of vistas for the firm and for Harry. Among other things it would mean an appointment to the Corporate Staff.

He had been working on it for six months, putting in endless hours and tremendous energy and creative imagination, and the final appointment, the yes or no appointment, was for tomorrow afternoon. He had everything together and was starting to review it again when he received a phone call advising him that his appointment for the following day would have to be cancelled, Mr. Ralston had to leave the country unexpectedly, and could Harry make the appointment for this afternoon at two, Mr. Ralston having no idea when he might be otherwise available.

Harry quickly agreed and automatically reached into his drawer for a fortune cookie. He read the fortune, frowned and threw it away. Who needs that: He who hesitates is lost, but it is better to be lost than dead. What kind of nonsense is that? He opened another … and another and another, becoming increasingly anxious and annoyed. He had been bothered by the ambiguity of some of the previous fortunes, but now they were being downright negative. He reached for the last one and it too was the same. If he took the advice of the cookies he opened today he would go home and lock himself in a closet. Right now he wished he could do just that. He hated the idea of trying to close this deal feeling so nervous and negative.

He frowned and looked at the pile of cookies and fortunes in his waste paper basket. What the hell was going on? Why was everything suddenly against him? Krist, he wished he could cancel the appointment! But if he did it would be all over. He would never get another chance. Not like this. He would not get the Corporate appointment. He had to see him today. But why was everything going wrong? He had lit his candles this morning. Why should this be happening to him? He looked through all his drawers for the third or fourth time hoping to find a stray fortune cookie, one that he had somehow overlooked, but to no avail. There just wasn't any left. He was completely out. And there was no way he could get any more before going uptown. Unless he had an early lunch in the Chinese restaurant next door. He brightened, Yeah. That's what I'll do. That's where it all started anyway. I'll have a quick lunch and get uptown in plenty of time. He brushed the cookie crumbs from his suit and left his office.

Something told him that he was not being too wise having lunch here today, having had lunch in a Chinese restaurant yesterday, but he was forced to dismiss the thought. He would be careful. He wouldn't eat much. He wouldn't take a chance on being victimized by the Chinese restaurant syndrome. Not today, and a faint voice way in the back of his head said: Famous last words.

He ate the soup and a little of the chop suey and quickly grabbed the fortune cookie when the waiter brought it and crushed it and read the fortune, then stared at it: There are times when the wisest thing to do is nothing. He could not believe it. This was insane. He waved to the waiter and asked him if he could bring him another fortune cookie. He nodded and when he brought it Harry cracked it open and almost moaned aloud as he read the fortune. Another one. I must be dreaming. Somebody must be playing some sort of trick.

He called the waiter again and asked for a dozen fortune cookies. The waiter looked at him for many seconds, Harry said excitedly that he would pay for them, breaking into a forced smile and explaining that it was for a joke. Eventually the waiter shrugged and brought another dozen fortune cookies. Harry stared at them for a moment, the waiter glancing at him from time to time, talking to the other waiters, then shrugging and shaking his head. Harry took a deep breath and relaxed as best he could and got ready to open the first one, girding his loins as if he were about to dive off a hundred foot tower into a tank of water through flaming oil. He opened the first one, read it quickly, tossed it aside and went to the next, repeating the same routine, his knot of anxiety growing with each one, becoming more and more sick, until he had opened them all (all the waiters were watching by this time, scratching their heads) and he sat staring at the pile of broken cookies and crumpled fortunes. Harry was on the verge of tears. He could not believe this was happening to him. All the way to the very brink of something great and then the entire world suddenly turns on him. He hadn't done anything to anyone. He lit his candles every morning. Why should this happen to him? It wasn't fair. Goddam it, it wasn't fair! I'm not going to put up with it! I'll be damned if I will! NO!!!! He spoke the last word aloud as he brought his fist down, hard and loud on a pile of broken cookies, the plates and little bottles jumping and clanging, people suddenly silent, sitting still, forks suspended in air, looking first at each other, then turning around to find the source of the disturbance; the waiters too stopping in mid-motion, looking at Harry and blinking as Harry ground his hand into the cookies and shouted, I'm not going to put up with it! That's it! Harry continued to mutter to himself as he paid his bill, unaware that everyone was staring at him, commenting that he was as mad as a hatter.

Harry was full of energy when he entered Mr. Ralston's office. The first thing Mr. Ralston did was to inform Harry that he was very busy and did not have time for superfluities. That was just fine with Harry as he was well prepared and wanted to get on with it too. He presented all the figures quickly, giving Mr. Ralston a copy of everything, noting the salient points, answering all questions easily and succinctly and when the meeting was concluded he left Mr. Ralston's office with the order.

When he got back Harry went directly to his office and plunked himself in his chair. By now his body was wet with perspiration and his insides were a turmoil of confusion and disbelief. He had the signed order right here but the fact seemed to be somewhere outside him. He knew it was real but it did not seem to have any pertinence to him, and the reality of the entire situation became increasingly vague the more he pondered it because he just could not believe it happened. How did it all come about? He could barely remember being in Mr. Ralston's office. He thought and thought and simply ended up increasing his confusion.

And what made it even more perplexing was the fact that he knew this would change his life. Every aspect of it. A house in Connecticut with trees and a garden. A summer place in Marthas Vineyard. Cars. A boat. Yeah … maybe a forty foot sloop and he would sail before the wind feeling the spray and breeze on his face …

But he would be functioning on the Corporate level now....

The thought was frightening. How could he possibly function on that level? How could he possibly make a speech before the Board of Directors (the mere thought sent tremors through his mind and body) giving them progress reports ... advising them of projected sales ... Oh krist, that's right. I'd have to continue making deals like this. I'd have a position to maintain! How could I do it? This one was a fluke. There's no way I can do this again ... Jesus, the Board wouldn't be satisfied for long they'd want it done again and again and again ...

Oh God, I can't do it. I could never take the pressure – he glanced at the pile of broken fortune cookies in his wastepaper basket – I wouldn't know what to do. Being a salesman is one thing, but Corporate Staff ... the responsibility ... and he'd be stuck with the house in Connecticut and the summer place in Marthas Vineyard and the boat and cars ... Oh God, no ... no ...

He felt icy cold and shivered as panic twisted itself through then around him; squeezing him tighter and tighter, making it almost impossible to breathe ... He struggled to gulp air into his lungs, then leaned forward and rested his elbows on his desk and held his head, sinking deeper and deeper into his despair ...

Then he noticed something in the newspaper on his desk. At first it was a blur but something forced his attention to that area and he found he could not move his gaze away from it. He blinked his eyes until his vision cleared and he realized he was staring at the daily horoscope, his horoscope for today: Today is the day to assert yourself. Great opportunities are yours if you just take the bull by the horns. Don't take no for an answer. He read it over ... then again ... at first just the words got through, and then their meaning, his body becoming more and more erect as he read, his face relaxing into a smile ... then he slammed his hand down, hard, on the paper and jumped to his feet, Of course! That's it! I knew it! I just knew it! I knew today was my day!!!! Thank God I'm not superstitious or I might have let those damn cookies ruin my life. Now I know how to do it – tapping the paper – right there all the time. Haha, there's no way I can be stopped now! He snatched the signed contract from his desk and went to the Executive Wing to advise the President in person that he had wrapped up the deal. After all, he may just as well start getting used to his new neighborhood!!!!

DEAD BABIES

Chapter XL

Whitehead

The Whiteheads have several claims to being the fattest family alive. At the time of writing you could go along Parky St, Wimbledon, any Sunday, one o'clock in the afternoon – and you'd see them, taking their seats in the Morris for the weekly Whitehead jaunt to Brighton.

'Get your huge fat arse out of the way' – 'Whose horrible great leg is this?' – 'Is this bit your bum, Keith, or Aggie's?' – 'I don't care whose guts these are, they've got to be moved' – 'That's not Dad's arm, you stupid great bitch, it's my leg!'

'Its no good.' says Whitehead Sr eventually, slapping his trotters on the steering-wheel. 'The Morris can't be expected to cope with this. You can take it in turns staying behind from now on.'

And indeed, as each toothpaste Whitehead squeezed into the Morris, the chassis drips two inches on its flattened tyres, and when Frank himself gets in behind the wheel, the whole car seems to sink imploringly to its knees.

'Flora, close that sodding door,' Frank tells his wife.

'I can't, Frank. Some of my leg is still out there.'

A crowd has gathered on the pavement. Neighbours lean with folded arms on half-washed cars. Curtains part along the terraced street.

'Oh, God.' says Whitehead Sr, 'they're all watching now, Keith! Give your mother a hand with her leg.'

Keith squats forward and fights his mother's thigh up into the car, while Frank leans sideways and tugs at the far door-strap with one hand and a fistful of Mrs Whitehead's hip with the other. Aggie, Keith's sister, sits crying with shame in the back seat; she sees her family conflate into one pulsing balloon of flesh.

'Come on – nearly home.'

'No!' shrieks Flora. 'There's still a bit of arm hanging out!'

'Got it,' pants Keith.

'The door closes noiselessly and to ironic cheers from the crowd the four grumpy pigs chug out into the street.

'Get your arse off the gear-lever, woman,' Frank demands as they pull up at the lights, 'How'm I expected to drive with arse all over the gear-lever? Keith! Move over, can't you, you fat little sod. You're weighing down the right rear wheel. I can feel her listing to the right.'

'Ah shut up, you fat old turd. How can I move with Aggie all over the place back here? It's you who's weighing it down, you great fat old fool.'

'I happen to have reduced considerably of late. And there's no cause for you to be so heavy – you're only four foot and a fart.'

'Ah shut up. You fat old bugger. You fat old cunt.'

'Keith,' said his mother, 'don't talk to your father like that.'

'Ah shut up. You fat old bitch. You fat old slag.'

'Keith,' said Aggie.

'Ah shut up.'

'This can't go on,' says Mrs Whitehead as the car wobbles down through the motorway heat-haze. 'Starvation diet, all of us, all next week. You too, Keith. All next week. Starvation diet. This can't go on.'

One hour later they sit in silence round a sea-front coffee shop table, paw-like hands dipping occasionally into a dome of cream, jam and custard slices. Warm sugary tea runs down their chins.

The four Whiteheads are ninety stone, heavier than the average rugby pack, a crazily over-glanded brood, their house a billowing cartoon world of sunken sofas, hammock-like beds and winded armchairs. They shuffle about it snarling and swearing at one another with the sheer thyrotoxic strain of keeping their bodies afloat.

Whitehead Sr, for instance, is a fabulously obese human being, better than thirty-five stone. As he trundles down the street school-parties are floored by his myriad stray fists of flab; bus platforms snap off should he climb on board; lifts whinny, shudder and stay where they are when he presses the UP button and plummet terrifyingly whether or not he is so foolish as to depress the DOWN; chairs splinter beneath him; tables somersault at a touch from his elbow; joists crack and floorboards powder. Frank's weight problem endangered, too, his position as cook at the bus terminal cafeteria: he would bend down in front of the cooker and – why

– his behind had swiped a shelf of pans off the opposite wall; he would turn round from the sink to find that his paunch had cleared the table; loaves, half-dozen cartons of margarine, even sides of beef would get lost for days in the fleshly gowns of his stomach. (Old Whitehead had been known also to eat the cafeteria bare while the manager went to the lavatory.) When it became quite impossible for Frank to enter the kitchen, without some of him being automatically – by definition – either on the hot-plate, under the grill, in the over or down the toaster, he was invited to pick up his cards. Frank had been a worthless cook anyway, hardly able to prepare an egg.

To make up the loss in income Mr Whitehead decided to expand the ailing family sweetshop. By compelling his wife to model eighteen hours a day at the Hornsey, Wimbledon and Baron's Court Art Polytechnics, he saved enough money to gut the sitting-room and have installed some bright steel ovens, a Fablon-decked counter, and a sign saying *Whitehead's Takeaway Fish and Chips*. The concern prospered, and eventually the sweetshop was phased out.

The turning-point was the turning-point also of little Keith's life.

He well remembered the transition. Keith would come home from school, a crimson-faced four-foot box in his sixth-form blazer, he refused a chocolate bar, snap at his father, then change into his white overalls. (He hated changing into these because they made him look appreciably more horrible than his school clothes did.) In hostile silence he and his father would serve the remaining children from the adjacent primary school – there would be more of them than usual because of the many while-stocks-last bargains featured in the closing-down sale. At five-fifteen or so, Frank's knuckle-less fingers were curling round a Mars Bar or a Turkish Delight. Keith would wait a few seconds then remove a few peppermint-creams from the high glass case. With slightly more hurried movements Frank might reach for a sachet of Poppets and Whitehead for a box of Maltesers. Now Frank whips his thumbnail down a carton of Savoy Truffles and upends it into his mouth; Keith's head fizzes with imploding sherbet-lemons. Bubbles of Caramac pop on Mr Whitehead's lip; his son is lock-jawed with fudge and Newberry Fruits. Frank skilfully flips a tray of violet creams on to the counter and laps them up like a dog. A runaway train of Toblerone shunts down the tunnel of little Keith's throat. By six-thirty they are engaged in a lurching, slow-motion alligator race to the downstairs lavatory-vomitorium. By seven, their batter-moist mouths gape beneath the fish-shop chip-chutes.

The family gained a hundredweight in five weeks.

Shortly afterwards, Keith went mad of a time.

Nothing seemed to precipitate it. One moment he was toddling out of the Mod. Lit, Library in Milton Avenue, London NW20; the next moment he was toddling into the Gregory Blishner Institute, Potters Bar, London NW36. What had happened in the interim was a rush of terror and confusion as solidly chemical as adrenalin, a telephone call and a bus ride.

Not that the preceding week had been entirely uneventful. For one thing it had included his inaugural few days at Wolfson College, London – days that had opened up whole new eras of ostracism, mortification and self-loathing. But Keith had been banking on that, and by and large he was agreeably surprised by the cordiality of his reception. On top of this, though, he had been independently menaced on the Monday by a traffic warden, an old man on the Underground and a floor-sweeper in a local pub. Keith had offered them no provocation and he accepted their threats and denunciations with respectful apologies. On the Tuesday he was denied service in a cafeteria – no reason given – and badly stoned by little boys in the park. The next day he crouched in his bedsitter drinking quarts of instant coffee. On the Thursday an entire Woolworth's shop-counter went into hysterics when he tried to buy a comb, a poker-faced conductor barred his entry on to an uncrowded bus, he found and removed a sheet on the lodge notice-board which read KEITH WHITEHEAD IS A HORROR SHOW, his tutor advised him – for personal reasons which he would as soon not disclose – to change subjects, and his father rang to say that he spoke for the whole family in asking Keith never to contact them again. A more or less average week, you'd have thought. But on the Friday Whitehead started to be insane.

For an hour he sat waiting in the Institute's arc-lit vestibule. He beguiled it in an examination of the back of his hand, trying hard not to look down the endless yellow corridor where mad persons now groped and slunk along the walls as wraith-like male nurses swept past them with throbbing steel-cylinders. 'Whitehead? This way.'

'How are you feeling?' the doctor asked.

'Sad and frightened.'

The doctor knitted his fingers together over the desk and leant forward. 'How long, would you say, you have felt this way?'

Keith looked at his watch. 'An hour and twenty minutes.'

The doctor, a slow-talking Ceylonese, went on to ask Keith about his background, in a patient but unimaginative attempt to reveal traumas, block, repressions, and so forth. Although Keith answered all the doctor's questions with grim candour it soon became clear that his life had been quite devoid of emotional incident.

'Look.' said Keith after a while, 'you don't have to do all this. I know what the trouble is. It's quite straightforward.'

The doctor sighed, 'O.K. What is it?

'No, I'm not telling you. You'll just think I've got paranoia.'

'No I won't.'

'Yes you will.'

'No I *won't.*'

The doctor had already seen twenty-one male university students that morning. Six had complained of impotence, five of cancelled sex, four of bedwetting, three of false memory, two of insomnia and one of somnolence. The doctor had prescribed Contentuless to every student except the one complaining of somnolence, whom he had instructed to go away.

'All right then,' said Keith. 'Well, as I told you, it's quite straightforward. No one likes me – actually most people dislike me instinctively, including my family – I'm not much good at my work, I've never had a girl-friend or a friend of any kind, I've got very little imagination, nothing makes me laugh, I'm fat, poor, bald, I've got a horrible spotty face, constipation, B.O., bad breath, no prick and I'm one inch tall. That's why I'm mad now. Fair enough?'

'Yes,' said the doctor.

Every life has its holidays, and Keith's month in the Institute was assuredly his. To begin with, he didn't go any madder. The panic and confusion receded at once, becoming a faint accusatory gibber at the nape of his neck. He found too that within a suspended community his sense of isolation could be turned to good account. He grew to think more coldly and shrewdly about his personal shortcomings. He found out what the average weight was for a five-foot man; he worked his way through the reading-room magazines, appreciatively noting down all instances of deformity and privation more acute than his own; a study of 'The Human Body.' Section of *The Guinness Book of Records* assured him how puny his problems really were. In time, the feeling he had carried around with him since the age of six or seven, the feeling that he ought to be dead, gradually began to fade.

And with every day that passed little Keith took solace and grateful encouragement from his fellow inmates, watching the old teddy-boys who yawned and snivelled in front of the common-room television, the fat forty-year-old infants who lay staked out with depressants in the wards, the mumbling bitches who leant slumped like rubbish bags along the corridors, the sparrow-like girls kneeling nervously on the lawn. Airy with barbiturates, Keith would rove the Institute grounds, every now and then his face folding into a sneer or lightening with a thrill of relish as his colleagues made their twitching way past him. He had overheard it said that you always went madder at the Institute because 'there was nothing to relate to.' But Keith didn't want to relate to anything; he felt only hatred and contempt for the mutants around him, and if ever he wished to remind himself of the true direction of his life he simply gazed at the high Institute walls, visualized the road that went to London, and listened with pleasant detachment to the sounds of buses and highheels in the street outside. The month did wonders for his confidence. Heck, he even got a girl.

Mapp and Lucia

5

Lucia was writing letters in the window of the garden-room next morning. One, already finished, was to Adele Brixton asking her to send to Mallards the Queen Elizabeth costume for the tableaux: a second, also finished, was to the Padre, saying that she found she would not have time to attend committees for the hospital fête, and begging him to co-opt Miss Mapp. She would, however, do all in her power to help the scheme, and make any little suggestions that occurred to her. She added that the chance of getting fruit gratis for the refreshment department would be far brighter if the owner of it was on the board.

The third letter, firmly beginning 'Dearest Liblib' (and to be signed very large, LUCIA), asking her to dine in two days' time, was not quite done when she saw dearest Liblib, with a fixed and awful smile, coming swiftly up the street. Lucia, sitting sideways to the window, could easily appear absorbed in her letter and unconscious of Elizabeth's approach, but from beneath half-lowered eyelids she watched her with the intensest interest. She was slanting across the street now, making a beeline for the door of Mallards ('and if she tries to get in without ringing the bell, she'll find the chain on the door,' thought Lucia).

The abandoned woman, disdaining the bell, turned the handle and pushed. It did not yield to her intrusion, and she pushed more strongly. There was the sound of jingling metal, audible even in the garden-room, as the hasp that held the end of the chain gave way; the door flew open wide, and with a few swift and nimble steps she just saved herself from falling flat on the floor of the hall.

Lucia, pale with fury, laid down her pen and waited for the situation to develop. She hoped she would behave like a lady, but was quite sure it would be a firm sort of lady. Presently up the steps to the garden-room came that fairy tread, the door was opened an inch, and that odious voice said:

'May I come in, dear?'

'Certainly,' said Lucia brightly.

'Lulu dear,' said Elizabeth, tripping across the room with little brisk steps. 'First I must apologize: so humbly. Such a stupid accident. I tried to open your front door, and gave it a teeny little push and your servants had forgotten to take the chain down. I am afraid I broke something. The hasp must have been rusty.'

Lucia looked puzzled.

'But didn't Grosvenor come to open the door when you rang?' she asked.

'That was just what I forgot to do, dear,' said Elizabeth. 'I thought I would pop in to see you without troubling Grosvenor. You and I are such friends, and so difficult to remember that my dear little Mallards — Several things to talk about!'

Lucia got up.

'Let us first see what damage you have done,' she said with an icy calmness, and marched straight out of the room, followed by Elizabeth. The sound of the explosion had brought Grosvenor out of the dining-room, and Lucia picked up the dangling hasp and examined it.

'No, no sign of rust,' she said. 'Grosvenor, you must go down to the ironmonger and get them to come up and repair this at once. The chain must be made safer and you must remember always to put it on, day and night. If I am out, I will ring.'

'So awfully sorry, dear Lulu,' said Elizabeth, slightly cowed by this firm treatment. 'I had no idea the chain could be up. We all keep our doors on the latch in Tilling. Quite a habit.'

'I always used to in Riseholme,' said Lucia. 'Let us go back to the garden-room, and you will tell me what you came to talk about.'

'Several things,' said Elizabeth when they had settled themselves. 'First, I am starting a little jumble-sale for the hospital, and I wanted to look out some old curtains and rugs, laid away in cupboards, to give to it. May I just go upstairs and downstairs and poke about to find them?'

'By all means,' said Lucia. 'Grosvenor shall go round with you as soon as she has come back from the ironmonger's.'

'Thank you, dear,' said Elizabeth, 'though there's no need to trouble Grosvenor. Then another thing. I persuaded Mr Georgie to send me a sketch for our picky exhibition. Promise me that you'll send me one too. Wouldn't be complete without something by you. How you get all you do into the day is beyond me; your sweet music, your sketching, and your dinner-parties every evening.'

Lucia readily promised, and Elizabeth then appeared to lose herself in reverie.

'There *is* one more thing,' she said at last. 'I have heard a little gossip in the town both today and yesterday about a fête which it is proposed to give in my garden. I feel sure it is mere tittle-tattle, but I thought it would be better to come up here to know from you that there is no foundation for it.'

'But I hope there is a great deal,' said Lucia. 'Some tableaux, some singing, in order to raise funds for the hospital. It would be so kind of you if you would supply the fruit for the refreshment booth from your garden. Apropos I should be so pleased to buy some of it every day myself. It would be fresher than if, as at present, it is taken down to the greengrocer and brought up again.'

'Anything to oblige you, dear Lulu,' said Elizabeth. 'But that would be difficult to arrange. I have contracted to send all my garden-produce to Twistevant's – such a quaint name, is it not? – for these months, and for the same reason I should be unable to supply this fête which I have heard spoken of. The fruit is no longer mine.'

Lucia had already made up her mind that, after this affair of the chain, nothing would induce her to propose that Elizabeth should take her place on the committee. She would cling to it through storm and tempest.

'I see,' she said. 'Perhaps then you could let us have some fruit from Diva's garden, unless you have sold that also.'

Elizabeth came to the point, disregarding so futile a suggestion.

'The fête itself, dear one,' she said, 'is what I must speak about. I cannot possibly permit it to take place in my garden. The rag-tag and bob-tail of Tilling passing through my hall and my sweet little sitting-room and spending the afternoon in my garden! All my carpets soiled and my flower-beds trampled on! And how do I know that they will not steal upstairs and filch what they can find?'

Lucia's blood had begun to boil: nobody could say that she was preserving a benevolent neutrality. In consequence she presented an icy demeanour, and if her voice trembled at all, it was from excessive cold.

'There will be no admission to the rooms in the house,' she said. 'I will lock all the doors, and I am sure that nobody in Tilling will be so ill bred as to attempt to force them open.'

That was a nasty one, Elizabeth recoiled for a moment from the shock, but rallied. She opened her mouth very wide to begin again, but Lucia got in first.

'They will pass straight from the front door into the garden,' she said, 'where we undertake to entertain them, presenting their tickets of admission or paying at the door. As for the carpet in your sweet little sitting-room, there isn't one. And I have too high an opinion of the manners of Tilling in general to suppose that they will trample on your flower-beds.'

'Perhaps you would like to hire a menagerie,' said Elizabeth, completely losing her self-control, 'and have an exhibition of tigers and sharks in the garden-room.'

'No: I should particularly dislike it,' said Lucia earnestly. 'Half of the garden-room would have to be turned into a seawater tank for the sharks and my piano would be flooded. And the rest would have to be full of horse-flesh for the tigers. A most ridiculous proposal, and I cannot entertain it.'

Elizabeth gave a dreadful gasp as if she was one of the sharks and the water had been forgotten. She adroitly changed the subject.

'Then again, there's the rumour – of course it's only rumour – that there is some idea of entertaining such inmates of the workhouse as are not bedridden. Impossible.'

'I fancy the Padre is arranging that,' said Lucia. 'For my part, I'm delighted to give them a little treat.'

'And for my part,' said Miss Mapp, rising (she had become Miss Mapp again in Lucia's mind), 'I will not have my little home-sanctuary invaded by the rag-tag –'

'The tickets will be half a crown,' interposed Lucia.

'— and bob-tail of Tilling,' continued Miss Mapp.

'As long as I am tenant here,' said Lucia, 'I shall ask here whom I please, and when I please, and – and how I please. Or do you wish me to send you a list of the friends I ask to dinner for your sanction?'

Miss Mapp, trembling very much, forced her lips to form the syllables:

'But, dear Lulu —'

'Dear Elizabeth, I must beg you not to call me Lulu,' she said. 'Such a detestable abbreviation—'

Grosvenor had appeared at the door of the garden-room.

'Yes, Grosvenor, what is it?' asked Lucia in precisely the same voice.

'The ironmonger is here, ma'am,' she said, 'and he says that he'll have to put in some rather large screws, as they're pulled out—'

'Whatever is necessary to make the door safe,' said Lucia. 'And Miss Mapp wants to look into cupboards and take some things of her own away. Go with her, please, and give her every facility.'

Lucia, quite in the grand style, turned to look out of the window in the direction of Mallards Cottage, in order to give Miss Mapp the opportunity of a discreet exit. She threw the window open.

'Georgino! Georgino!' she called, and Georgie's face appeared above the paling.

'Come round and have 'ickle talk, Georgie,' she said. 'Sumfin I want to tell you. Presto!'

She kissed her hand to Georgie and turned back into the room. Miss Mapp was still there, but now invisible to Lucia's eye. She hummed a gay bar of Mozartino, and went back to her table in the bow-window where she tore up the letter of resignation and recommendation she had written to the Padre, and the half-finished note to Miss Mapp, which so cordially asked her to dinner, saying that it was so long since they had met, for they had met again now. When she looked up she was alone, and there was Georgie tripping up the steps by the front door. Though it was standing open (for the ironmonger was already engaged on the firm restoration of the chain) he very properly rang the bell and was admitted.

'There you are,' said Lucia brightly as he came in. 'Another lovely day.'

'Perfect. What has happened to your front door?'

Lucia laughed.

'Elizabeth came to see me,' she said gaily. 'The chain was on the door, as I have ordered it always shall be. But she gave the door such a biff that the hasp pulled out. It's being repaired.'

'No!' said Georgie, 'and did you give her what for?'

'She had several things she wanted to see me about,' said Lucia, keeping an intermittent eye on the front door. 'She wanted to get out of her cupboards some stuff for the jumble-sale she is getting up in aid of the hospital, and she is at it now under Grosvenor's superintendence. Then she wanted me to send a sketch for the picture exhibition, I said I would be delighted. Then she said she could not manage to send any fruit for our fête here. She did not approve of the fête at all, Georgie. In fact, she forbade me to give it. We had a little chat about that.'

'But what's to be done then?' asked Georgie.

'Nothing that I know of, except to give the fête,' said Lucia. 'But it would be no use asking her to be on the committee for an object of which she disapproved, so I tore up the letter I had written to the Padre about it.'

Lucia suddenly focused her eyes and her attention on the front door, and a tone of warm human interest melted the deadly chill of her voice.

'Georgie, there she goes,' she said. 'What a quantity of things! There's an old kettle and a boot-jack, and a rug with a hole in it, and one stair-rod. And there's a shaving from the front door where they are putting in bigger screws, stuck to her skirt.... And she's dropped the stair-rod.... Major Benjy's picking it up for her.'

Georgie hurried to the window to see these exciting happenings, but Miss Mapp, having recovered the stair-rod, was already disappearing.

'I wish I hadn't given her my picture of the Land-gate,' said he. 'It was one of my best. But aren't you going to tell me all about your interview? Properly, I mean: everything.'

'Not worth speaking of,' said Lucia. She asked me if I would like to have a menagerie and keep tigers and sharks in the garden-room. That sort of thing. Mere raving. Come out, Georgie. I want to do a little shopping. Coplen told me there were some excellent greengages from the garden which he was taking down to Twistevant's.'

THEATRE OF BLOOD

There's no doubt that the advent of video libraries provided an unhealthy boost to my interest in horror. My brother and I, both in our mid-teens, would make the trip on our bikes and scour the shelves with the all-important question: "How many killings?" A high body count was essential, otherwise there might be the danger of plot, or 'talking'. Zombies ate flesh, the moon was bloody and graves were spat on – no bother. Only two scenes freaked me out as a kid: Regan's head-turning in *The Exorcist* and Robert Morley's death in *Theatre of Blood*. Douglas Hickox's film is the perfect mixture of comedy and horror, and as such can be seen as a major influence on *The League of Gentlemen*. Like *The Wicker Man*, this was one of the first "have you seen?" conversations I'd have in order to root out the people worth knowing, and sure enough all four of us love this film.

THEATRE OF BLOOD

EDWARD LIONHEART: Perfect, absolutely perfect. Thank goodness no-one can get near enough to notice the dazed, glazed, drunken, idiotic expression in his eyes. Now you are to obey my orders, do you hear?

LIONHEART LOOK-ALIKE: Yessir!

LIONHEART: Now let us see what that stupid cretin Mr Meredith Merridew had to say about my Titus Andronicus. [reads from newspaper cutting] "Mr Lionheart's rendering of the role can only be described as villainous. Laid between the delicately underplayed performances of Miss Lillywhite as Lavinia and Miss Mole as Tamora, one is irresistibly reminded of a ham sandwich." My reputation. Hark villain! I will grind your bones to dust and make two pasties of your shameful head.

[…]

MEREDITH MERRIDEW: Woo-hoo, woo-hoo, woo-hoo – where are my babies, eh? Ha ha ha. Daddy's home. Woo-hoo. Where are my doggie-woggies, my doggie-woggies? Oo – ha ha – come to Daddy. I know where you are. I know where you're hiding!

LIONHEART: Meredith Merridew, this is your dish [fanfare and applause].

MERRIDEW: Oh, oh! What a divine surprise! I've often thought, 'What if I was on *This Is Your Dish*?', and now that I am, I can't think of anything to say, except, this is a very great honour.

LIONHEART: Merci. Please be seated, monsieur. And now we will make you, make you comfortable. There we go.

MERRIDEW: Which is the camera?

LIONHEART: That one, right over there.

MERRIDEW: For what we about to receive, may the Lord make us truly thankful. Amen.

[…]

LIONHEART: This is the very best vintage, monsieur. *Soixante-six.*

MERRIDEW: Mmm-hmm.

LIONHEART: Oh, I hope everything is to monsieur's satisfaction.

MERRIDEW: Simply delicious. I wonder where my babies have got to? My doggies, you know. I always think of them as my babies.

LIONHEART: Of course you do, monsieur – and so do we. That is part of your surprise.

MERRIDEW: All the same, I wish they were here to share this with me.

LIONHEART: But there they are – both baked in the pie. Whereof their mother daintily has fed, eating the flesh which she herself has bred. [Pulls a hair out of pie] Tut, tut, tut.

MERRIDEW: What was that? Where are my dogs? Where are my babies?

LIONHEART: Well, if monsieur cannot do without his dogs, then he shall have his dogs.

The others start to whistle and laugh.

LIONHEART: You see, monsieur, two dogs, two pies. We knew that monsieur would be hungry. You do remember, monsieur, how in *Titus Andronicus,* the Queen Tamora was served her own children baked in a pie. Of course in your case we've used only the tenderest morsels. Do have some more!

Pushes him on to table.

LIONHEART: Now – will you ever again ruin the reputation of an honest man?

MERRIDEW: No.

They forcefeed him.

LIONHEART: Have you learnt your lesson?

MERRIDEW: Yes.

LIONHEART: Can I be certain that you will never again offend me?

MERRIDEW: Yes.

LIONHEART: You can be sure, detestable more, gorged with the dearest morsel of life, thus I enforce force thy wrathen jaws t'open, and you despite, I'll cram you with more food.

Stuffs him full of food using brass pipe.

EDWARD LIONHEART: Pity – he didn't have the stomach for it.

DEAD FUNNY

L ike many people, I've spent hundreds, probably thousands of pounds on theatre tickets and yet would struggle to recall the smallest fraction of the shows I'd seen. On a strictly cash-for-laughs basis, Terry Johnson's *Dead Funny* has to be my most profitable theatregoing experience. I was in fits from start to finish and went to see it five times. The line between comedy and pain has rarely been so well drawn, and the brilliant writing can turn in an instant, leaving you howling with laughter, then sadness. I took Reece to a performance, knowing it would also be his cup of tea, and we were dismayed to find ourselves sitting next to a blind woman whose companion was describing all the events onstage. "There's a woman, sitting on the floor, glass in hand. Oop, the husband's home. Moustache. Smiling…" Luckily once the dialogue started the companion stopped nattering and allowed the play to speak for itself.

I think I'll do likewise. Enjoy.

Dead Funny

SCENE TWO

The same. One week later. Richard alone.

RICHARD: The comic traditions of this small island are the envy of the world. France has its rural whimsy. America its Jewish wit. Belgium its Belgians. No, but seriously. One nation stands out when it comes to comedy. Ask a Norwegian, a Canadian, a native Australian, they'll all tell you; the English are funny.

ELEANOR: *appears listening.*

RICHARD: And the undisputed King of British comedy was of course, indeed still is … Benny Hill. But it's not only those Joe Soaps, those Mr and Mrs Averages who number themselves among his fans. Mention should also be made of Greta Garbo. Michael Jackson. The Queen Mother.

ELEANOR: The Ayatollah Khomeni. Saddam Hussein.

RICHARD: I didn't know you were in.

ELEANOR: I fell asleep.

RICHARD: Have you been drinking?

ELEANOR: I only drink at mealtimes.

RICHARD: What did you have for lunch?

ELEANOR: Three martinis and an orgasm.

RICHARD: Are you going out?

ELEANOR: Tonight's the night is it? Farewell Fred Scuttle?

RICHARD: Yes.

ELEANOR: I wouldn't miss it for the world. I've got a class at seven, but I'll be back!

RICHARD: You're drinking too much.

ELEANOR: I'm drinking just enough. For a Wednesday.

RICHARD: Don't start.

ELEANOR: When are the anoraks arriving?

RICHARD: They don't all wear anoraks.

ELEANOR: They do.

RICHARD: That is a generalization.

ELEANOR: Every one of them wears an anorak.

RICHARD: Inaccurate stereotyping.

ELEANOR: I know they don't call them anoraks any more, but if it's day-glo and padded and makes you look like a cuddly hand grenade then as far as I'm concerned it's an anorak.

RICHARD: I'm willing to admit not all of them have an IQ of a hundred and fifty ...

ELEANOR: Put together.

RICHARD: ... and it's very easy to take the mickey out of a group of people bonded by a common interest ...

ELEANOR: Sorry.

RICHARD: ... but there's no need for this unending stream of abuse.

ELEANOR: I'm sorry. I've got a surprise for you later.

RICHARD: What?

Doorbell.

ELEANOR: Hello Brian.

RICHARD *goes to the door.*

ELEANOR *drinks.*

RICHARD: Hello, Brian.

BRIAN *enters with shopping.*

BRIAN: I'm very upset. I've just had a dreadful row and you know me; I don't have arguments, but he's really upset me.

RICHARD: Who?

BRIAN: Who do you think? Les Rollins.

RICHARD: Ah.

BRIAN: Anyway, I've been to Tescos and I've baked a cake. Hello Ellie.

ELEANOR: Hello Brian.

BRIAN: What's this?

ELEANOR: A key to the door; you'll be in and out all evening.

BRIAN: Ooh, only if my luck changes. Ta. Anyway, Rollins phoned me about tonight and says, what's all this he hears about fancy dress? I said it's not fancy dress, it's a token gesture. Token gesture my arse, he says. I'm not coming dressed up! I tried to explain it's a little tradition

177

the society likes to uphold and that it wasn't fancy dress, it was just a visual tribute and you didn't have to go the whole hog. Just a beret or some rimless specs or slicked back hair and Chinese glasses, whatever … a *tribute.*

RICHARD: That's right.

BRIAN: Well, he wouldn't have it. Said it was farcical. I was a bit rude, I said, if you don't like it, don't come.

ELEANOR: Maybe he's got a point.

BRIAN: What?

ELEANOR: Well. It's a bit undignified, isn't it?

BRIAN: There is nothing undignified about humbling oneself and donning the symbolic garb of a great clown.

RICHARD: Of course not.

ELEANOR: It's just that some people look a bit funny dressed up in a bald wig and baggy trousers; not you Brian, but some people.

BRIAN: You think he's right? You think we should just abandon one of our silliest traditions just because Les Rollins 'feels a bit peculiar'?! He likes Ben Elton, you know. Les Rollins is a big fan of Ben Elton. What does that tell you?

RICHARD: Don't get upset, Brian.

BRIAN: I am upset. I'm very upset. Ever since he joined there's been contention in the air. I knew he was going to be trouble when he turned up to his first meeting with that video of Tommy Cooper's last performance, and his fatal collapse. I was appalled.

RICHARD: There was quite a healthy majority wanted to see it, Brian.

ELEANOR: Seventeen to one, wasn't it?

BRIAN: I was ashamed of you. I thought you at least had good taste. That upset me, that show of hands. I couldn't watch.

RICHARD: You should have. It was actually very dignified.

ELEANOR: A man holding a rubber chicken having a coronary in front of fifteen hundred people? Dignified?

BRIAN: Exactly.

RICHARD: He was plying his craft, he paused, and then he fell like an oak. Yes. Dignified.

ELEANOR: First trick he ever got right, I know that.

BRIAN: It wasn't even a first generation tape; it was a grainy old bootleg.

RICHARD: Bit of history though.

BRIAN: It was a snuff movie. I knew we'd rue the day we voted Les Rollins in. I'm not at all sure any more about a lot of the membership, to tell you the truth. I've seen the *Bottom* videos surreptitiously passed during coffee break. There doesn't seem to be any discrimination any more between good old bawdy innuendo and filth. Between good old slapstick and sick physical violence. Maybe I'm getting old. He hasn't said anything to you has he? Rollins?

RICHARD: What about?

BRIAN: Me?

RICHARD: No.

BRIAN: Anyway, that's the bad news.

ELEANOR: There's good news is there?

BRIAN: There's very good news. We've got a guest of honour. Don't ask me how I got his phone number, but I did. And you know my philosophy; if you don't ask you don't get. So I phoned and I asked and he said he'd be honoured.

RICHARD: Who?

BRIAN: Honoured. I nearly fell off my chair.

RICHARD: Who?

BRIAN: Henry McGee.

RICHARD: No.

BRIAN: Yes.

RICHARD: Henry McGee?

BRIAN: Yes.

RICHARD: I don't believe you.

BRIAN: Henry McGee.

ELEANOR: In my house?

BRIAN: He was totally charming. He said of course he'd heard of us. He'd seen us on the news doing Hattie's plaque. And he said he'd be honoured to join with us in remembering Benny.

RICHARD: That's extraordinary.

BRIAN: Then he went a bit quiet. You know.

RICHARD: Right.

BRIAN: Then he said ... I miss him, of course.

RICHARD: Did he?

BRIAN: 'I miss him, of course.' Then he asked if I'd like to see *It Runs in the Family.* He's currently appearing in *It Runs in the Family.*

ELEANOR: Benny Hill?

BRIAN: Henry McGee.

ELEANOR: Oh. I was going to say. In fact, I was going to go.

BRIAN: He said I should definitely see it, Ray Cooney being a master of the genre. And let him know I was coming.

RICHARD: He offered you tickets?

BRIAN: No, just to let him know when I'd got tickets, I suppose to see him afterwards.

RICHARD: That's …

BRIAN: He was very charming on the phone.

RICHARD: I'm not surprised though.

BRIAN: A charming man. 'I miss him, of course.'

ELEANOR: Well, that's a bit of a coup isn't it, Brian?

BRIAN: I know.

ELEANOR: Step up from Bella Emberg.

BRIAN: Oh, now, now. Bella was …

RICHARD: Ellie.

ELEANOR: Oh, she was.

BRIAN: She was very kind to fit us in to what was for her a pretty hectic Madhouse season.

ELEANOR: I know. I know. She was very kind. And startlingly articulate. I think Bella Emberg was almost as articulate as she was thin.

BRIAN: Can I unpack this lot in the kitchen?

RICHARD: Of course.

Exit Brian.

ELEANOR: I shouldn't have said that.

RICHARD: You're getting very cruel.

ELEANOR: I know.

RICHARD: I mean; poor Brian.

ELEANOR: I mean poor Bella. She was sweet.

BRIAN: [off] I've catered for twenty.

ELEANOR: Twenty?

BRIAN: But if they all turn up there should be enough.

ELEANOR: You said half a dozen.

BRIAN: [off] Oh, and I had a bit of a stroke in Tescos.

ELEANOR: I bet that had them rolling in the aisles. Where can I get the video?

BRIAN: Look. Custard pies.

ELEANOR: What for?

BRIAN: Just a joke. I shouldn't think anyone'll actually throw one.

ELEANOR: I should bloody well hope not.

BRIAN: Do you think it's living dangerously? Because I needn't put them out.

RICHARD: No, it's a nice idea.

ELEANOR: So was the *Titanic*.

BRIAN: Can I help myself to plates?

RICHARD: Yes.

Exit Brian.

RICHARD: This means a lot to Brian.

ELEANOR: So?

RICHARD: Why are you trying to spoil it for him?

ELEANOR: Time of the month.

RICHARD: Couldn't we call a truce, just for tonight?

Pause.

ELEANOR: I suppose a fuck's out of the question?

RICHARD: If you're that desperate, have an affair.

Enter Brian.

BRIAN: It's very good of you both. I gave serious thought to using my flat now that Mum's not there. But it's so small. I thought if I opened it out and used Mum's room, but that'd feel very strange because I'm not using Mum's room yet. I'm still in the small back room, but I have laid out the dining area in the living room as my office area now. I use the big table and to eat I use the television table I got Mum from Argos. All in all it's nice to have the extra space; I know she wouldn't mind me saying that; she used to say much the same herself. But her room's much as she left it. Which reminds me Ellie, I keep forgetting to bring you that perfume ...

ELEANOR: Oh, that's all right.

BRIAN: No no, I've remembered.

Gives her a bottle of stale 4711 and a minuscule bottle of Chanel no 4.

BRIAN: She'd have liked you to have it. She liked you.

ELEANOR: Thank you.

BRIAN: I've got some sausage rolls. Can I pop them in the oven?

ELEANOR: You can pop anything in my oven any time you like, Brian.

BRIAN: Oh well, if you weren't spoken for.

ELEANOR: I'm not even spoken *to*. Richard wouldn't mind.

BRIAN: Oh well then, I'll whisk you away.

ELEANOR: Yes please. Thanks for this.

BRIAN *exits.*

ELEANOR: Who with?

RICHARD: What?

ELEANOR: An affair?

RICHARD: Well, that would be your choice, wouldn't it?

ELEANOR: Oh, thanks. All right. I'll have an affair with Nick.

RICHARD: Nick? You always said he had a face like a turtle.

ELEANOR: You don't have to look at the mantelpiece Richard, when you're sitting on it.

BRIAN *enters.*

BRIAN: Right, that's me done for now. I'm just going to nip home and put my frock on. Nick is bringing the wine now, isn't he?

RICHARD: I hope so.

BRIAN: I'll see you later then. What a performance.

BRIAN *leaves.*

RICHARD: What I meant was you don't have to lead a celibate life just because I choose to. You are allowed to choose.

ELEANOR: I chose you. We're supposed to have chosen each other. We're supposed to be a couple. Couples make love.

RICHARD: Not the couples I know.

ELEANOR: Yes they do.

RICHARD: They don't you know.

ELEANOR: Well the couples I know do. It's normal.

RICHARD: It doesn't feel normal.

ELEANOR: It's perfectly normal for most people.

RICHARD: I'm not most people.

ELEANOR: Exactly; you're not normal.

RICHARD: I'm perfectly normal.

ELEANOR: If you were normal, we'd have a sex life!

RICHARD: I can't stand these conversations going round and round …

ELEANOR: We have to discuss things; it's part of the process.

RICHARD: Part of the pressure.

ELEANOR: There is no pressure.

RICHARD: Pressure from Miriam, pressure from you.

ELEANOR: I don't want to pressure you.

RICHARD: Don't then.

ELEANOR: But I can't ignore this … misery I feel.

RICHARD: This is my body. It's not yours. It's mine. It doesn't want to be touched. That doesn't make me particularly happy, but it feels perfectly normal.

Doorbell.

ELEANOR: I'm going to rip that doorbell out with my teeth. I gave you the key, Brian!

She goes to the door. Nick and Lisa enter, with carry cot.

ELEANOR: [off] Oh. Hello.

LISA: I know we're early, I know. I told him we were going to be early.

NICK: Sorry.

ELEANOR: That's all right; the party's started.

RICHARD: Hi, Nick.

NICK: Hi.

LISA: Can I take him straight upstairs?

ELEANOR: Sure.

LISA *exits.*

NICK: Sorry we're early. Bit of a snag. I couldn't get any cash out of the machine for the booze.

RICHARD: Been embezzling the funds, have you?

NICK: No, no. I don't know; it just ate the card. Thing is, we're a bit short ourselves at the moment.

RICHARD: I'll give you some.

NICK: Cheers mate: There's a second card you see, that Brian used to have, but he swears he gave it back to me. Oh, it'll sort itself out. Ta, mate. I'd better rush; I've left the car running.

ELEANOR: If you're going to Threshers, you can give me a lift to the Poly.

NICK: Sure.

ELEANOR: I'll give you a blow job on the way.

NICK: Splendid. She's a wonderful woman, your wife. Nothing's too much trouble, is it?

RICHARD: See you later.

NICK: Right. Come on then; let's hope we don't hit any potholes.

Exit Nick.

ELEANOR: It'd give him a hell of a shock if I did, wouldn't it?

RICHARD: Go to work, Ellie.

Exit Ellie as Lisa comes downstairs.

ELEANOR: [off] Bye, Lisa!

LISA: [off] Oh. Bye. She go with him?

RICHARD: She's got a class.

LISA: Oh, I see.

She takes off her coat; dressed in a severe woollen twin-set and pearls.

LISA: Da da! Nick wanted me to come as a Hill's Angel of course, but I told him he'd got another think coming. So I've come as a spinster. Well, it was either bimbo, battle-axe or spinster and I'm certainly not a battle-axe, am I?

She poses. Richard sips his drink. She sits.

Norman Wisdom was very good, wasn't he? I'd have enjoyed it more if I hadn't been stuck on the end next to Les Rollins. He kept saying whatever it was Norman was going to say just before he said it, and he's a very tactile person, isn't he, Les? Very wide to sit next to. Squeezes past when there's bags of room. Holds his glass at nipple height so he can brush you with his knuckles. He's been paying me quite a lot of attention actually; I've been wondering if I should mention it to Nick.

Richard goes to her. She stands. He lifts his hand to fondle her breast. She moves away.

LISA: I've had this headache threatening me all day. Did you see 'It'll Be Alright on the Night'? Dennis Norden said something very interesting. He said apparently Sigmund Freud said there were only four kinds of joke.

Richard closes the door, gently bends her over the back of the sofa.

LISA: I taped it actually. Apparently, let's see if I can get this right …

Richard pulls down her knickers and unzips his fly.

LISA: There's … Concealment of Knowledge Later Revealed, Substitution of One Concept for Another. Um … Unexpected Conclusion to a Hitherto Logical Progression, and um …
He enters her.
Oh. Something else.
They fuck.
Hard.

Enter Benny Hill in long mac, beret and pebble glasses.

BRIAN: Here I am then.

Lisa head first over the sofa, Richard zips up fly before first securing penis.

BRIAN: Only me.

Reece's Pieces

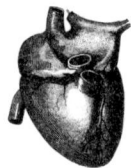

'THE TELL-TALE HEART'

Edgar Allan Poe can sometimes, I feel, be a bit of a torturous read. I could never get through 'The Gold Bug' for example. But when he's good, he's really good, and I think 'The Tell-tale Heart' is classic Poe. A bullet point of great Poe. The story is a simple one, told with clarity and justification by a man who has lost his mind. The terror is in the detail of what has driven this man to murder, and the ensuing guilt and paranoia that overwhelm and undo him. I remember as a child – and here is an insight of me as a child, making the room from 'The Tell-tale Heart' with removable floorboards to hide the old man's body under. I made the old man and his horrid white eye from plasticine, and hid him – in bits – under floorboards made from a cereal packet. Whilst others were cutting out the daleks on the back, I had other uses for my Weetabix box.

The stealth with which the murderer, slowly, over a number of nights, dares to open up the old man's door and peep inside at his sleeping victim, is particularly creepy. And his crumbling under the polite smiles of the police that come to visit him is a brilliant denouement to a quietly powerful story.

'THE TELL-TALE HEART'

TRUE! – nervous – very, very dreadfully nervous I had been and am; but why will you say that I am mad? The disease had sharpened my senses – not destroyed – not dulled them. Above all was the sense of hearing acute. I heard all things in the heaven and in the earth. I heard many things in hell. How, then, am I mad? Hearken! and observe how healthily – how calmly I can tell you the whole story.

It is impossible to say how first the idea entered my brain; but once conceived, it haunted me day and night. Object there was none. Passion there was none. I loved the old man. He had never wronged me. He had never given me insult. For his gold I had no desire. I think it was his eye! yes, it was this! He had the eye of a vulture – a pale blue eye, with a film over it. Whenever it fell upon me, my blood ran cold; and so by degrees – very gradually – I made up my mind to take the life of the old man, and thus rid myself of the eye forever.

Now this is the point. You fancy me mad. Madmen know nothing. But you should have seen me. You should have seen how wisely I proceeded – with what caution – with what foresight – with what dissimulation I went to work! I was never kinder to the old man than during the whole week before I killed him. And every night, about midnight, I turned the latch of his door and opened it – oh so gently! And then, when I had made an opening sufficient for my head, I put in a dark lantern, all closed, closed, that no light shone out, and then I thrust in my head. Oh, you would have laughed to see how cunningly I thrust it in! I moved it slowly – very, very slowly, so that I might not disturb the old man's sleep. It took me an hour to place my whole head within the opening so far that I could see him as he lay upon his bed. Ha! would a madman have been so wise as this. And then, when my head was well in the room, I undid the lantern cautiously – oh, so cautiously – cautiously (for the hinges creaked) – I undid it just so much that a single thin ray fell upon the vulture eye. And this I did for seven long nights – every night just at midnight – but I found the eye always closed; and so it was impossible to do the work; for it was not the old man who vexed me, but his Evil Eye. And every morning, when the day broke, I went boldly into the chamber, and spoke courageously to him, calling him by name in a hearty tone, and inquiring how he has passed the night. So you see he would have been a very profound old man, indeed, to suspect that every night, just at twelve, I looked in upon him while he slept.

Upon the eighth night I was more than usually cautious in opening the door. A watch's minute hand moves more quickly than did mine. Never before that night had I felt the extent of my own powers – of my sagacity. I could scarcely contain my feelings of triumph. To think that there I was, opening the door, little by little, and he not even to dream of my secret deeds or thoughts. I fairly chuckled at the idea; and perhaps he heard me; for he moved on the bed suddenly, as if startled. Now you may think that I drew back – but no. His room was as black as pitch with the thick darkness, (for the shutters were close fastened, through fear of robbers,) and so I knew that he could not see the opening of the door, and I kept pushing it on steadily, steadily.

I had my head in, and was about to open the lantern, when my thumb slipped upon the tin fastening, and the old man sprang up in bed, crying out – "Who's there?"

I kept quite still and said nothing. For a whole hour I did not move a muscle, and in the meantime I did not hear him lie down. He was still sitting up in the bed listening; – just as I have done, night after night, hearkening to the death watches in the wall.

Presently I heard a slight groan, and I knew it was the groan of mortal terror. It was not a groan of pain or of grief – oh, no! – it was the low stifled sound that arises from the bottom of the soul when overcharged with awe. I knew the sound well. Many a night, just at midnight, when all the world slept, it has welled up from my own bosom, deepening, with its dreadful echo, the terrors that distracted me. I say I knew it well. I knew what the old man felt, and pitied him, although I chuckled at heart. I knew that he had been lying awake ever since the first slight noise, when he had turned in the bed. His fears had been ever since growing upon him. He had been trying to fancy them causeless, but could not. He had been saying to himself – "It is nothing but the wind in the chimney – it is only a mouse crossing the floor," or "It is merely a cricket which has made a single chirp." Yes, he had been trying to comfort himself with these suppositions: but he had found all in vain. All in vain; because Death, in approaching him had stalked with his black shadow before him, and enveloped the victim. And it was the mournful influence of the unperceived shadow that caused him to feel – although he neither saw nor heard – to feel the presence of my head within the room.

When I had waited a long time, very patiently, without hearing him lie down, I resolved to open a little – a very, very little crevice in the lantern. So I opened it – you cannot imagine how stealthily, stealthily – until, at length a simple dim ray, like the thread of the spider, shot from out the crevice and fell full upon the vulture eye.

It was open – wide, wide open – and I grew furious as I gazed upon it. I saw it with perfect distinctness – all a dull blue, with a hideous veil over it that chilled the very marrow in my bones; but I could see nothing else of the old man's face or person: for I had directed the ray as if by instinct, precisely upon the damned spot.

And have I not told you that what you mistake for madness is but over-acuteness of the sense? – now, I say, there came to my ears a low, dull, quick sound, such as a watch makes when enveloped in cotton. I knew that sound well, too. It was the beating of the old man's heart. It increased my fury, as the beating of a drum stimulates the soldier into courage.

But even yet I refrained and kept still. I scarcely breathed. I held the lantern motionless. I tried how steadily I could maintain the ray upon the eye. Meantime the hellish tattoo of the heart increased. It grew quicker and quicker, and louder and louder every instant. The old man's terror must have been extreme! It grew louder, I say, louder every moment! – do you mark me well I have told you that I am nervous: so I am. And now at the dead hour of the night, amid the dreadful silence of that old house, so strange a noise as this excited me to uncontrollable terror. Yet, for some minutes longer I refrained and stood still. But the beating grew louder, louder! I thought the heart must burst. And now a new anxiety seized me – the sound would be heard by a neighbour! The old man's hour had come! With a loud yell, I threw open the lantern and leaped into the room. He shrieked once – once only. In an instant I dragged him to the floor, and pulled the heavy bed over him. I then smiled gaily, to find the deed so far done. But, for many minutes, the heart beat on with a muffled sound. This, however, did not vex me; it would not be heard through the wall. At length it ceased. The old man was dead. I removed the bed and examined the corpse. Yes, he was stone, stone dead. I placed my hand upon the heart and held it there many minutes. There was no pulsation. He was stone dead. His eye would trouble me no more.

If still you think me mad, you will think so no longer when I describe the wise precautions I took for the concealment of the body. The night waned, and I worked hastily, but in silence. First of all I dismembered the corpse. I cut off the head and the arms and the legs.

I then took up three planks from the flooring of the chamber, and deposited all between the scantlings. I then replaced the boards so cleverly, so cunningly, that no human eye – not even his – could have detected anything wrong. There was nothing to wash out – no stain of any kind – no blood-spot whatever. I had been too wary for that. A tub had caught all – ha! ha!

When I had made an end of these labors, it was four o'clock – still dark as midnight. As the bell sounded the hour, there came a knocking at the street door. I went down to open it with a light heart, – for what had I now to fear? There entered three men, who introduced themselves, with perfect suavity, as officers of the police. A shriek had been heard by a neighbour during the night; suspicion of foul play had been aroused; information had been lodged at the police office, and they (the officers) had been deputed to search the premises.

I smiled, – for what had I to fear? I bade the gentlemen welcome. The shriek, I said, was my own in a dream. The old man, I mentioned, was absent in the country. I took my visitors all over the house. I bade them search – search well. I led them, at length, to his chamber. I showed them his treasures, secure, undisturbed. In the enthusiasm of my confidence, I brought chairs into the room, and desired them here to rest from their fatigues, while I myself, in the wild audacity of my perfect triumph, placed my own seat upon the very spot beneath which reposed the corpse of the victim.

The officers were satisfied. My manner had convinced them. I was singularly at ease. They sat, and while I answered cheerily, they chatted of familiar things. But, ere long, I felt myself getting pale and wished them gone. My head ached, and I fancied a ringing in my ears: but still they sat and still chatted. The ringing became more distinct: – It continued and became more distinct: I talked more freely to get rid of the feeling: but it continued and gained definiteness – until, at length, I found that the noise was not within my ears.

No doubt I now grew very pale; – but I talked more fluently, and with a heightened voice. Yet the sound increased – and what could I do? It was a low, dull, quick sound – much such a sound as a watch makes when enveloped in cotton. I gasped for breath – and yet the officers heard it not. I talked more quickly – more vehemently; but the noise steadily increased. I arose and argued about trifles, in a high key and with violent gesticulations; but the noise steadily increased. Why would they not be gone? I paced the floor to and fro with heavy strides, as if excited to fury by the observations of the men – but the noise steadily increased. Oh God! what could I do? I foamed – I raved – I swore! I swung the chair upon which I had been sitting, and grated it upon the boards, but the noise arose over all and continually increased. It grew louder – louder – louder! And still the men chatted pleasantly, and smiled. Was it possible they heard not? Almighty God! – no, no! They heard! – they suspected! – they knew! – they were making a mockery of my horror! – this I thought, and this I think. But anything was better than this agony! Anything was more tolerable than this derision! I could bear those hypocritical smiles no longer! I felt that I must scream or die! and now – again! – hark! louder! louder! louder! louder!

"Villains!" I shrieked, "dissemble no more! I admit the deed! – tear up the planks! here, here! – It is the beating of his hideous heart!"

THE HAUNTING OF
HILL HOUSE

When I first happened upon *The Haunting*, the Robert Wise film adaptation of Shirley Jackson's novel, late one night on BBC2, (as most of the great horrors were discovered when I was a boy), I remember sitting through it like an endurance test, barely able to keep watching. I was really, really frightened. I didn't like it. I mean, I did, I loved horror films, but when they actually scared me – they became something else. The pounding "like a cannon ball" on the door, as the "thing" outside terrorises Claire Bloom and Julie Harris in their bedroom is, to this day, one of the most frightening scenes of cinema. The thing that kept me awake though, was the muttering through the walls during the night, and the shapes and faces that seem to appear in the wall paper. Indeed, it is the descriptions of Hill House itself, and the madman that designed it, that make the novel such a frightening one. Shirley Jackson introduces us to her haunted house brilliantly as Eleanor Lance, one of a team of invited psychics, lays eyes on the monstrosity for the first time. The moment makes your blood run cold, and I'll never forget reading it. It stops you in your tracks – just like Eleanor Lance: "The house was vile". That passage is reproduced here.

The Haunting of Hill House

The house was vile. She shivered and thought, the words coming freely into her mind. Hill House is vile, it is diseased; get away from here at once.

No human eye can isolate the unhappy coincidence of line and place which suggests evil in the face of a house, and yet somehow a maniac juxtaposition, a badly turned angle, some chance meeting of roof and sky, turned Hill House into a place of despair, more frightening because the face of Hill House seemed awake, with a watchfulness from the blank windows and a touch of glee in the eyebrow of a cornice. Almost any house, caught unexpectedly or at an odd angle, can turn a deeply humorous look on a watching person; even a mischievous little chimney, or a dormer like a dimple, can catch up a beholder with a sense of fellowship; but a house arrogant and hating, never off guard, can only be evil. This house, which seemed somehow to have formed itself, flying together into its own powerful pattern under the hands of its builders, fitting itself into its own construction of lines and angles, reared its great head back against the sky without concession to humanity. It was a house without kindness, never meant to be lived in, not a fit place for people or for love or for hope. Exorcism cannot alter the countenance of a house; Hill House would stay as it was until it was destroyed.

I should have turned back at the gate, Eleanor thought. The house had caught her with an atavistic turn in the pit of the stomach, and she looked along the lines of its roofs, fruitlessly endeavoring to locate the badness, whatever dwelt there; her hands turned nervously cold so that she fumbled, trying to take out a cigarette, and beyond everything else she was afraid, listening to the sick voice inside her which whispered, *Get away from here, get away.*

But this is what I came so far to find, she told herself; I can't go back. Besides, he would laugh at me if I tried to get back out through that gate.

Trying not to look up at the house – and she could not even have told its color, or its style, or its size, except that it was enormous and dark, looking down over her – she started the car again, and drove up the last bit of driveway directly to the steps, which led in a forthright, no-escape manner onto the veranda and aimed at the front door. The drive turned off on either side, to encircle the house, and probably later she could take her car around and find a building of some kind to put it in; now she felt uneasily that she did not care to cut off her means of departure too completely. She turned the car just enough to move it off to one side, out of the way of later arrivals – it would be a pity, she thought grimly, for anyone to get a first look at this house with anything so comforting as a human automobile parked in front of it – and got out, taking her suitcase and her coat. Well, she thought inadequately, here I am.

It was an act of moral strength to lift her foot and set it on the bottom step, and she thought that her deep unwillingness to touch Hill House for the first time came directly from the vivid feeling that it was waiting for her, evil, but patient. Journeys end in lovers meeting, she thought, remembering her song at last, and laughed, standing on the steps of Hill House, journeys end in lovers meeting, and she put her feet down firmly and went up to the veranda and the door. Hill House came around her in a rush; she was enshadowed, and the sound of her feet on the wood of the veranda was an outrage in the utter silence, as though it had been a very long time since feet stamped across the boards of Hill House. She brought her hand up to the heavy iron knocker that had a child's face, determined to make more noise and yet more, so that Hill House might be very sure she was there, and then the door opened without warning and she was looking at a woman who, if like ever merited like, could only be the wife of the man at the gate.

"Mrs. Dudley?" she said, catching her breath. "I'm Eleanor Vance. I'm expected."

Silently the woman stood aside. Her apron was clean, her hair was neat, and yet she gave an indefinable air of dirtiness, quite in keeping with her husband, and the suspicious sullenness of her face was a match for the malicious petulance of his. No, Eleanor told herself; it's partly because everything seems so dark around here, and partly because I expected that man's wife to be ugly. If I hadn't seen Hill House, would I be so unfair to these people? They only take care of it, after all.

The hall in which they stood was overfull of dark wood and weighty carving, dim under the heaviness of the staircase, which lay back from the farther end. Above there seemed to be another hallway, going the width of the house; she could see a wide landing and then, across the staircase well, doors closed along the upper hall. On either side of her now were great double doors, carved with fruit and grain and living things; all the doors she could see in this house were closed.

When she tried to speak, her voice was drowned in the dim stillness, and she had to try again to make a sound. "Can you take me to my room?" she asked at last, gesturing toward her suitcase on the floor and watching the wavering reflection of her hand going down and down into the deep shadows of the polished floor, "I gather I'm the first one here. You – you *did* say you were Mrs. Dudley?" I think I'm going to cry, she thought, like a child sobbing and wailing, *I don't like it here....*

Mrs. Dudley turned and started up the stairs, and Eleanor took up her suitcase and followed, hurrying after anything else alive in this house. No, she thought, I don't like it here. Mrs. Dudley came to the top of the stairs and turned right, and Eleanor saw that with some rare perception the builders of the house had given up any attempt at style – probably after realizing what the house was going to be, whether they chose it or not – and had, on this second floor set in a long, straight hall to accommodate the doors to the bedrooms; she had a quick impression of the builders finishing off the second and third stories of the house with a kind of indecent haste, eager to finish their work without embellishment and get out of there, following the simplest possible pattern for the rooms. At the left end of the hall was a second staircase, probably going from servants' rooms on the third floor down past the second to the service rooms below; at the right end of the hall another room had been set in, perhaps, since it was on the end, to get the maximum amount of sun and light. Except for a continuation of the dark woodwork, and what looked like a series of poorly executed engravings arranged with unlovely exactness along the hall in either direction, nothing broke the straightness of the hall except the series of doors, all closed.

Mrs. Dudley crossed the hall and opened a door, perhaps at random. "This is the blue room," she said.

From the turn in the staircase Eleanor assumed that the room would be at the front of the house; sister Anne, sister Anne, she thought, and moved gratefully toward the light from the room. "How nice," she said, standing in the doorway, but only from the sense that she must say something; it was not nice at all, and only barely tolerable; it held enclosed the same clashing disharmony that marked Hill House throughout.

Mrs. Dudley turned aside to let Eleanor come in, and spoke, apparently to the wall. "I set dinner on the dining-room sideboard at six sharp," she said. "You can serve yourselves. I clear up in the morning. I have breakfast ready for you at nine. That's the way I agreed to do. I can't keep the rooms up the way you'd like, but there's no one else you could get that would help me. I don't wait on people. What I agreed to, it doesn't mean I wait on people."

Eleanor nodded, standing uncertainly in the doorway.

"I don't stay after I set out dinner," Mrs. Dudley went on. "Not after it begins to get dark. I leave before dark comes."

"I know," Eleanor said.

"We live over in the town, six miles away."

"Yes," Eleanor said, remembering Hillsdale.

"So there won't be anyone around if you need help."

"I understand."

"We couldn't even hear you, in the night."

"I don't suppose—"

"No one could. No one lives any nearer than the town. No one else will come any nearer than that."

"I know," Eleanor said tiredly.

"In the night," Mrs. Dudley said, and smiled outright. "In the dark," she said, and closed the door behind her.

Eleanor almost giggled, thinking of herself calling, "Oh, Mrs. Dudley, I need your help in the dark," and then she shivered.

A BIT MORE FRY
AND LAURIE

I was delighted when finally, you could get this series on DVD. Truly hilarious, it is as inventive and subvertive as I remember it to be when I first watched and loved it in the 1980s. I remember how shocked I was at sketches that would break down, or suddenly betray the fact they *were* sketches by Stephen Fry accidentally stepping off the set. It seemed very daring to me – but most of all I loved Fry and Laurie's use of language. Sketches that started out as one thing and turned into another – the rhythm of their writing is a great joy to read, as well as watch – and the sketch I have chosen here is a great example of that. It is 'traditional' without being traditional at all. And you can hear their voices immediately when you read it.

A Bit More Fry & Laurie

Society

A sitting room. A doorbell rings. A woman gets up and answers the door to Stephen and Hugh. Most of the way through Hugh is repeating everything Stephen says, a fraction of a second later.

STEPHEN: Morning.

HUGH: Morning.

STEPHEN: We're from the Westminster Society ...

HUGH: Society ...

STEPHEN: We wondered if we could come in and talk to you about our aims, and the possibility of you joining us.

HUGH: ... joining us, possibly, who knows?

WOMAN: Well ...

STEPHEN: Thank you ...

HUGH: So much.

STEPHEN: I'm Mr Willis. And this is Mr Barraclough.

HUGH: Barraclough ...

STEPHEN: No relation, in case you're wondering.

WOMAN: Sorry?

STEPHEN: We're not related to each other, in case you thought we were.

WOMAN: Well why should you be?

STEPHEN: Well we shouldn't, that's what I'm saying. We shouldn't be related and we're not. Hence the totally different names.

WOMAN: So, what can I do for you?

STEPHEN: As I say, my colleague and I are thinking of founding this society ...

HUGH: Society ...

STEPHEN: Would you be interested in joining us?

HUGH: ... perhaps joining us?

WOMAN: And what is this society for?

STEPHEN: It's ...

HUGH: Well ...

They look at each other.

STEPHEN: Well obviously this is one of the things we need to look at ...

HUGH: Look at it very carefully indeed ...

STEPHEN: And I think you've already shown that you would be a very useful member ...

HUGH: Useful member of the society.

WOMAN: But you said you had some aims.

STEPHEN: I don't think we did.

HUGH: ... did say that, we may have done ...

WOMAN: But when I answered the door, you said could you come in and talk about the aims of your society.

They look uncomfortable.

STEPHEN: Well that's a matter of opinion ...

HUGH: Subjective opinion, really ...

WOMAN: Well all right, but what is the point of this society? I mean you've got to have a point, otherwise ... there's no point.

STEPHEN: Hmm. That's a good point.

HUGH: Well made ...

WOMAN: I mean are you going to collect postage stamps?

STEPHEN: Yes.

HUGH: Definitely. Collect postage stamps.

WOMAN: Or are you going to practise Highland dancing?

STEPHEN: Yes. Stamps and Highland dancing are very high on the society's agenda.

HUGH: Hardly anything higher on the agenda than those two.

WOMAN: Or talk about Roman ruins in Shropshire?

STEPHEN: Definitely that.

HUGH: That's even higher on the agenda. That's right up at the top.

WOMAN: But you don't know?

STEPHEN: Know what?

HUGH: Know what, precisely?

WOMAN: You don't know for certain what the society is going to be for?

STEPHEN: Well, we have made one or two notes ...

HUGH: Just one or two ...

WOMAN: Yes?

STEPHEN: But unfortunately, not to do with the society.

HUGH: On a completely separate matter.

STEPHEN: However, to answer your question in the spirit in which it was asked ...

HUGH: In that very selfsame spirit ...

STEPHEN: My view is that the society should be run in the interests of its members.

HUGH: Brilliant. That's my view too. Members.

STEPHEN: But you see, until we have some members, we don't really have any interests.

HUGH: You might say that our hands are tied ...

STEPHEN: So. Will you help us?

WOMAN: Can I make a suggestion?

STEPHEN: Of course. Suggestions.

HUGH: Eureka. Suggestions.

STEPHEN: Tuesdays and Thursdays could be suggestion evenings.

WOMAN: No, can I make a suggestion now. And that is that you come back when you've decided what this society is supposed to be for. I can't stand here talking all day.

STEPHEN: Now there's an idea.

HUGH: Definitely an idea there.

STEPHEN: A society for people who can't stand here talking all day.

HUGH: All day and all night.

STEPHEN: I think that would be a very popular society....

HUGH: Flock to join that society ...

STEPHEN: When you think of all the people who knock on your door.

HUGH: Knock on your bell ...

STEPHEN: Jehovah's witnesses ...

HUGH: Witnesses to the Jehovah's incident ...

STEPHEN: Charity collectors ... estate agents ... small boys wanting their ball back ...

HUGH: The ball which incidentally went over the fence back ...

STEPHEN: Could we interest you in joining that society?

WOMAN: I'm going to shut the door now.

STEPHEN: Excellent.

WOMAN: What?

STEPHEN: Shutting the door indicates a definite interest in joining a society for people who can't stand here talking all day ...

HUGH: Total commitment to the society.

She slams the door. Cut to a shot of them outside the door.

STEPHEN: Well that's one member for our society, then ...

HUGH: One member for definite member ...

STEPHEN: Shall we try next door?

HUGH: Next door, why not?

EXORCIST III

This is one of the great horror films of the past twenty years and is always criminally overlooked. Truly terrifying with a magnificent central performance by George C Scott, the screenplay by William Peter Blatty crackles with fabulously sharp dialogue that would not be out of place in a Shane Black script. I've picked this particular excerpt though, to show just how funny his writing can be. Indeed, in 1964, Blatty penned the second Pink Panther installment *A Shot in The Dark*. When Bill Kinderman visits his old friend Father Dyer in hospital, their exchange is so quickfire and funny it almost seems to come from a different film. You don't expect this warmth and humour. All the more horrifying then, when Father Dyer is murdered and Kinderman loses a friend and a friendship that we have already grown to care about. Ed Flanders as Father Joseph Dyer is particularly deadpan in this role, getting not only great humour, but great pathos from his small part in the film.

Exorcist III: Legion

Through an open door he sees merriment, a birthday cake, patient and visitors, a family. He pauses at one room number long enough for us to see the legend 'Neurology' painted on the wall. In the background, another large statue of Christ. Kinderman continues on. He looks into a room opposite the charge desk, almost passes, then takes a half-step back, stares into.

INT. PRIVATE ROOM IN NEUROLOGY WARD. DAY

The footsteps approach off-screen. Dyer is sitting up reading a newspaper. Kinderman enters and walks hurriedly to the bedside, agitated.

KINDERMAN: And so what is this nonsense?
DYER: Look, there's nothing really wrong. They're just doing some tests.
KINDERMAN: You mean they couldn't find a rabbit?
DYER: [picking up paper and burying face in it] I don't know you.

Kinderman grabs top of paper and folds it back to see banner:

KINDERMAN: [incredulous] This is *Women's Wear Daily* you're reading?
DYER: So what! Am I supposed to give spiritual advice in a vacuum? [his gaze flicks to the bear] Is that for me?
KINDERMAN: [as Dyer takes bear] I just found it in the street. I thought it might suit you.
Dyer embarks upon a fit of delicate coughing.
    [as he sits] Oh, so we're doing Anastasia today. I thought you told me that there's nothing really wrong with you.
DYER: There isn't. My brother Eddie had these same stupid symptoms for years.
KINDERMAN: [exploding] Your brother Eddie died at thirty!
DYER: So what? He got killed in Vietnam.

KINDERMAN: There could be some connection!
DYER: [incredulous] A connection?

Kinderman rubs a hand over face, abashed.

KINDERMAN: I'm just tired.
DYER: [gesturing at phone] Call the desk and book a room.

A young nurse [Nurse Hara] has hurried down the hall and now pokes her head into the room.

NURSE HARA: Things okay in here, guys?
KINDERMAN: [a little sharp and defensive] Yes, I'm fine!

And as Hara withdraws with raised eyebrows:

Now, you're sure it's not serious, Father.

DYER: Well, with Eddie—
KINDERMAN: Don't mention Eddie!
DYER: With my brother it was nerves.
KINDERMAN: Yes, you do make people nervous.
DYER: Only sinners.
KINDERMAN: Everybody!

Kinderman glowers, reaches over and plops the bag of burgers on to the bed next to Dyer.

KINDERMAN: Here, I brought you a hamburger, Father.
DYER: I'm not hungry.
KINDERMAN: Eat half. It's White Castle.
DYER: Where'd the other half come from?
KINDERMAN: Space, your native country.

A short, stout nurse [Nurse Bierce] waddles into the room with a tourniquet and hypodermic needle. She is a veteran. Tough.

NURSE BIERCE: Come to take a little blood from you, Father.
DYER: Again?

NURSE BIERCE: What's 'again'?
DYER: Someone took it twenty minutes ago.
NURSE BIERCE: Are you kidding me, Father?

He points to a little round piece of tape on his inner forearm.

DYER: There's the hole.

She has already turned away, grim and gimlet-eyed as:

NURSE BIERCE: There it sure as hell goddamn ratshit is.
KINDERMAN: Eat the burger. It's got pickles.
DYER: I will.
KINDERMAN: Couldn't hurt.

Bierce stands outside the door to room and bellows down the hallway:

NURSE BIERCE: Who stuck this guy?
DYER: Nice and peaceful here, isn't it?
KINDERMAN: Idyllic.
DYER: I've been thinking.
KINDERMAN: This is new.
DYER: You'd better start being nice to me.
KINDERMAN: The bear is only garbage then, I gather.

Kinderman picks up the newspaper as:

DYER: I was thinking. Being here in the hospital …
KINDERMAN: Being here in the hospital with not a thing wrong with you.
DYER: I thought about things that I've heard about surgery.
KINDERMAN: [staring at photo layout in paper] These people have almost no clothes on, did you know that?

As we hear the drug cart approaching in the hallway:

DYER: They say that when you're under anesthesia, your unconscious is aware of everything. It hears the doctors and nurses talking about you; it feels the pain of the scalpel. But when you wake up from the anesthesia it's as if it had never happened. So maybe when we all go back to God, that's how it will be with all the pain of the world.

Nurse Keating has entered, pushing a drug cart in before her. The cart's wheels are very squeaky and make a very distinctive ominous sound. She plucks a chart front the cart.

NURSE KEATING: Mr Horowitz?

As Kinderman gives Dyer an inscrutable look:

DYER: No.
NURSE KEATING: This is 402?
DYER: 404.

Withdrawing cart and imitating Saturday Night Live's *Emily:*

NURSE KEATING: 'Never mind.'

Kinderman's gaze is fixed thoughtfully on the cart as:

DYER: Go in peace, and may the Schwartz be with you, my child.

Dyer has picked up the newspaper and is into it as:

KINDERMAN: That's a drug cart?
DYER: Why not?
KINDERMAN: Almost anyone could steal something from it.
DYER: I heard about what happened in the church.
KINDERMAN: [playing dumb] Beg your pardon?
DYER: [pretending absorption in the newspaper] Father Kanavan.
KINDERMAN: We found some kind of drug in him, Father. He didn't feel a thing. He had no pain.
DYER: Oh, well, that's good.

We know from his voice that he knows Kinderman is lying.

KINDERMAN: Don't you think you should be reading from the gospels or something?
DYER: They don't give you all the fashions.
KINDERMAN: This is true.
DYER: Damn right. Gooey gowns are getting boring. Could you get me something serious to read?

KINDERMAN: [checking watch; getting up] I should be going.
DYER: Can't you pick me something up?
KINDERMAN: [burying face in hand] My God, the grammar!
DYER: Be a pal. I want the *Star* and the *National Enquirer.*

INT. NEUROLOGY WING. HALLWAY. DAY

We are shooting long from outside Dyer's door. Kinderman rounds a far corner and strides toward us, red-faced and laden with trash newspapers. He enters.

INT. DYER'S ROOM. DAY

Angle through door from hallway. Kinderman marches to Dyer's bed, drops the armload of papers on to it.

KINDERMAN: As you ordered. *The Life of Monet* and *Conversations with Wolfgang Pauli.*
DYER: Thanks.
KINDERMAN: There are Jesuit missions in India, Father. Couldn't you find one to work in? The flies are not as bad as they say. They're very pretty. They're all different colors.

Dyer indifferently sorts through newspapers, magazines spread on his bed messily.

DYER: See, these are all last week's editions. I've read them.

KINDERMAN: You'll forgive me if I leave now this mystical discussion? Too much of esthetics always gives me a headache. Plus I'm visiting two patients in another ward, both priests: Joe DiMaggio and Jimmy the Greek. [turns and starts out] I am leaving.
DYER: Is it something I said?
KINDERMAN: Mother India is calling you, Father.

Dyer watches fondly as Kinderman disappears from view. Staring at empty open doorway:

DYER: 'Bye, Bill.

HANNIBAL

Mark and I waited for years to have new lines for Lecter to speak. Since *The Silence of the Lambs* we had used up, and just about done to death every brilliant phrase he said. We couldn't imagine a time when we would be treated to whole new passages and scenarios for us, and the good doctor, to get our teeth into. So to speak. And so along came *Hannibal*. A monster of a book, with several monsters at its heart. Operatic, daring and a bit of a "fuck you" to people who thought they knew what they wanted from their next visit from Hannibal and Clarice, Thomas Harris had other plans. I have chosen this extraordinary passage from near the end of the book, as the memory of first reading it, will I think always stay with me. I had to re-read it to be sure of what I thought I'd just read. I was 'shocked' – properly shocked, and from reading words in a book! How about that! Apparently medically accurate, Dr Lecter takes the top off nasty bigot Paul Krendler's head and slices off morsels of his brain which he fries and eats before him! As more and more is cut away, Krendler is less and less coherent as his frontal lobe is destroyed. I love the detail that he unknowingly starts shouting rather than speaking and the finale as Lecter scrapes the dirty dishes into Krendler's empty head like a kitchen sink before the washing up, is just incredible.

Hannibal

Chapter 100

The breeze of their entry into the dining room stirred the flames of the candles and the warmers. Starling had only seen the dining room in passage and it was wonderful to see the room transformed. Bright, inviting. Tall crystal repeating the candle flames above the creamy napery at their places and the space reduced to intimate size with a screen of flowers shutting off the rest of the table.

Dr Lecter has brought his flat silver from the warmer at the last minute and when Starling explored her place setting, she felt in the handle of her knife an almost feverish heat.

Dr Lecter poured wine and gave her only a tiny *amuse-gueule* to eat for starters, a single Belon oyster and a morsel of sausage, as she had to sit over half a glass of wine and admire in the context of his table.

The height of his candlesticks was exactly right. The flames lit the deeps of her décolleté and he did not have to be vigilant about her sleeves.

"What are we having?"

He raised his finger to his lips. "You never ask, it spoils the surprise."

They talked about the trimming of crow quills and their effect on the voice of a harpsichord, and only for a moment did she recall a crow robbing her mother's service cart on a motel balcony long ago. From a distance she judged the memory irrelevant to this pleasant time and she deliberately set it aside.

"Hungry?"

"Yes"

"Then we'll have our first course."

Dr Lecter moved a single tray from the sideboard to a space beside his place at the table and rolled a service cart to tableside. Here were his pans, his burners, and his condiments in little crystal bowls.

He fired up his burners and began with a goodly knob of Charante butter in his copper *fait-tout* saucepan, swirling the melting butter and browning the butterfat hazelnut, he set the butter aside on a trivet.

He smiled at Starling, his teeth very white.

"Clarice, do you recall what we said about pleasant and unpleasant remarks, and things being very funny in context?"

"That butter smells wonderful. Yes, I remember."

"And do you remember who you saw in the mirror, how splendid she was?"

"Dr Lecter, if you don't mind my saying so this is getting a little *Dick and Jane.* I remember perfectly."

"Good. Mr Krendler is joining us for our first course."

Dr Lecter moved the large flower arrangement from the table to the sideboard.

Deputy Assistant Inspector General Paul Krendler, in the flesh, sat at the table in a stout oak armchair. Krendler opened his eyes wide and looked about. He wore his runner's headband and a very nice funeral tuxedo, with integral shirt and tie. The garment being split up the back. Dr Lecter had been able to sort of tuck it around him, covering the yards of the duct tape that held him to the chair.

Starling's eyelids might have lowered a fraction and her lips slightly pursed as they sometimes did on the firing range.

Now Dr Lecter took a pair of silver tongs from the sideboard and peeled off the tape covering Krendler's mouth.

"Good evening, again, Mr Krendler."

"Good evening." Krendler did not seem to be quite himself. His place was set with a small tureen.

"Would you like to say good evening to Ms Starling?"

"Hello Starling." He seemed to brighten. "I always wanted to watch you eat."

Starling took him in from a distance, as though she were the wise old pier glass watching. "Hello, Mr Krendler." She raised her face to Dr Lecter, busy with his pans. "How did you ever catch him?"

"Mr Krendler is on his way to an important conference about his future in politics." Dr Lecter said "Margot Verger invited him as a favour to me. Sort of a quid pro quo. Mr Krendler jogged up to the pad in Rock Creek Park to meet the Verger helicopter. But he caught a ride with me instead. Would you like to say grace before our meal, Mr Krendler. Mr *Krendler?*"

"Grace? Yes." Krendler closed his eyes. "Father, we thank thee for the blessings we are about to receive and we dedicate them to Thy service. Starling is a big girl to be fucking her daddy even if she is southern. Please forgive her for that and bring her to my service. In Jesus' name, amen."

Starling noted that Dr Lecter kept his eyes piously closed throughout the prayer.

She felt quick and calm. "*Paul* I have to tell you, the Apostle *Paul* couldn't have done better. He hated women too. He should have been named *Appall*."

"You really blew it this time, Starling. You'll never be reinstated."

"Was that a *job* offer you worked into the blessing? I never saw such tact."

"I'm going to Congress." Krendler smiled unpleasantly. "Come around the campaign headquarters. I might find something for you to do. You could be an office girl. Can you type and file?"

"Certainly."

"Can you take dictation?"

"I use voice-recognition software," Starling said. She continued in a judicious tone. "If you'll excuse me for talking shop at the table, you aren't fast enough to steal in Congress. You can't make up for a second-rate intelligence just by playing dirty. You'd last longer as a big crook's gofer."

"Don't wait on us, Mr Krendler," Dr Lecter urged.

"Have some of your broth while it's hot." He raised the covered *potager* and straw to Krendler's lips.

Krendler made a face. "That soup's not very good."

"Actually, it's more of a parsley and thyme infusion." The doctor said. "and more for our sake than yours. Have another few swallows, and let it circulate."

Starling apparently was weighing an issue, using her palms like the Scales of Justice. "You know, Mr Krendler, every time you ever leered at me. I had the nagging feeling I had done something to deserve it." She moved her palms up and down judiciously, a motion similar to passing a Slinky back and forth. "I *didn't* deserve it. Every time you wrote something negative in my personnel folder, I resented it, but still I searched myself. I doubted myself for a moment and tried to scratch this tiny itch that said Daddy knows best."

"You *don't* know best, Mr Krendler. In fact, you don't know anything." Starling had a sip of her splendid White Burgundy and said to Dr Lecter, "I *love* this. But I think we should take it off the ice." She turned again, attentive hostess to her guest. "You are forever an . . . an oaf, and beneath notice," she said in a pleasant tone. "And that's enough about you at this lovely table. Since you are Dr Lecter's guest, I hope you enjoy the meal."

"*Who are you anyway?*" Krendler said. "You're not Starling. You've got the spot on your face, but you're not Starling."

Dr Lecter added shallots to his hot browned butter and at the instant their perfume rose he put in minced caper berries. He set the saucepan off the fire, and set his sauté pan on the heat. From the sideboard he took a large crystal bowl of ice cold water and a silver salver and put them beside Paul Krendler.

"I had some plans for that smart mouth," Krendler said, "but I'd *never* hire you now. What gave you an appointment anyway?"

"I don't expect you to change your attitude entirely as the other Paul did, Mr Krendler." Dr Lecter said.

"You are not on the road to Damascus, or even on the road to the Verger helicopter."

Dr Lecter took off Krendler's runner's headband as you would remover the rubber band from a tin of caviar.

"All we ask is that you keep an open mind." Carefully, using both hands, Dr Lecter lifted off the top of Krendler's head, put it on the salver and removed it to the sideboard. Hardly a drop of blood fell from the clean incision, the major blood vessels having been tied and the others neatly sealed under a local anaesthetic, and the skull sawn around in the kitchen a half-hour before the meal.

Dr Lecter's method in removing the top of Krendler's skull was as old as Egyptian medicine, except that he had the advantage of an autopsy saw with cranial blade, a skull key and better anaesthetics. The brain itself feels no pain.

The pinky-grey dome of Krendler's brain was visible above his truncated skull.

Standing over Krendler with an instrument resembling a tonsil spoon, Dr Lecter removed a slice of Krendler's prefrontal lobe, then another, until he had four. Krendler's eyes looked up as though he were following what was going on. Dr Lecter placed the slices in the bowl of ice water, the water acidulated with the juice of a lemon, in order to firm them.

"*Would you like to swing on a star.*" Krendler sang abruptly. "*Carry moonbeams home in a jar.*"

In classic cuisine brains are soaked and then pressed and chilled overnight to firm them. In dealing with the item absolutely fresh, the challenge is to prevent the material from simply disintegrating into a handful of lumpy gelatine.

With splendid dexterity, the doctor brought the firmed slices to a plate, dredged them lightly in seasoned flour, and then in fresh brioche crumbs.

He grated a fresh black truffle into his sauce and finished it with a squeeze of lemon juice.

Quickly he sautéed the slices until they were just brown on each side.

"Smells great!" Krendler said.

Dr Lecter placed the browned brains on broad croutons on the warmed plates, and dressed them with the sauce and truffle slices. A garish of parsley and whole caper berries with their stems, and a single nasturtium blossom on watercress to achieve a little height, completed his presentation.

"How is it?" Krendler asked, once again behind the flowers and speaking immoderately loud, as persons with lobotomies are prone to do.

"Really excellent." Starling said. "I've never had caper berries before."

Dr Lecter found the shine of butter sauce on her lip intensely moving.

Krendler sang behind the greens, mostly day-care songs, and he invited requests.

Oblivious to him, Dr Lecter and Starling discussed Mischa. Starling knew of the doctor's sister's fate from their conversations about loss, but now the doctor spoke in a hopeful way about her possible return. It did not seem unreasonable to Starling on the evening that Mischa might return.

She expressed the hope that she might meet Mischa.

"You sound like a cornbread country cunt." Krendler yelled through the flowers.

"See if I sound like Oliver Twist when I ask for *MORE*," Starling replied, releasing in Dr Lecter glee he could scarcely contain.

A second helping consumed most of the frontal lobe, back nearly to the premotor cortex. Krendler was reduced to irrelevant observations about things in his immediate vision and the tuneless recitation behind the flowers of a lengthy lewd verse called "Shine."

Absorbed in their talk, Starling and Lecter were no more disturbed than they would have been by the singing of happy birthday at another table in a restaurant, but when Krendler's volume became intrusive, Dr Lecter retrieved his crossbow from a corner.

"I want you to listen to the sound of this stringed instrument, Clarice."

He waited for a moment of silence from Krendler and shot a bolt across the table through the tall flowers.

That particular frequency of the crossbow string, should you hear it again in any context, means only your complete freedom and peace and self-sufficiency," Dr Lecter said.

The feathers and part of the shaft remained on the visible side of the flower arrangement and moved at more or less the pace of a baton directing a heart.

Krendler's voice stopped at once and in a few beats the baton stopped too.

"It's about a D below middle C?" Starling said.

"Exactly."

A moment later Krendler made a gargling sound behind the flowers. It was only a spasm in his voice box caused by the increasing acidity of his blood, he being newly dead.

"Let's have our next course," the doctor said, "a little sorbet to refresh our palates before the quail. No, no, don't get up. Mr Krendler will help me clear, if you'll excuse him."

It was all quickly done. Behind the screen of the flowers, Dr Lecter simply scraped the plates into Krendler's skull and stacked them in his lap. He replaced the top of Krendler's head and, picking up the rope attached to a dolly beneath his chair, towed him away to the kitchen.

There Dr Lecter rewound his crossbow. Conveniently it used the same battery pack as his autopsy saw.

The quails' skins were crisp and they were stuffed with foie gras. Dr Lecter talked about Henry VIII as composer and Starling told him about computer-aided design in engine sounds, the replication of pleasing frequencies.

Dessert would be in the drawing room, Dr Lecter announced.

GLENGARRY GLEN ROSS

I first saw the film of *Glengarry Glen Ross* in a little cinema in West Virginia on the year of its release, 1992. The lady who sold me my ticket warned me that there was a lot of profanity in the movie. I found it so strange to be made aware of such a thing... and it actually made me more aware of the swearing than had it not been flagged up in the first place. David Mamet's searing play has too many brilliant set pieces to choose from, but I have picked Ricky Roma's devastating attack against Williamson, the boss of the agency where these salesmen spend their days. After losing him a potentially huge contract, Roma begins a tirade against his incompetent boss that is so savage and so cruel, it leaves you open-mouthed at the elegance of the vitriol. It is also, of course, extremely funny – and like all the language Mamet uses, it's just so enjoyable to listen to. He relishes the extravagance of the abuse, not only of the salesmen to one another, but also the salesmen to their potential victims down the telephone lines. Their sales pitches and insidious patter – whilst desperately trying to gain a client's confidence – is just as ugly as the swear words they use when addressing each other.

GLENGARRY GLEN ROSS

Play 3

WILLIAMSON: Your contract went out to the bank.

Pause

LINGK: You cashed the check?
WILLIAMSON: We...
ROMA: ... Mr Williamson...
WILLIAMSON: Your check was cashed yesterday afternoon. And we're completely insured, as you know, in any case.

Pause

LINGK [to **ROMA**]: You cashed the check?
ROMA: Not to my knowledge, no ...
LINGK: Oh, Christ ... [he starts out the door.] Don't follow me ... Oh Christ... [Pause to Roma.] I know I've let you down. I'm sorry. For... Forgive... for... I don't know anymore. [Pause] Forgive me. [Lingk exits] [Pause]
ROMA: [to Williamson] You stupid fucking cunt. *You* Williamson... I'm talking to you, shithead ... You just cost me six thousand dollars. [Pause] Six thousand dollars. And one Cadillac. That's right. What are you going to do about it? What are you going to do about it, asshole. You're fucking *shit*. Where did you learn your *trade*? You stupid fucking *cunt* you *idiot*. Whoever told you you could work with *men*?
BAYLEN: Could I...
ROMA: I'm going to have your *job*, shithead. I'm going *downtown* and talk

218

to Mitch and Murray, and I'm going to Lemkin. I don't care *whose* nephew you are, who you know, whose dick you're sucking on. You're going *out*, I swear to you, you're going...

BAYLEN: Hey, fella, let's get this done...

ROMA: Anyone in this office lives on their wits ... [To Baylen:] I'm going to be with you in a second. [To Williamson:] What you're hired for is to *help* us – does that seem clear to you? To *help* us. Not to fuck us up... to help men who are going *out* there to try to earn a *living*. You *fairy*. You company man ... I'll tell you something else. I hope you knocked the joint off, I can tell our friend here something might help him to catch you. [He starts into the room.] You want to learn the first rule you'd know if you ever spent a day in your life, you never open your mouth till you know what the shot is. [*Pause*] You fucking *child*...[Levene has come out during the diatribe with Lingk and has sat at the back listening. To Levene.] Don't leave. I have to talk *to you*. [To Williamson] You fucking *child*... [Roma goes into the inner room]

LEVENE: You *are* a shithead, Williamson ... [Pause]

LEVENE: You can't think on your feet you should keep your mouth closed. [Pause] You hear me? I'm talking to you Do you hear me...?

WILLIAMSON: Yes. [Pause] I hear you.

LEVENE: You can't learn that in an office. Eh? He's right. You have to learn it on the streets. You can't buy that. You have to live it.

WILLIAMSON: Mmm.

LEVENE: Yes Mmm. Yes Precisely. Precisely. 'Cause your partner depends on it. [Pause.] I'm talking to you, I'm trying to tell you something.

WILLIAMSON: You are?

LEVENE: Yes, I am

WILLIAMSON: What are you trying to tell me?

LEVENE: What I was trying to tell you yesterday. Why you don't belong in this business.

WILLIAMSON: Why I don't—

LEVENE: You listen to me, someday you might say, 'Hey...'
No, fuck that, you just listen what I'm going to say: Your partner depends on you. Your partner... a man who's your 'partner' depends on you... you have to go with him and for him... or you're shit, you're shit, you can't exist alone...

WILLIAMSON: [brushing past him] Excuse me...

LEVENE: ... excuse you, nothing, you be as cold as you want, but you just fucked a good man out of six thousand dollars and his goddam bonus cause you didn't know the shot, if you can do that and you aren't man enough that it get you, then I don't know what, if you can't take some thing from that.... [Blocking his way] you're scum, you're fucking white-bread. You be as cold as you want. A child would know if he's right. [Pause] You're going to make something up, be sure it will help or keep your mouth closed.

Pause

WILLIAMSON: Mmm.

Levene: Lifts up his arm.

LEVENE: Now I'm done with you

Pause

WILLIAMSON: How do you know I made it up?
LEVENE: [pause] What?
WILLIAMSON: How do you know I made it up?
LEVENE: [pause] What are you talking about?
WILLIAMSON: You said 'You don't make something up unless it's sure to help [Pause] How did you know that I made it up?
LEVENE: What are you talking about?
WILLIAMSON: I told the customer that his contract had gone to the bank.
LEVENE: Well hadn't it?
WILLIAMSON: No [Pause] It hadn't.
LEVENE: Don't *fuck* with me, John, don't *fuck* with me... what are you saying?
WILLIAMSON: Well, I'm saying this, Shel: Usually I take the contracts to the bank. Last night I didn't. How did you know that? One night a year that I left a contract on my desk. Nobody knew that but you. Now how did you know that? [Pause]
You want to talk to me, you want to talk to someone *else*... because this is *my* job on the line, and you're going to *talk* to me: Now how did you know that contract was on my desk?
LEVENE: You're so full of shit.

WILLIAMSON: You robbed the office.

LEVENE: [laughs] Sure!

WILLIAMSON: What'd you do with the leads? [Pause. He points to the Detective's room.] You want to go in there? I tell him what we know, he's going to dig up *something*… You got an alibi last night? You better have one. What did you do with the leads? If you tell me what you did with the leads, we can talk.

LEVENE: I don't know what you are saying.

WILLIAMSON: If you tell me where the leads are, I won't turn you in. If you *don't* I am going to tell the cop you stole them, Mitch and Murray will see that you go to jail.

LEVENE: They wouldn't do that.

WILLIAMSON: They would and they will. What did you do with the leads? I'm walking in that door – you have five seconds to tell me: or you are going to jail.

LEVENE: I…

WILLIAMSON: I don't care. You understand? *Where are the leads?* [*Pause*] Alright [Williamson goes to open the office door.]

LEVENE: I sold them to Jerry Graff.

WILLIAMSON: How much did you get for them? [*Pause*] How much did you get for them?

LEVENE: Five thousand. I kept half.

WILLIAMSON: Who kept the other half?

Pause

LEVENE: Do I have to tell you? [Pause. Williamson starts to open the door] Moss.

WILLIAMSON: That was easy wasn't it?

Pause

LEVENE: It was his idea.

WILLIAMSON: *Was* it?

LEVENE: I… I'm sure he got more than the five, actually.

WILLIAMSON: Uh Huh?

LEVENE: He told me my share was twenty-five.

Pause

WILLIAMSON: Mmm.

LEVENE: Okay: I, look: I'm going to make it worth your while. I am. I turned this thing around. I closed the *old* stuff, I can do it again. *I'm* the one's going to close 'em. *I* am! *I* am! Cause I turned this thing a… I can do *that*, I can do *anyth*…

Last night. I'm going to tell you, I was ready to Do the Dutch. Moss gets me. 'Do this, we'll get well… 'Why not? Big fuckin' deal. I'm hoping to get caught. To put me out of my … [Pause] But it taught me something. What it taught me, that you've got to get *out* there. Big deal. So I wasn't cut out to be a thief. I *was* born for a salesman. And now I'm back, and I got my *balls* back… and, you know, John, you have the *advantage* on me now. Whatever it takes to make it right, we'll make it right. We're going to make it right.

WILLIAMSON: I want to tell you something, Shelly. You have a big mouth.

Pause

LEVENE: What?

WILLIAMSON: You've got a big mouth, and now I'm going to show you an even bigger one. [He starts toward the Detective's door.]

LEVENE: Where are you going, John? … you can't do that, you don't want to do that … hold, hold on… hold on… wait… wait…wait… [He pulls money out of his pockets.] Wait…uh, look… [He starts splitting the money.] Look, twelve, twenty, two, twen… twenty-five hundred, it's…take it. [Pause.] Take it… [Pause] Take it!

WILLIAMSON: No, I don't think so, Shel.

LEVENE: I…

WILLIAMSON: No, I think I don't want your money. I think you fucked up my office. And I think you're going away.

LEVENE: I… what? Are you, are you, that's why …? Are you nuts? I'm… I'm to *close* for you, I'm going to [Thrusting money at him.] Here, here, I'm going to *make* this office…I'm going to be back there Number One… Hey, hey, hey! This is only the beginning… List… list… listen. Listen. Just one moment. List… here's what…here's what we're going to do. Twenty per cent. I'm going to give you twenty per cent of my sales... [Pause] Twenty per cent. [Pause] For as long as I am with the firm. [Pause] Fifty per cent [Pause] You're going to be my partner. [Pause] Fifty per cent. Of all my sales.

WILLIAMSON: What sales?

LEVENE: What sales...? I just *closed* eight-two *grand*... Are you fuckin'... I'm *back*... I'm *back*, this is only the beginning.

WILLIAMSON: Only the beginning...

LEVENE: Abso...

WILLIAMSON: Where have you been, Shelly? Bruce and Harriett Nyborg. Do you want to see the *momos*...? They're nuts,,, they used to call in every week. When I was with Webb. And we were selling Arizona... they're nuts... did you see how they were *living*? How can you delude yours...

LEVENE: I've got the check...

WILLIAMSON: Frame it. It's worthless.

Pause

LEVENE: The check's no good?

WILLIAMSON: You stick around I'll pull the memo for you [He starts for the door.] I'm busy now...

LEVENE: ... their check's no good? They're nuts...?

WILLIAMSON: Call up the bank. *I* called them.

LEVENE: You did?

WILLIAMSON: I called them when we had the lead... four months ago. [Pause] the people are insane. They just like talking to salesmen. [Williamson starts for the door.]

LEVENE: Don't.

WILLIAMSON: I'm sorry.

LEVENE: Why?

WILLIAMSON: Because I don't like you.

LEVENE: John: John:... my *daughter*...

WILLIAMSON: Fuck you.

Roma comes out of the Detective's door. Williamson goes in.

ROMA: [to Williamson] Asshole... [To Levene] Guy couldn't find his fuckin' couch in the *living-room*... Ah, Christ... what a day, what a day... and I haven't even had a cup of *coffee*... Jagoff John opens his mouth he blows my Cadillac... [He sighs.] I swear... it's not a world of men... it's not a world of men, Machine... it's a world of clock watchers, bureaucrats, office holders... What it is, it's a fucked-up world... there's no adventure *to* it...[Pause] Dying breed. Yes it is. [Pause] We are the members of a dying breed. That's... that's... I want to talk to you. I've wanted to talk to you for some *time* actually... seriously. Did you eat today?

LEVENE: Me?

ROMA: Yes.

LEVENE: No.

ROMA: No? Come on, we're going to swing by the Chinks, we got to talk.

LEVENE: I think I'd better stay here for a while.

ROMA: Okay: Two things, then One... I been thinking about this for a *month*, I said 'the Machine...There's a fellow I could *work* with,' never, isn't that funny? I never did a thing. Now: That shit that you were slinging on the guy today was *very* good, and excuse me it isn't even my *place* to *say* that to you that way; I've been on a hot streak, so big deal. What I'm saying, it was *admirable* and, so was the *deal* that you closed. Now listen: there's things I could *learn* from you - you see I knew we'd work well together – Here's what I was thinking: we Team Up. We team up, we go out together, we split everything right down the middle...

Baylen sticks his head out of the room.

BAYLEN: Mr *Levene*...?

ROMA: ... fifty-fifty. Or we could go down the street. You know, we could go *anywhere*...

BAYLEN: Would you step in here please...?

ROMA: So let's put it *together*? Okay? [Pause] Shel? Say 'okay'.

LEVENE: [pause] Hmm.

BAYLEN: Mr Levene, I think we have to talk.

ROMA: I'm going to the Chinks. You're done, come down, we're going to smoke a cigarette.

LEVENE: I...

Baylen comes over to him and forcefully leads him into the room.

BAYLEN: ... get in the room.

ROMA: Hey, hey, hey, *easy* friend. That's the 'Machine', That is Shelly 'The Machine' Lev...

BAYLEN: Come on. Get in the goddamn *room*...

LEVENE: I...

ROMA: I'll be at the resta...

Baylen and Levene have disappeared into the next room and the door is slammed. Pause.

ROMA: Williamson: listen to me: when the *leads* come in... listen to me: when the *leads* come in I want my top two off the list. For *me* my usual two. Anything you give *Levene*...

WILLIAMSON: ... I wouldn't worry about it.

ROMA: Well I'm going to worry about it, and so are you, so you shut up and listen. [Pause] I GET HIS ACTION. My stuff is mine whatever he gets, I'm taking half. You put me in with him.

Aaronow enters.

AARONOW: Did they?

ROMA: You understand?

AARONOW: Did they catch...?

ROMA: Do you understand? My stuff is mine, his stuff is ours.

WILLIAMSON: Mmm.

AARONOW: Did they find the guy who broke into the office yet?

ROMA: No *I* don't know.

Pause

AARONOW: Did the leads come in yet?

ROMA: No.

AARONOW: [settling into a desk chair] Oh, god I hate this job.

ROMA: [simultaneous with 'job', going out of the office] I'll be at the restaurant.

RUMPELSTILTSKIN

E ver since reading the Ladybird book of the Grimm Brothers classic, I have been afraid of the little man in stripy tights whose name turns out to be Rumpelstiltskin. I think a lot of my fear came from the illustrations of the funny little man who appeared in the room of the poor miller's daughter, smiling and listening to her plight, before offering his assistance. It was the underlying notion that at some point in the future he would want to be repaid for his help; and when he asks for her baby the horror is only made worse when he is spied dancing round a little camp fire, singing about how he will soon have the miller's baby to bake! The other nightmarish image comes after she correctly guesses his name, and Rumpelstiltskin shouts at the miller's daughter: "The fairies must have told you!", stamps his foot so hard that it goes through the floor and then he pulls himself in two while trying to get it out. It's a ghoulish end to a horrid little character that I never fail to find a little bit too frightening.

RUMPELSTILTSKIN

There was once a miller who was very poor, but he had a beautiful daughter; and a thought struck him that he would speak about her to the king, and get some situation for her. So he obtained an audience, and told the king that he had a daughter who could spin straw into gold.

'Then' said the king, 'that is a quality which pleases me well. If your daughter is, as you say, so very skilful, bring her to the castle tomorrow morning, and I will try what she can do.'

The miller next day took his daughter to the castle, and as soon as she arrived the king led her into a chamber which was quite full of straw. And placing a spinning-wheel before her, said:

'Now set to work at once, for if all this straw is not spun into gold before sunrise, you shall die.'

Then he locked the door himself, and left her alone.

The poor maiden sat for some time looking at the straw in despair. She had never in her life been taught to spin, and she had not the least idea how to turn straw into gold. Every moment her fear became greater, and at last she began to weep bitterly.

As evening came on, the door opened, and a little man entered, who said:

'Good-evening, young daughter of the miller. Why do you weep so sadly?'

'Oh!' she replied. 'I have all this straw to spin into gold, and I know not how to do it.'

'What will you give me,' said the little man, 'if I spin it for you?'

'My neck ribbon,' she said.

The man took the ribbon, seated himself before the spinning-wheel, and as the wheel went whirr, whirr, whirr, three times, the spool was full of gold. Then he fastened on more straw, and after three turns of the wheel the spool was a second time full; and so he went on all night, and before the morning dawned the straw was all spun and the spools full of gold. Then he left her.

At sunrise the king came to the chamber, but when he caught sight of the glittering gold, he was first astonished and then full of joy. But his heart was greedy for gold, so he led the miller's daughter into another chamber

227

full of straw, and much larger than the former, and ordered her, as she valued her life, to spin that into gold before sunrise next morning.

The maiden, when left alone, could only weep, for she knew it was an impossible task. But in the evening the same little man again appeared, and said, 'What will you give me if I spin all this straw into gold?'

'My ring from my finger,' answered the maiden.

The little man took the ring, set to work at the spinning-wheel, and before morning the whole of the straw was spun into gold.

The king gloated with delight over the glittering heap, but he was not yet satiated with gold. So he led the maiden into a still larger room full of straw, and said, 'You must spin for me during one more night, and if all this straw is spun into gold by the morning, then you shall be my wife.'

'Although she is a miller's daughter,' thought the king, 'I could not find a richer wife in the whole world.'

No sooner was the maiden alone, than the manikin again appeared for the third time, and said, 'What will you give me if I spin the straw for you this time?'

'I have nothing more that I can give,' answered the maiden.

'Then promise when you are queen to give me your first child,' said the little man.

'Who knows if I shall ever be queen,' thought the maiden; and she knew also that in her trouble there was no other help for her. So she promised what he wished.

Immediately he set to work, and very soon spun all the straw into gold.

In the morning when the king came and found that what he required was done, he ordered preparations to be made for a splendid wedding and in a few days the miller's beautiful daughter became a queen. About a year after this a beautiful little child was born to the queen, who never thought of her promise to the little man, till one night he stepped suddenly into her chamber, and said, 'Now give me what you have promised.'

In great terror the queen offered him all the treasures in the kingdom if he would leave her the child.

But the little man said, 'No; something living I like better than all the treasures in the world.' Then the queen began to mourn and weep so bitterly, that the little man had compassion on her, and said, 'I will give you three days, and if in that time you can find out my name, then you shall keep your child.'

After he was gone, the queen lay awake till morning, thinking over all the names she had ever heard of, and determined to send a messenger all over the country to enquire far and wide what names had been given to people formerly.

The next night the little man came again, and she repeated all the names she could think of, Casper, Melchior, Balzar, and many others that she knew, in every rank of society. But the little man said, 'No, I have not one of these names.'

The next day she made every inquiry among the neighbours, and when the little man came at night for the second time, she mentioned most unearthly names, such as Brown-ribs, Dicky-calf, and Spindle-leg. But he answered always, 'No, it is none of these.'

On the third day the messenger returned and related his adventures. He had not been able to find a single new name, but on his way home he crossed a high mountain, and came to the borders of a wood, in which the foxes and the hares wished him 'good night.' After this he came to a tiny little house, and saw before it a fire burning, and hopping round it, on one leg, was a ridiculous-looking little man, who cried:

'To-day I brew, to-morrow I bake
Next morning I shall the queen's child take;
How glad I am that she does not dream
That Rumplestiltskin is my name!'

The messenger could not think what made the queen so overjoyed when she heard this name, but she rewarded him handsomely and dismissed him.

On the third and last night, the little man appeared for the last time, and said. 'Now then, queen-mother, what is my name?

'Well.' she replied, 'are you called Conrad?

'No,'

'Henry?'

'No,'

'Then your name is Rumplestiltskin!'

'The fairies must have told you that!' screamed the little man, and in his rage struck the ground so fiercely with his right foot that it sunk in deeply into the earth, dragging his body after it. Then in his fury, he laid hold of his left foot with both hands, and tore himself completely in half.

HANNAH AND
HER SISTERS

A lifelong fan of Woody Allen, I had *that* poster from Manhattan in my room at college, my favourite film of his has to be this one. It is such an affecting film because there is such heart to it. The characters' ache is so real here, and Michael Caine gives, in my opinion, his best screen performance. This scene is where Caine, in a very funny sequence, contrives to bump into Lee (Barbara Hershey) on the streets of New York. Caine is married to her sister, Hannah (Mia Farrow), but find he has feelings for Lee. Look at the dialogue here, and notice how Allen writes the "ums and ahhs" very precisely. The blossoming of their mutual attraction is beautifully played out in this New York bookshop; and the end of the scene with Lee reading the poem by E. E. Cummings is so emotionally powerful. Since this film, I have been at several weddings where that very same poem has been read out. It is very moving, and a great choice if you're stuck for a eulogy.

Hannah and her Sisters

EXTERIOR. STREET OUTSIDE FREDERICK'S LOFT – DAY.

The movie briefly holds on a ripped, red, paint-splattered door as Elliot, wearing a raincoat, appears nearby. He looks down the street and the film cuts to his point of view: Frederick's loft building.

The movie goes back to the impatient Elliot; he's looking around him. He glances at his watch as the film cuts back once again to the loft building, where Lee finally appears, walking down the street away from Elliot. A truck passes down the street. Lee doesn't see him. She walks further and further away; she turns a corner.

Elliot frantically looks around again; then, in a burst of decision, he runs around a garbage dump, crossing the street, and still running, he moves down an adjacent street, past The Canal Lumber Company and several other buildings, as the film cuts back to Lee, walking down a different street, oblivious.

The jazz plays on as the movie cuts back and forth between the fast-moving Elliot, rushing down the SoHo streets, past a truck waiting for the a light to change, past some pedestrians, some garbage cans, turning corners, and the strolling Lee, walking up different streets, past different buildings.

Lee eventually crosses a street, lost in thought, looking right and left, as Elliot, pretending nonchalance, waits on the corner, looking at his watch. She looks up in surprise; the music stops.

ELLIOT: [Trying not to sound out of breath] Oh, my goodness!

LEE: [Overlapping, smiling in surprise] Oh, Elliot!

ELLIOT: Hi.

LEE: [smiling] What are you doing here?

ELLIOT: [Looking around, gesturing] Well, I'm- I'm looking for a bookstore.

LEE: [Shaking her head] Oh, what, in this section of town?

ELLIOT: Yes. Yeah, I- I'm kill –

LEE: [Overlapping] You're out looking here?

ELLIOT: [Glancing at his watch again] Well, yes, I'm killing time. I have a client near here and I ... I'm quite early.

LEE: [Laughing] Ohhhh!

ELLIOT: [Gesturing] How about you?

LEE: Oh. Well, I live –

ELLIOT: [Interrupting, chuckling] Oh, yes! You live near here, don't you?

LEE: [Overlapping, chuckling] Yes, I do.

ELLIOT: [Putting his hands behind his back] Where are you headed?

LEE: Oh, I was just going to my AA meeting.

ELLIOT: Oh my goodness. Well, why do you still go to those? You never touch alcohol.

They begin to walk down the street.

LEE: [Laughing] Well, listen, you didn't know me before Frederick. I'd ... I'd start with a beer at about ten in the morning, and ... go on.

ELLIOT: [Looking at Lee] Oh. You must have been, uh, very unhappy.

LEE: Yeah, unhappy and fat. [Chuckling] And I still find the meetings very comforting, you know.

She shrugs.

ELLIOT: I'll never understand it. You're so bright and charming and beautiful.

LEE: [Laughing] Oh, God

ELLIOT: [Overlapping, chuckling] I think to myself [Laughing] what problems could she possibly have?

LEE: [Gesturing, laughing] Don't let me get started on my childhood. [Stopping in her tracks, remembering] Oh, you know what? There is a bookstore.

ELLIOT: [Stopping alongside her] Yes?

LEE: [Overlapping, pointing] A couple of blocks from here. If you don't know about it, you should. You'd really love it.

ELLIOT: Yes?

LEE: [Nodding] Yeah, you would.

ELLIOT: [Looking around for a moment, then gesturing to Lee] Well, i-if-if you have some free time ...

LEE: [Nodding] Yeah, sure. [Chuckling]

ELLIOT: Thank you.

They begin to walk again as the movie cuts to the interior of the Pageant Book & Print Shop, an old serious bookstore. A nude print hangs at the end of one of the library shelf-like bookcases, which are packed, row after row, with books. An unseen Elliot and Lee carry on a conversation as the camera moves down an aisle, past the rows of books. A piano playing "Bewitched" is heard. Pictures hang on the aisle ends of the shelves.

LEE: [Offscreen] Isn't this great? [Chuckling] They have everything here.

ELLIOT: [Offscreen, distracted] Yes, it's-it's wonderful.

LEE: [Offscreen] What book did you want to buy?

ELLIOT: [Offscreen] What? Book?

LEE: [Offscreen] Your book? You wanted to buy a book?

The camera moves past another aisle of books to reveal Lee, browsing through a shelf.

ELLIOT: [Offscreen] Oh, book? Oh, no, I ... [Laughing] I'm killing time. I ...I-I just, uh, w-want to browse, uh...

LEE: [Looking up at a row of books] Well, you sure picked the right place. I mean, you can stay here all afternoon, not buy anything and just read.

She walks down a centre aisle, the camera still in it's parallel aisle, following her.

ELLIOT: [Offscreen] Unless, of course, if-if you had some time. I mean, we could get some coffee.

LEE: No, I don't have time

Lee stops at the row where Elliott has been browsing. She is hidden by a shelf; only Elliot is seen as he talks to the offscreen Lee.

ELLIOT: [Gesturing] No, no. I-I understand completely. No problem. Y-you're busy. I-I-I...

LEE: [Offscreen, chuckling] You seem tense, Is everything alright? You feel okay?

ELLIOT: [Overlapping] No! No...

LEE: [Offscreen] No?

ELLIOT: [Gesturing, looking at books] Uh, yes!

LEE: [Offscreen] Yes?

Elliot starts walking down the centre aisle, in the same direction Lee had walked up. He continues to talk to her as she remains offscreen in a nearby row.

ELLIOT: [Offscreen momentarily, hidden by a shelf as he talks] Yes.

LEE: [Offscreen] Everything's okay? [Chuckling]

ELLIOT: Yeah. How are you?

LEE: [Offscreen] I'm... all right.

ELLIOT: [Offscreen momentarily, hidden by another shelf as he walks] How- how's Frederick?

Elliot stops walking to browse through some books. "Bewitched" still plays.

LEE: [Offscreen] Fine. Oh, we went to the Caravaggio exhibition at the Met. It's such a treat to go through a museum with Frederick. I mean... you learn so much. Do you like Caravaggio?

ELLIOT: [Turning to talk to the offscreen Lee] Oh, yes. Who doesn't? [Pointing] Look!

Elliot turns and walks back down the centre aisle to a row of books he'd already passed.

ELLIOT: [Pointing to a book on a shelf, continuing] E.E. Cummings. I'd like to get you this.

LEE: [Offscreen laughing] Oh, no, I can't let you get me that. That's too much.

ELLIOT: [Pulling the book off the shelf and browsing through it] Oh, oh, yes. I- I- I'd like to, uh, uh, very much.

LEE: [Offscreen] No, I don't think so,

ELLIOT: [Gesturing with the book, looking at the offscreen Lee] I- I read a poem of you and thought of his last week. [Nervously laughing trying to correct his mistake]. A poem of [laughing] his and thought of you last – [laughing]. You'll be fine, though. [Chuckling]

Lee walks over to Elliot in the centre aisle. She looks at the book.

LEE: [Overlapping] Uh, uh, this is great. I mean, I love E.E. Cummings, but I can't let you get this.

ELLIOT: [Overlapping, patting the book] Yes, I'd I- I- I'd love, I'd love to get you this.

LEE: [Looking down at the book] Well, sure.

ELLIOT: [Overlapping] And – and maybe, um… maybe we could discuss it sometime.

He hands Lee the book. She thumbs through it as the movie cuts to the street outside the bookstore. Lee, holding the book in a brown bag, and Elliot are walking out.

LEE: [Laughing, holding up the bag] Well, thanks a lot.

ELLIOT: [Pointing to the bookstore] Thanks for showing me the bookstore. Perhaps you could, uh, take me to an AA meeting sometime. Uh… uh, I'd love to see what goes on.

LEE: [Nodding] Well, yeah, yeah. You'd love it. It's really entertaining. You'd have a good time [stepping closer to the curb and hailing a cab]. I know you would.

ELLIOT: [Pointing to the book] And, uh, d- don't forget the poem on page a hundred and twelve. It reminded me of you.

A taxi pulls over to the curb; they walk over to it.

LEE: [Laughing] Really? Well…

Elliot opens the rear door for Lee. She laughs as she gets in.

ELLIOT: [Leaning down to talk to Lee in the cab] Page a hundred and twelve.

LEE: Bye.

ELLIOT: [Closing the taxi door for Lee] Bye.

He watches the taxi pull away.

CUT TO:

INTERIOR. FREDERICK'S LOFT BEDROOM – NIGHT

Lee, in slacks and shirt, is curled up on the bed, her back to the camera, as she reads the E.E.Cummings poem in the glow of a night-table lamp. The piano music is still heard.

LEE'S VOICE-OVER: [Reading] "your slightest look easily will/unclose me/though I have closed myself as/fingers,/you open always petal by petal /myself…"

As Lee continues to read aloud, the movie cuts to Elliott's dark den, lit by a light in the hallway. Elliot enters, wearing a robe, crossing the room in the dark.

LEE'S VOICE-OVER: [Continuing reading] "…as Spring opens/Touching skilfully, mysteriously/her first rose/I do not know what it is about you/that closes and opens;/only something in me understands/the voice of your eyes is deeper than/all roses] …"

Elliot turns on a light. The camera stays on his face as he looks off into the distance, mouthing indistinctly the line of poetry Lee next reads aloud.

LEE'S VOICE-OVER: [Continuing reading] "nobody, not even the rain, has such small hands."

The film leaves Elliot's face and cuts back to the loft, where Lee, having finished the poem, sits up in the bed, staring pensively, lost in her thoughts.

I, AN ACTOR

Nicholas Craig is the brilliant creation of Nigel Planer and Christopher Douglas. The book *I, An Actor* is the best parody of po-faced theatrical biographies there has ever been. The book is so bitingly cruel and wicked towards "luvvies" and all their theatrical kind, it has on the back of it, this quote from the late Sheridan Morley, reviewing it for *The Times* – "Disloyal, vindictive, bitter, scandalous and insulting". Fabulously, the book IS all those things, and Craig the biggest twat you would ever have to share a rehearsal room with, but I love it and him. The 'art' of acting is sometimes cloaked in mystery by certain actors, and Planer and Douglas go about bursting that particular bubble with their prick, Craig. There are so many gems you just have to read it, but visually it is hysterical too. The rehearsal photos, and Craig donning his overblown theatrical make-up ("sketching the nuances") is all hysterical stuff.

The Chinese Meal

If actors are a noble priestly caste of Fakir magician poets with the theatre as their temple and the stage their altar, the Chinese restaurant is where they have their dinner after the show.

The Chinese meal is essential to the nourishment of 'Actor-Family-Oneness' and is actually rather a complicated ritual. To start with, there will always be one or two people in my theatre company who, between you and me, are irretrievably naff and boring. It is obviously important that these 'Nafferoonnies' remain unaware of any plans to 'go chinky after the perf'. They wouldn't enjoy it and so it is kinder not to ask them. It may be necessary for everyone to say false goodnights to each other and leave the stage door in different directions.

There is a special skill in timing your arrival at the Chinese restaurant: too early and you'll have a long hungry wait; too late and you'll find yourself stuck right on the end of a table with someone from wardrobe. The right time to arrive is when the first table has been filled up and another one is being dragged across to make an extension. Plonk yourself down at the point of the join – you are then bang in the middle of the group, handily placed to leave or join conversations and to help yourself to a wide range of other people's food.

Always, always, *always* suggest that everyone digs into everyone else's and argue hard for the bill to be equally split at the end. It ought to be perfectly possible to consume £20 worth of food and drink while still only paying £10.37[1] like everyone else.

---

1 Of course these prices are a bit out of date but the principles of post-perf chinky etiquette are as infrangible now as when they were first codified – an as thy will be for actors a thousand years hence. Although, in fact, I tend to eat far less Chinese food than in the past – they say they don't put MSG into things but they do and of course you end up totally dehydrated and spend the rest of the night gulping down gallons of Evian. Lebanese would be my post-perf cuisine of choice. Or Moroccan, but I always insist on an assurance from the kitchen that the rice will be gluten-free and that they must never, EVER, mix cumin with harissa, or use modified starch in the stock. I find that a lengthy discussion about my diet is a wonderful way to get the conversation off to a flying start.

Actor's conversation, being unfettered and life-affirming will usually cause other diners to fall silent, ashamed of their bourgeois values and enchanted by the exuberance of the 'theatre folk'. A kindly act is to draw them into your group by waving or going over to their tables, kneeling down before them and begging for forgiveness in extravagant language. Try to sing the theme tunes from obscure Seventies TV shows, quote from other plays, and – of course – lots and lots of regional accents and silly voices.

MONTY PYTHON, *The Brand New Monty Python Bok* (Methuen, 1973). Reprinted by permission of Methuen; **VIZ**, The Shittish Isles, (2001). Reprinted by permission of *Viz* magazine; **ERIC CHAPPELL** 'Things That Go Bump in the Night' from *Rising Damp: The Complete Scripts*, (Granada Media, 2002). Reprinted by permission of Bryan Drew Ltd on behalf of the author; **ALAN BENNETT**, 'A Chip in the Sugar' from *The Complete Talking Heads*, (BBC Books, 1998). Reprinted by permission of The Random House Group Ltd; **ROBERT AICKMAN**, 'Wood' from *Tales of Love and Death*, (Gollancz, 1977). Reprinted by permission of Artellus Ltd; **MICHAEL PALIN AND TERRY JONES**, *Ripping Yarns* (Methuen, 1978) Reprinted by permission of Methuen; **PHILIP ROTH**, *Portnoy's Complaint* (Vintage). Reprinted by permission of The Random House Group Limited; **TERRY RAVENSCROFT**, The Cissy and Ada Sketches. Reprinted by permission of the author, http://www.razza.fsnet.co.uk; **JOHN SHUTTLEWORTH**, *Pillock of the Community*, (2003). Reprinted by permission of the author; **JOEL COEN AND ETHAN COEN**, *Barton Fink*, (Faber, 1991). Reprinted by permission of Faber and Faber; **DAVID RENWICK**, 'Mastermind' sketch from *The Two Ronnies*. Reprinted by permission of the author; **ALAN BENNETT**, *Prick Up Your Ears* (Faber and Faber, 1987). Reprinted by permission of Faber and Faber; **NOËL COWARD**, "Mad About the Boy" (1932). Reprinted by permission of A&C Black; **JULIA DAVIS AND ROB BRYDON**, 'All Over my Glasses' from *Human Remains* (Baby Cow, 2003); **ROBERT HOLMES**, *The Talons of Weng-Chiang*, (BBC, 1977); **MIKE LEIGH**, *Nuts In May* from the film directed by Mike Leigh (1977) is reproduced by permission of PFD (www.pfd. co.uk) on behalf of Mike Leigh; **RUFUS WAINWRIGHT**, 'Dinner at Eight' from *Want One*, (Dreamworks, 2003). Courtesy of Warner Chappell Music; **DICK CLEMENT AND IAN LA FRENAIS**, 'A Night In' from *Porridge: The Complete Scripts*, (Headline, 2002). Reprinted by permission of the publishers; **VICTORIA WOOD**, 'Self-Service' from *Barmy: The New Victoria Wood Sketchbook*, (Methuen, 1987). Reprinted by permission of the author; *A Change of Sex*, produced by Roger Mills, directed by David Pearson, (BBC, 1979); **JEREMY DYSON, MARK GATISS, STEVE PEMBERTON AND REECE SHEARSMITH**, *The League of Gentlemen: Scripts and That*, (BBC Books, 2003). By permission of the Random House Group Limited; **CHRISTOPHER DOUGLAS & NIGEL PLANER**, *I, An Actor*, (Methuen, 2001 Rev. Ed.). Reproduced by permission of PFD on behalf of the authors; **LUPINO LANE**, *How to Become a Comedian* (Frederick Muller, 1945); **HUBERT SELBY JNR**, 'Fortune Cookie' from *Song of the Silent Snow*, (Marion Boyars, 1986). By permission of Marion Boyars Publishers, London and New York; **MARTIN AMIS**, *Dead Babies*, (Jonathan Cape, 1975). Reprinted by permission of the Random House Group Ltd; **E.F. BENSON**, *Mapp and Lucia* (Hodder & Stoughton, 1931). Reprinted by permission of A P Watt Ltd on behalf of the Executors of the Estate of K S P McDowall; **ANTONY GREVILLE-BELL**, *Theatre of Blood*, (MGM, 1973); **TERRY JOHNSON**, *Dead Funny* from *Plays: Two* (Methuen Drama, 1998). Reprinted by permission of A&C Black; **EDGAR ALLAN POE**, 'The Tell-tale Heart' (1843); **SHIRLEY JACKSON**, *The Haunting of Hill House*, (Michael Joseph, 1960). Reprinted by permission of A.M. Heath on behalf of the Estate of Shirley Jackson; **STEPHEN FRY AND HUGH LAURIE**, 'Society' from *A Bit More Fry and Laurie*, (Random House, 1991). Reprinted by permission of David Higham Associates Ltd; **WILLIAM PETER BLATTY**, *The Exorcist*, (Faber and Faber, 1999). Reprinted by permission of Faber and Faber; **THOMAS HARRIS**, *Hannibal*, (William Heinemann, 1999). Reprinted by permission of the Random House Group Ltd; **DAVID MAMET**, *Glengarry Glen Ross* from *Plays: Three*, (Methuen Drama, 1996). Reprinted by permission of A&C Black; **THE BROTHERS GRIMM**, "Rumpelstiltskin" from *Grimm's Fairy Tales*, (Frederick Warne, 1884); **WOODY ALLEN**, *Hannah and her Sisters*, (Faber and Faber, 1988). Reprinted by permission of Faber and Faber.

Every effort has been made to trace copyright holders. The publishers would be happy to correct any errors or omissions that are brought to their attention in subsequent editions.